CASE STUDIES IN CULTURAL ANTHROPOLOGY

SERIES EDITORS

George and Louise Spindler

STANFORD UNIVERSITY

THE RASHAAYDA BEDOUIN
Arab Pastoralists of Eastern Sudan

THE RASHAAYDA BEDOUIN
Arab Pastoralists of Eastern Sudan

WILLIAM C. YOUNG

Georgia Southern University

CASE STUDIES IN CULTURAL ANTHROPOLOGY

HARCOURT BRACE COLLEGE PUBLISHERS

Fort Worth Philadelphia San Diego New York Orlando Austin San Antonio
Toronto Montreal London Sydney Tokyo

Publisher	**Ted Buchholz**
Editor in Chief	**Christopher P. Klein**
Senior Acquisitions Editor	**Stephen T. Jordan**
Assistant Editor	**Linda Wiley**
Project Editor	**Louise Slominsky**
Production Manager	**Diane Gray**
Art Director	**Burl Dean Sloan**

Cover photo by William C. Young.

Address for Editorial Correspondence:
Harcourt Brace College Publishers
301 Commerce Street, Suite 3700
Fort Worth, TX 76102

Address for Orders:
Harcourt Brace & Company
6277 Sea Harbor Drive
Orlando, FL 32887-6777
1-800-782-4479, or 1-800-433-0001 (in Florida)

Photo and Figure Credits: Photo on p. 134 courtesy of Tim Keating. Figure 2 (p. 32) after Sadr, 1991: pp. 28–29. All other photos and figures by the author.

Library of Congress Catalog Card Number: 95-76767

ISBN 0-15-501513-3

Printed in the United States of America

5 6 7 8 9 0 1 2 3 4 016 9 8 7 6 5 4 3 2 1

Foreword

ABOUT THE SERIES

These case studies in cultural anthropology are designed for students in beginning and intermediate courses in the social sciences, to bring them insights into the richness and complexity of human life as it is lived in different ways, in different places. The authors are men and women who have lived in the societies they write about and who are professionally trained as observers and interpreters of human behavior. Also, the authors are teachers; in their writing, the needs of the student reader remain foremost. It is our belief that when an understanding of ways of life very different from one's own is gained, abstractions and generalizations about the human condition become meaningful.

The scope and character of the series has changed constantly since we published the first case studies in 1960, in keeping with our intention to represent anthropology as it is. We are concerned with the ways in which human groups and communities are coping with the massive changes wrought in their physical and sociopolitical environments in recent decades. We are also concerned with the ways in which established cultures have solved life's problems. And we want to include representation of the various modes of communication and emphasis that are being formed and reformed as anthropology itself changes.

We think of this series as an instructional series, intended for use in the classroom. We, the editors, have always used case studies in our teaching, whether for beginning students or advanced graduate students. We start with case studies, whether from our own series or from elsewhere, and weave our way into theory, and then turn again to cases. For us, they are the grounding of our discipline.

ABOUT THE AUTHOR

William C. Young was born in Minneapolis, Minnesota. His first interest in the Arab world was sparked by his high school Spanish teacher, Virginia Gagan, who taught him about Arab civilization in Spain. After finishing high school he studied chemistry briefly at the University of Southern California and then transferred to Cornell University, where he majored in anthropology and earned his B.A. While at Cornell he also learned German, began studying Arabic, and was introduced to linguistics and Middle Eastern history, two subjects which he still enjoys studying. He completed his graduate work at the University of California–Los Angeles, under the guidance of Fadwa El Guindi. He received his Ph.D. in anthropology in 1988.

Dr. Young's major research interests are in the anthropology of ritual, kinship, and pastoral peoples. He has lived for long periods in Tunisia, Egypt, Sudan, and Jordan, and was a Fulbright Lecturer at Yarmouk University (in Jordan) from 1991 to 1994. Young believes in the ultimate unity of the natural and human sciences but also finds inspiration in the humanistic perspectives of the historian and philosopher of religion. He tries to keep up with new developments in physical anthropology, linguistics, and history as well as in his own specialities. He enjoys studying foreign languages and is always working on this never-ending project. Dr. Young is currently teaching anthropology at Georgia Southern University in Statesboro, Georgia.

ABOUT THIS CASE STUDY

For years we have tried to acquire a case study of a nomadic Bedouin culture. In fact, several case studies were contracted, but all these efforts were cut short. Authors turned to other projects, lost interest in the Bedouin research they had done, or died. Finally William Young came to our rescue. The series, and the instructors and students it serves, have benefited greatly.

The Rashaayda Bedouin: Arab Pastoralists of Eastern Sudan is a remarkable case study. It takes the reader into the Rashaayda's world, furnishing it with vivid detail about domestic affairs inside the tent and the social landscape outside. It shows us a protocol of daily life that strikes the American reader as ceremonious and complex, affecting all social interaction. This life is described from the perspective of one who has lived it. Bill Young learned the Rashaayda's language, donned their costume, and for a while became a member of one of their families. He learned to respond to events and problems like one of the Rashaayda. When reading his study one has the sense at times that their way of life is being described by a Rashiidi.

This impression is dispelled when one encounters Young's sophisticated interpretation of the symbolism in the Rashiidi behavior. A man's partial unsheathing of his sword, a woman's adjusting her veil, the placement of the tents—in short, the use of every object—all deliver social messages that are as specific as well-formulated sentences. The author explores this symbolic process with a keen eye and an anthropologically trained mind. The texture of a way of life emerges that is complex, full of ceremony, and leavened by rituals that reward those who carry them out.

The author also explores some fundamental issues concerning the Rashaayda's ecological adaptation. The environment in which they move is surely not the world's most hospitable. For much of the year it is dry and hot and its plant life is scanty; rain and vegetation appear during only two short seasons. Careful planning, foresight, and expert understanding of that environment in all its variability is essential for survival. The animals, too, must be handled properly. Goats, sheep—even the camels that the Rashaayda depend upon for transporting people and moving household goods—all yield useful goods: milk, meat, and hair (which the Rashaayda weave into tent cloth). And the Rashaayda are not only nomadic herders; they are also horticulturalists. They plant their crops in places where rain sometimes falls, working the soil, sowing, and reaping in step with the seasons. Managing all of this productively requires expertise, and the Rashaayda display it abundantly.

The Rashiidi way of life is both exotic and mundane, as are all ways of life. The Rashaayda are different from "us" (whoever and wherever "we" are), but like "us" they face a number of universal problems: the struggle for security and material needs; the trials of raising children and teaching them right from wrong; the hardships of sickness and separation from loved ones. They deal with these problems in ways that are different but understandable. In fact, once we are over the first shock of unfamiliarity, we can appreciate their unique approaches and empathize with them.

This case study is an expression of what most anthropologists try to convey to their students, particularly when they teach an introductory course. The dramatic cultural differences exhibited by the human species need not obscure our common humanity, but they certainly do make humanity more interesting.

We are fortunate to have *The Rashaayda Bedouin* in the series. We urge a careful and receptive reading of it, for what it has to teach us.

George and Louise Spindler
Series Editors
Ethnographics
Box 38
Calistoga, CA 94515

Acknowledgments

This case study is based on research that was funded by the Social Science Research Council and the Fulbright-Hayes Commission. I am very grateful indeed for their generous support and would like to thank them for it here. I am also much indebted to the von Grunebaum Center for Near Eastern Studies, UCLA, for the NDEA Title VI grants I received through the Center and for the office space they gave me while I was writing my doctoral dissertation. The Center was a most congenial place for me to work. I must also thank the East-West Foundation for the grant they gave me to support my writing.

I owe a great deal, as well, to Fadwa El Guindi. Dr. El Guindi was my friend and counselor as well as my professor during my years of graduate study. She took special interest in my research and was extremely generous with her time, spending hours going over my rough drafts and suggesting improvements. While I was in the field she answered my many letters faithfully and even came to Sudan to visit and encourage me. Her energetic lectures were both intellectually stimulating and inspiring; they are models that I have followed now that I myself am teaching. She often invited me and her other students to her home, where we would discuss our work, our hopes for anthropology, and our hopes for ourselves. It has been very good, indeed, to know Dr. El Guindi all these years. I am also very much indebted to Dwight Read for his willingness to read the many drafts of my dissertation and for the patient and positive comments on it that he made. Both he and Dr. El Guindi suffered through the bulky first drafts and made them readable by telling me where and how to cut. Dr. Read also helped me in many other ways, by listening attentively and without condescension to my arguments, pointing out my mistakes and showing me what new areas of study would benefit me. I am grateful for his unfailing good humor and kindness.

Georges Sabagh, Director of the von Grunebaum Center for Near Eastern Studies, UCLA, also deserves my special thanks for his constant interest in my work and welfare. Without his support I would often have felt lost at UCLA. He made the Center my home away from home. Although I have not made the same weighty demands of my other professors, they have always been more than willing to help me. I would like to thank Laura Nader for agreeing so readily to serve on my doctoral committee, for her moral support, and for her thoughtful comments on my dissertation. Philip Newman also was of great help to me. He showed me how to teach and also helped me with my writing; he made me feel welcome in his office and at his home. I also must thank Gerry Hale for his efforts to keep factual errors out of my research; I have benefited greatly from his wide-ranging knowledge of Sudan and Sudanese society. Robert Edgerton and Michael Moerman both showed me new ways of studying human societies that enriched my understanding of anthropology. Afaf Lutfi al-Sayyid Marsot was also very helpful, both in developing my sense of historical analysis and in keeping my writing clear of unnecessary jargon. Finally, Marjorie Franken, Anne Jennings, David Kronenfeld, and Victor de Munck gave me new perspectives on my field data and helped me develop my thinking.

There are many others upon whom I depended during my years in graduate school. I would especially like to thank Nicole Sault, my friend since we began our studies at UCLA and my colleague, now, as well, for her interest and encouragement. I also want to express my gratitude to Mary Murrell, administrative assistant at the Near Eastern Center, for her kindness and constant good cheer. She also gave generously of her time and energy. My good friend Abdlaziz Shebl kept me company and inspired me while I labored on my dissertation. Vincent J. Cornell, Harry Bernstein, and Khalid al-Dakhil have also been faithful and good companions and, each in his own way, has encouraged me and has helped me deal with the problems that have come my way.

I must thank my colleagues in Sudan, as well, for their warm welcome, for including me in the activities of their departments whenever I came to Khartoum, and for their useful and insightful discussions about my research. They include Abdel Ghaffar Mohammad Ahmed, Taj al-Anbiya' 'Ali al-Dawi, and Hasan Mohammad Salih (in the Department of Sociology and Anthropology) and Salih al-'Arifi (in Geography). I also have not forgotten the late 'Omar Bilal Siddiq, my first friend from Sudan, who was always very generous with his time and considerate of my feelings and opinions. He was the best example of Sudanese ethics and character that I have ever met, always sincere and moderate. He is sorely missed; *Allah yarḥamuhu* ("God have mercy on his soul"). I must also thank Tim Keating for allowing me to use one of his photographs and Thomas Stevenson for his very useful technical advice.

My greatest debt, of course, is to the Rashaayda themselves. I feel especially grateful to the families of Ḥaamid ibin 'Aayiḍ, Aḥmad ibin Ḥasan, and 'Abdallah ibin Ḥasan, who became my family while I was in the field. I will never forget them. I feel both gratitude and pleasure when I recall my friends and neighbors in the camp of Naafi' Barakaat. They kept me company; without them life in the desert would have been hard indeed. I also thank the family of Saliim Sa'd Saliim and the Rashaayda of 'Aṭbara and al-Daamir for their hospitality. So many others shared their homes and lives with me unselfishly that I cannot mention them all here by name. They know, however, that I have not forgotten them.

List of Figures

Contents

Introduction

This book is an ethnography of the Rashaayda Bedouin, an Arabic-speaking people who live in northeastern Sudan. It is based on anthropological fieldwork that I carried out among the Rashaayda between 1978 and 1980. Like all ethnographies, it is selective. It does not tell the reader everything there is to know about the Rashaayda; that would be an impossible goal for any book. Rather, it concentrates on some of the issues that are currently being discussed by American anthropologists and Americans in general. These include: How much does gender identity differ from one society to the next? What are the causes of racism? What are the causes of an unequal distribution of wealth in a given society and how does it affect social relations? I have tried to address these issues by presenting illustrations of how gender, race, and political-economic differences are constructed among the Rashaayda. Thus the monograph is very much a product of its time; perhaps these concerns will seem outdated in twenty or thirty years. I will not apologize for this focus; to be readable, every book must have definite points to make.

Nevertheless, I have endeavored to do more than contribute to current debates about gender, race, and class. I have also tried to convey, as faithfully as I can, what it was like to live with the Rashaayda. They are nomadic pastoralists and spend half of each year in small, cramped tents. Living with them during the rainy seasons meant moving with them, learning their techniques of pastoral migration, using their scarce water sparingly, sharing the meals that they made from grain they planted and from the milk and meat that they took from their own animals. My first chapter recounts two days during December 1978 when the Rashaayda were moving from winter pastures to dry-season campsites. It provides a picture of their nomadic life.

The book also contains numerous short studies—almost vignettes—of incidents I witnessed that gave me insight into the Rashaayda's values, attitudes, and ideas. These incidents reveal the structure of their social world, showing how the members of a household work together to obtain the material necessities of life and realize other valued goals. Chapter Two describes households and larger social units (extended households, camps, "tribal branches," and "tribes") as well, showing how each has its distinctive tasks. The household has important roles in production but also carries out life-crisis rituals, offers hospitality to guests, arranges marriages, and regulates the transmission of property from one generation to the next. Coresident households help each other during pastoral migrations, and the members of camps "elect" leaders, celebrate Islamic holidays, and help keep the peace in times of conflict. The case studies also indicate the limits of the Rashaayda's social world and show how they deal with outsiders. These latter data, in particular, are useful for those interested in the social construction of race and ethnicity. Most of this information appears in Chapters Two and Four.

Chapter Three of this monograph contains information on the Rashaayda's cosmology. By utilizing Pierre Bourdieu's notion of *habitus* (see also p. 73), it links the Rashaayda's religious practices with their perception of the environment, their encoding and decoding of the body, and the structure of their living space. It shows how their variety of Islamic ritual practice is integrated with their everyday life. This chapter also explores the construction of personal identity, explaining how people are given their names and genealogical affiliations, how they marry, and how they resolve conflicts.

Chapter Four deals with the social identities of groups and shows how these have changed historically. It points out that the Rashaayda's Bedouin identity is not immutable and depends largely on the economic and political conditions which have made nomadic pastoralism profitable for them. It also explores the history of inter-ethnic relations between the Rashaayda and other groups in eastern Sudan, all of whom are called "tribes" (*gabaayil*) in Sudanese Arabic. The historical data in this chapter call into question the idea that "tribes" are stable, clearly-bounded units based entirely on patrilineal descent. It also raises the issue of whether "tribe" is the best translation of the Arabic term *gabiila.* The word "tribe" appears between scare-quotes in this chapter and, indeed, in every other part of this book. This is partly because "tribe" is a very inexact translation of the Arabic term and party because "tribe" has been used in so many different ways that it no longer seems to have any definite meaning. Sometimes "tribe" refers to a large population whose members speak a nonwritten language (such as the Navaho); sometimes it refers to a local group of people who claim descent from a common ancestor (for instance, the "tribes of Israel" named in the Old Testament); and sometimes it names an intermediate stage (between the "band" and the "chiefdom") in sociocultural evolution (cf. Sahlins 1968). Because it has so many contradictory connotations, some anthropologists (e.g. Fried 1975) now reject it completely. To keep readers aware of the problematic connotations of "tribe" I have enclosed it between quotation marks in every passage where it appears. At the end of this chapter there is a discussion of historical changes in gender identity and the processes which have prevented women from becoming politically prominent.

The Epilogue is a discussion of how I collected my data and what my personal relationships with the Rashaayda were like. I describe in some detail how I entered the field, how I established rapport with some Rashiidi families, and how I tried to come to terms with the Islamic faith and values of the Rashaayda. I also reflect on the difficulties of returning from the field after having adopted a Muslim identity and point of view, on the ethical aspects of writing an ethnography about the Rashaayda, and on the problems involved in maintaining contact with (and keeping faith with) the people who sheltered and supported me while I was in Sudan.

Throughout the book I have tried to back up my ethnographic generalizations with concrete examples. Where possible, I have provided photographs of unfamiliar objects and actions. I also show how difficult it is to translate key Arabic terms accurately. When necessary, I include transcribed Arabic terms along with their glosses. I found this especially important when discussing objects (such as items of clothing) and social categories (such as "free," "slave," and "the offspring of slave women and free men") that have no exact English equivalents.

In this connection I should explain how I have transcribed words in the Rashaayda's dialect of Arabic. There are many systems for transcribing spoken Arabic dialects. I have adopted a system similar to one used by specialists for transliterating written Arabic. In this system, dots are placed below some letters (*ṭ, ṣ*) to distinguish emphatic (dark) consonants from their nonemphatic (apico-alveolar, clear) counterparts (*t, s*). I also use a dot to distinguish the voiceless pharyngeal fricative (*ḥ*), which has no counterpart in English, from the voiceless laryngeal fricative (*h*), that is, English "h." The symbol (') stands for a glottal stop, while (') stands for a voiced pharyngeal fricative, *'ayn*. There are also pairs of letters which should be easy for an English speaker to identify: *sh* stands for the voiceless alveopalatal fricative in "she"; *ch* stands for the voiceless alveopalatal affricate in "rich"; *th* stands for the voiceless interdental fricative in "bath"; and *dh* stands for the voiced interdental fricative in "bathe." I use *ḍ* to transcribe the emphatic counterpart of *dh;* there is no emphatic counterpart of *d* in Rashiidi Arabic. Two other letter pairs have no equivalent in English: *kh* represents the voiceless dorso-velar fricative in German "ach", while *gh* represents a voiced dorso-velar fricative that sounds something like an untrilled, French "r." The letter *ǧ* represents a voiced palatal affricate which, in the Rashaayda's dialect of Arabic (see Chapter Two, p. 29), is an allophone of the phoneme /g/; it contrasts phonemically with the voiced alveopalatal fricative *j*. Long vowels (uu, ii, aa) are doubled while short vowels (u, i, a) are transcribed with one letter.

1 / The Daily Life of Some Rashaayda at the End of the Migratory Season

APPROPRIATE UNITS OF OBSERVATION AND DESCRIPTION FOR AN ETHNOGRAPHY OF NOMADIC PASTORALISTS

All ethnographers begin, implicitly or explicitly, by choosing a frame of reference for presenting their data. Somehow the data must be made comprehensible for the reader, to fit together in some logical sequence without, at the same time, losing their novelty and freshness. One organizing device is based on time. The ethnographer may choose to describe his or her first day in the field or may select a particular day as a typical one in the lives of the people being described. This device can work well. Ethnographers often find that "one day in the life" is a good unit of observation because it accurately reflects the way the people themselves divide up their time and organize their work. Most people do not choose to stay awake more than 18 hours at a stretch, so for them the unit "one day plus one night" is fundamental. It also fits the working schedule of many nonindustrial societies, if for no other reason that cooked food does not keep overnight in most climates without refrigeration; new meals must be cooked every day. Thus the 24-hour period is the most suitable unit of observation for many studies.

This general rule does not hold for all societies, however, especially pastoralist societies. From the perspective of pastoralism, sleeping, eating, and other daily activities are secondary; what matters is how the livestock are cared for and utilized. As we will see, among the Rashaayda the move from one nomadic campsite to another during the final weeks of the migratory season takes more than 24 hours. To depict the Rashaayda's daily life during this time, then, I have decided to describe two days, not just one. This decision is based on a methodological principle, one which Karl Heider, who teaches ethnographic film, put very succinctly: Always record "whole people in whole acts." In other words, do not stop the camera (or, in my case, the narrative) until the action itself has stopped. This ensures that you will capture all of the data which are directly relevant to the action being studied, even if their relevance is not obvious at the time the record is made.

Bearing this in mind, let us turn to my ethnography. I should point out that it is not an exact rendering of those particular two days in December 1978. They do form the framework of the narrative, and most of the events I describe actually took place during those days. Some events, however, occurred a few days earlier. Although I have not changed the content of my notes for December 1978, I have sometimes changed the dates. A strictly faithful, mechanical reproduction of my field notes would not have served the reader well; a more orderly narrative is necessary.

Some of the details presented concern the technology of nomadic pastoralism, some are related to "tribal" identity, and others serve to represent the members of my Rashiidi[1] family not as "tribesmen" but as individuals with distinctive personalities and styles. Still others provide some insight into what it means to be a man or a woman in this society. I have not tried to sort out these various kinds of data; they are presented much as I recorded them. My goal in this chapter is not to explain or analyze the Rashaayda's way of life; systematic analysis will come in subsequent chapters. Rather, I want to show how their attitudes, values, cultural categories, and aspirations are all interconnected in the course of daily activities. Their traditions are simultaneously Arab, Bedouin, Islamic, and purely local. These heterogeneous elements form a cultural whole which is integrated, to some extent logically and to a large extent practically. It is certainly possible, and for some purposes necessary, to separate "Bedouin" customs from Islamic or Arab traditions. The lesson of this chapter is that the Rashaayda themselves do not separate them, and that when we want to speak of them only as "Bedouin" or Muslims, we do so at the risk of distorting their experience.

DAY ONE: BREAKING CAMP

Although the sun had not yet appeared in the morning sky, Suluum was already up and working; I could see her fanning the embers of last night's fire. Only her silhouette was visible in the faint light of early dawn. She crouched at the side of her portable hearth, a two-foot-wide, concave piece of scrap metal, and peered over her drawn-up knees at the ashes and coals in its center. She was wielding a small fan made of plaited straw with one hand and breaking up twigs and bits of wood with the other. When the coals finally glowed into life, she piled her tinder on top and snapped the fan rapidly up and down until they caught fire. Then she paused to breathe, pushing her long, wide sleeves farther up her arms and adjusting the "married woman's mask" that covered her nose, mouth, and cheeks.

The family water skins and a blackened cooking pot were on her right. She untied the leather thong that bound the neck of one water skin and pumped a measure of water into the pot, pressing the top of the bulging skin gently. Once she had enough water for our morning tea, she deftly closed the water skin, sealing the neck by twisting it tight and tying it with the thong. She put more wood on the fire, and when it flared up she arranged three tin cans around its periphery that would support the cooking pot. Then she put the pot on the fire and called to her children to wake them.

We had to rise early that morning because we were moving to a new campsite. Last night Suluum and her twenty-year-old daughter Faḍiyya[2] had taken down her

[1] "Rashiidi" is the adjectival form of "Rashaayda." A man belonging to the Rashaayda "tribe" is a Rashiidi; the dialect of Arabic that he speaks is "Rashiidi Arabic."

[2] I have changed the names of all women mentioned in this case study. Rashiidi women do not reveal their names to strangers, and the Rashaayda would object if I published them. The only exception is Suluum, who died two years after my return to the United States. I have left her name unchanged to keep alive her memory.

*A woman wearing the married woman's mask (*ğinaaʿ*). The mask covers her mouth and nose. She has also thrown the end of one of her sleeves over her head because she is being photographed; ordinarily she would not cover her head while inside a tent. She is cooking a pancakelike bread (*ʿabbuud*) on an iron griddle.*

small, rainy-season tent. They had unpinned the canvas liner that formed the innermost layer of the tent and then had pulled up some of the tent pegs, freeing the outer layer of tent cloth so that they could take it down and roll it up. The heavy, black-and-white tent cloth now lay in piles around our campsite, ready to be dragged over to where the camels were couched and tied to their saddles. The household furnishings—Suluum's grindstone, her large leather storage bag, the family's sacks of grain, our clothes—were also ready to go. But first we had to eat breakfast.

I sat up on my bed—a short, rectangular cot made of roughly hewn wood, with a cotton-stuffed mattress and a taut web of tightly stretched rope underneath it that served as springs—and said good morning. Suluum replied in kind and then resumed her efforts to rouse her children. Her teenaged son Naafi‘ lay stretched out on the ground beside me on a reed mat. His face was covered by the thin white length of cloth that he wore as a turban during the daytime. Suluum called to him: *yaa naafi‘! guum yaa naafi‘, guum, uṭlub rabbak* ("Naafi‘! Get up, Naafi‘; get up, ask for your Lord's favor [i.e., perform the dawn prayer])." Naafi‘ groaned but did not sit up. I could see that his eyes were screwed shut beneath his gauzy, unrolled turban. I slipped on my sandals, stood up, and walked behind the campsite to urinate. I took our *ibriiǧ*—a tall tin can equipped with a handle and spout—with me, so that I could wash with a little water and make sure that no urine would dirty my clothes. When I returned Naafi‘ was awake and his father, Ḥaamid, was making his ablutions for prayer. Ḥaamid poured a few drops of our scarce water from a bowl into his right hand and splashed it across his face, reciting "I witness that there is no god but God" softly as he did so. Ḥaamid's other sons, ‘Abd al-Ḥamiid and Ḥamiid, were also awake, and Ḥamiid (the youngest boy) had gotten up to milk the goats that were tethered near our beds.

This was just the beginning of what was to be a long day. I had been migrating with Suluum, Ḥaamid, and their children on and off for the previous six months, since the beginning of July 1978. It was now mid-December 1978, and the rains which first had turned the dry soil of northeastern Sudan into a layer of thick mud—and then had transformed it into a green carpet of grasses and herbs—were over. We could no longer find pasture for our animals in the parched savanna regions that we had been crossing. Yesterday we had decided to move to a more permanent campsite near a well where we could spend the dry season. It would take us most of two days to "move our tents (*nishidd buyuutnaa*)" to our dry-season campsite.

Suluum and Ḥaamid's family—my family, for the next two years—were members of an Arabic-speaking society known as *gabiilat ar-Rashaayda,* "the Rashaayda tribe." They were also nomadic pastoralists. As they said, *ḥinna ‘arab nishidd wa niḥuṭṭ,* "We are people/Arabs who take up their tents and put them down again in a new place." Many of their relatives also lived a nomadic life, moving through desert pastures during the rainy seasons to exploit wild vegetation and rain pools and staying in one place only during the dry seasons. Suluum's newly married son, for example, had also been migrating this year; we would see him when we reached our new campsite, where about twenty other families had already arrived. But Suluum's married daughter would not be there. She and her family now lived in Khashm al-Girba, a nearby agricultural scheme run by the Sudanese government. Although she had given up migration, she still kept sheep and goats, letting them graze on crop stubble after her wheat and cotton had been harvested. Sometimes her children would come to visit us.

By the time the sun had appeared on the horizon the adults had finished their prayers and Ḥamiid had finished milking the goats; we were ready to drink our tea. Suluum tossed a small handful of black tea into the pot of boiling water and stirred it with a spoon; Ḥamiid added the bowl of milk; and when this mixture boiled Suluum poured half of it into the family teapot. Then she washed the glasses with a little water, set them on a metal tray, and filled them to the brim. We gathered around the hearth to drink, picking up the hot glasses gingerly, with the tips of our fingers.

We were not migrating by ourselves; there were too many goats, sheep, and camels for Ḥaamid and his sons to handle on their own. Suluum's eldest son, 'Abdallah, and his wife and two small children were moving with us. They were camped to our right. I could see them sitting around their hearth, drinking their morning tea. Sometimes 'Abdallah's wife 'Aabda would forget to bank her fire at night and would have no live coals to work with in the morning. Then she would have to ask for some coals from our fire, much to Suluum's disgust, or worse, would have to waste matches and kerosene in order to start a new fire. But today Suluum had no cause to complain about her daughter-in-law; her fire was lighted, her family's belongings were packed, and her tent cloth was properly folded.

Suluum did not sit and drink tea with us; she was busy cooking our breakfast. She began by starting another fire on the ground, ten feet away from the hearth, using some of the wood that was already burning under the teapot. She beat the burning firewood with a stick to break it into small, glowing embers. Then she greased the flat metal sheet that she used for baking, spreading a few drops of sesame seed oil on its clean side. Next she uncovered a bowl filled with moist sorghum dough; she had ground the sorghum on her grindstone the day before. She pressed the wet dough onto the metal sheet, shaping it to form a flat, circular loaf. Finally she inverted the sheet and laid it on top of the embers. After covering the topmost side of the sheet with sand, she left it and came back to our hearth for her tea. The dough would take half an hour to bake.

'Abdallah came over to our hearth while we were still drinking our third glass of tea. He was eager to get started, so that we could finish migrating before noon and rest during the hot afternoon hours. But he did not even suggest that we hurry with our breakfast. His mother's husband, Ḥaamid, was the most senior man in our small camp, and although 'Abdallah did not owe him quite the same respect that he had once owed his own father (who had been killed some twenty years earlier), Ḥaamid still had the final word, at least formally, when the two families made decisions about migration. So 'Abdallah was merely coming to see whether Ḥaamid was prepared to begin moving. He was dressed casually, wearing only a tee-shirt and the long, wide, lightweight cotton pants (*sirwaal*) that all men in the area wore. He chatted with us while Ḥaamid ordered his sons to fetch our burden camels and prepare to load them.

Ḥaamid's family gathered up their cooking pots and bedding, dragged the heavy rolls of tent cloth closer to the camels, and tied it all to the baggage saddles. All that I could do was watch. As usual, when they began to work I told them I wanted to help, but they would not hear of it. "Relax," Ḥaamid told me, "you're our guest. There's no need to wear yourself out." I protested that I wanted to do my fair share of the work but Ḥaamid just said "No, no . . ." and went to help his son lift a sack of flour onto one camel's back. I was distressed that they would not allow me to work with them. I wanted to be part of their family, as much as possible, and felt guilty sitting while they worked. In fact, however, this was what they wanted. I was still a guest, and guests never do the slightest amount of work for their hosts in the Arab world.

Months would pass before they started giving me work. Each time that Ḥaamid or Suluum assigned me a simple chore I became more like a family member. By the end of my stay with them I was doing children's tasks, helping to fill water skins at the well, catching a goat—grabbing it by one long, floppy ear—so that it could be milked, and chasing small stock out of the tent. I still had not learned the more difficult tasks, like branding, but I was doing enough to feel like one of the family. On that December morning, however, I was still an outsider, even though not a complete stranger. They had invited me to migrate with them and could see that I was doing my best to adjust. But they did not yet want me to work and doubted that, even if I tried, I could help them load their camels properly.

Like all aspects of migration, loading the camels required experience. If the load were not balanced it would wound the camel or make pressure sores on its back. The square, sturdy baggage saddles had to be properly cushioned and the saddle cinches had to be tight. While the boys tied their family's belongings to the baggage saddles, 'Abdallah walked from one camel to the next, testing the weight of their burdens and the tightness of their knots. The heaps of baggage were gradually transferred to the backs of the women's burden camels. The finishing touch was the three beds (mine and the beds belonging to Ḥaamid's family and 'Abdallah's family), which were set on top of everything and covered with brightly colored red and blue quilts. These served as platforms on which the women could ride and where 'Aabda could sit with her little children. The men's camels, however, were equipped with lightweight riding saddles, not baggage saddles; they would need them to ride quickly and keep control of the herd as we moved.

'Abdallah put on his white turban and *thawb* (a long, loose shirtlike garment that reached below the knees). We were all dressed up. The women (Suluum, Faḍiyya, and 'Aabda) wore decorated masks made of black cloth that were half-covered by silvery lead beadwork. They had put on their best dresses early in the morning, before I was awake. Their long, wide sleeves, with their alternating panels of black cotton cloth and brilliantly colored rayon, would make a fine impression on anyone we passed (and on the people at our next camp, as well).

Two of the boys saddled up my camel—a huge, aging bull named Jum'a (Arabic for "Friday")—and helped me mount, keeping the camel's head down by holding the reins so he would not jump up as soon as he felt my weight on his back. I was irritated with myself for not having learned to mount unassisted. I was also not very happy with Friday but tried not to show it. He was so stolid that no matter how much I goaded him with my feet and whip, he could hardly keep up with the women's camels, much less the faster mounts of the men. Yet I was also excited to be riding again.

It had been three weeks since I had last ridden. In late November I had hitched a ride into the nearby town of Kassala on a pickup truck. I had spent a week at one of the town's small hotels, writing up my new field notes, washing my clothes, having a few good meals, and buying coffee beans and ginger for Suluum. Then I had asked the Rashiidi truck drivers in Kassala where Ḥaamid's family had moved during my absence. One of them had known and had offered to take me (and fifteen other passengers) back to them. When I rejoined them I found that they had just pitched their tents in a new location and would not be moving again for as long as the pasture held out. So another week had gone by before I had a chance to migrate with them.

While Naafi' held Friday's bridle, I hooked my right leg around the pommel of his saddle and pushed myself up with my left leg, holding onto the saddle with my hands. Friday got up immediately, with a low rumble of complaint, but I was in the seat before he had stood. Although I had ridden him many times before, I still needed to pay special attention while riding to stay in the saddle. His uneven gait was not like a horse's; whenever I managed to get him to move at an easy canter, he would literally throw me an inch or so into the air with every step. The other men were accustomed to this jarring ride and adopted the proper posture (back straight, head erect, right leg curled around the saddle pommel) without thinking, but I had to concentrate to avoid being tossed off my perch on Friday's back.

Suluum walked over and handed me a big piece of steaming bread, which she had just extracted from her simple oven. I reached down to take it and almost dropped it; it was still hot, and my hands were not as callused as hers. "Don't eat it now," she said, "wait until you are hungry." I put it inside the breast pocket of my *thawb* and watched Faḍiyya and 'Aabda clambering up on top of their burden camels. Their camels, weighted down by the baggage and the beds, did not stand up as quickly as mine had.

'Abd al-Ḥamiid helped his mother mount. He handed Suluum the long piece of cane that she liked to use for goading her camel. Then he pulled on his reins and urged him to rise, making a loud, slurping sound with his tongue and lips. The animal responded to this cue by getting up. Once the camel was standing, Ḥaamid cast a critical eye on its load, checking it for balance and stability; it looked all right. In the meantime 'Abdallah was urging 'Aabda's camel to stand. Finally the men and boys got on their mounts, and we were ready to go.

It was good to get moving, once the hard work of packing and loading up was done. All of us were in fine spirits. We set out and 'Abdallah started singing. He had a good voice and could glide rapidly from the low, almost spoken parts of the song to the high notes, which he practically shouted. He sang like this only when we were migrating, and each time I heard him I wished I could turn on a tape recorder. But I could not observe and participate at the same time. We enjoyed the song. Although the women's mouths were covered, I could tell by the crinkling of their eyes that they were smiling.

After a few minutes 'Abdallah left us, prodding his mount with his left heel to make him break into a run. He rode about three hundred feet in front of us, where his mother's husband Ḥaamid and his half-brother Naafi' joined him. I could see them consulting with each other, heads up and backs straight as they rode. 'Abdallah was going ahead to look for pasture—even though there was not much vegetation left in the area at this time of year—and to choose our temporary camping site. He was our scout (*ṭarraash*). Once he had found a good spot he would come back and guide us to it. This way, when we stopped moving for the night, the camels would find something to eat. 'Abdallah rode off, leaving Ḥaamid and Naafi' at the head of our party for the time being.

But they also left us after a few minutes. They had to catch up with 'Abd al-Ḥamiid and Ḥamiid, who had gathered the small herd of ten goats and five sheep together with the camels and who were now urging them onwards, some distance to our left. I watched them depart. Once they reached the boys and their animals, Ḥaamid, 'Abd al-Ḥamiid, and Naafi' would take charge of their herd of fifteen milking camels and calves. The camels could move quickly and had to be guided by riders on camelback, but the goats and sheep were slow. Ḥamiid, about eight years old, was not too young to take care of these small stock. He rode on our donkey and pitched stones at goats that strayed too far from the herd, keeping them in check. The older boys and men were riding on young male camels (*ǧi'daan*), much faster than the donkey and able to outpace the camels in the herd.

Suluum, her daughter Faḍiyya, and her daughter-in-law 'Aabda rode on the large, lumbering bulls (*ba'aariin*), which were slow but strong enough to carry our belongings. They chatted as they rode but although I was close enough to hear them I found them hard to understand. First of all, their voices were muffled by the tight masks which they wore over their mouths. Second, I was still not used to their dialect of Arabic, which was very different from the Egyptian dialect that I had studied three years before in Cairo. They could understand me well enough, because the Cairene Arabic that I spoke was similar to the dialect spoken in the large cities of northern Sudan. Suluum sometimes spoke to me in a simplified Sudanese Arabic but when she spoke to Faḍiyya and 'Aabda she reverted to the Rashaayda's own dialect, which sounded very strange to me. Finally, when they began a new conversation I seldom knew who they were talking about. I did not want to annoy them with tiresome and intrusive questions about these people and knew from experience that direct questions like these would seldom get answers. So I kept quiet and just listened, trying to make some sense of their conversation and enjoy the ride.

An hour passed and the heat of the coming day began to make itself felt. Naafi' came back to make sure that everything was going all right. He had no real cause for worry at this time of year, when there was little pasture and the camels were frequently hungry—hence, docile! But four months earlier, when the pastures had still been good and the camels' stomachs were full, they had been frisky and hard to control. One had tried to bolt and had thrown off part of his load of clothing. Two months before that, when we had been moving north from the summer pastures near the town of al-Showak, we had had to cross an asphalt road built on top of a five-foot-high gravel embankment. The camels were afraid of this road because of its slippery surface, and we had been worried that one might fall. Yet all had gone well.

Naafi' asked me whether I was getting tired, and I said no. He lingered with us for a while, perhaps to get a break from his father's close supervision. He was a skinny and laconic 17-year-old who chafed under the sometimes brusk orders of his father and mother. He told me how he was looking forward to reaching our dry-season camp, where there were other families to visit and, especially, other young men his own age. Although he liked the activity and bounty of the migratory season—when there was plenty of camel's milk, and when he would go hunting for birds at night with 'Abdallah and Ḥaamid—he was weary of having no one to talk to other than his immediate family. After a few minutes he rode off in the direction of the herd, which by now was too far away for me to see.

We made our way across what was for me a barren landscape, without trees, rivers, or even much ground cover. True, there were patches of scrubby bushes, about four feet high, which the Rashaayda called "trees" (*shajar*). But I never learned to think of them as trees; for me, "trees" were oaks, elms, and maples! There were also shallow water courses that collected rain water during the wet season, where leafy green herbs sprouted and where the Rashaayda planted grain. By now these had dried up and the wild vegetation was turning yellow. I could hardly distinguish one stretch of ground from another; all that I knew for sure was that we were heading north (*mitshaamiliin*), keeping the sun on our right. Suluum, however, who had been crossing and re-crossing these lands for some sixty years, could recognize landmarks that were invisible to me. She could spot faint depressions in the land that had been shallow rain pools four months earlier, and she could identify the different species of bushes that distinguished one area from another. I asked her where we were. She said that we were on course, heading towards the wells at al-'Udeyd, and pointed to her evidence: *shuuf haadhiich il-chitir, hinuu* ("Look at those *chitir* bushes, over there"). When Naafi' came and went without telling her to change direction, she was doubly reassured.

Once we saw the camp of some other pastoralists about 300 yards to the west but we did not move in their direction. Those people belonged to the Hadendowa "tribe" (*gabiilat al-hadandowa*). We could tell who they were, even at a distance, from the shapes of their dwellings. They did not use goats' hair tents like we did; they lived in portable shelters made of palm-frond mats. The Hadendowa were the Rashaayda's traditional enemies. If we met one of them, we would not even greet him with *as-salaamu 'aleykum* (as Muslims should) but would pass by without speaking. The Rashaayda had been competing with the Hadendowa for pasture land and water for generations, and the old men could recall many armed clashes between Rashiidi camps and groups of Hadendowa. They were also *'ujmaan* (non-Arabic speakers), whereas we were Arabs and spoke good Arabic. So I was not surprised when we passed them by. They ignored us, just as we ignored them.

I wondered where 'Abdallah and Ḥaamid were now, and whether they had also seen the Hadendowa. As always when we migrated, I felt a little uncomfortable to have been left trailing behind the men. It was not that I did not want to talk to the women. I liked Suluum, especially, and she was becoming one of my best informants. But I could also see that the Rashaayda had a fairly sharp division of labor between the sexes, and that a man who did women's work or a woman who did man's work could be fiercely ridiculed. I was still not completely certain what the basis for the sexual division of labor was, and I was afraid of making mistakes that would make me look ridiculous. Was it proper for me to be riding with the women?

As I found out months later, I was partly right to be concerned and partly wrong. I was wrong, first of all, because as a guest in a Rashiidi household I was not supposed to work. Riding per se was not categorized as "work," and since I was not performing either men's work or women's work I was not violating the sexual division of labor. Second, the Rashaayda had much lower expectations of me than I did for myself. As 'Abdallah told me once, when I was stubbornly insisting on carrying out a task that adult men normally performed without a second thought, *laachin manta mithilnaa:* "But you're not like us." The task seemed simple: It was just a matter of walking some 800 feet from one camp to another on a moonless night. It was too dark to see any landmarks on the ground, and I could not see the tents that I wanted to visit, but I thought if I just proceeded in a straight line in the right direction I would reach them. I did not realize how easy it might be to lose my way, nor did I know that the Rashaayda themselves had learned to navigate by the stars at night, relying on their knowledge of the constellations and their changing positions in the night sky. 'Abdallah at first tried to steer me in the right direction but in the end sent a five-year-old boy with me as a guide. Although my pride was hurt, I had to admit he was right; no matter how hard I tried, I could not master every chore that the Rashaayda thought appropriate for my sex. Yet I was not wrong to assume that the division of our group into a team of men and a team of women during migration was significant. This division had as much to do with relations between the "tribes" of the region as it did with the relations between the sexes.

It was no accident that the men always rode ahead of the women and children, nor was it just a matter of the technical requirements of nomadic pastoralism. True, someone had to manage the herd, and the men on their faster camels were better equipped to do this than the women. But it was not just a question of livestock management; the men were also equipped for defending us. They all had swords, and one of them had a rifle, stashed in their saddlebags below their saddles. At the time I did not pay this much thought, since I was already accustomed to seeing men carrying swords while they rode. Almost every nomadic man in the area carried a sword, usually keeping it in a scabbard and slinging it over one shoulder on a strap. Later, however, when I had acquired more of the practical skills of everyday life, and when Suluum and Ḥaamid had begun to assign me more of the chores given to family members, I began to see some things through their eyes.

Once, about one year after my first migratory season with the Rashaayda, I went into Kassala with two neighbor women. They surprised me by lingering 15 and 20 yards behind me as we walked through the streets. I thought at first that I was walking too quickly and stopped to let them catch up, but one of them just waved me on with a languid upward flip of her hand. I walked ahead again, a little slower this time, thinking that they were just enjoying their shopping and wanted to stroll. They clearly did not want me to stroll with them, however, and this did not surprise me, since men and women did not usually walk in mixed groups. As we proceeded through the market it dawned on me that, for the Rashaayda, the crowded streets were much like the nearly empty desert. Both were potentially dangerous, since the enemies of the Rashaayda were present there and could in theory attack us. Of course the streets were less dangerous than the desert, since it was against the law for men to carry swords while they were in town, but the potential for violence was still there. It was my job to stay on the alert, watch for possible troublemakers, and confront (*yugaabil*) them if they bothered us.

The partial equivalence between the streets of a town and the open desert (*il-khalaa*) was brought home to me on another occasion, when I was taking photographs of three women and their children who had camped at the foot of a small, low hill. The women had put on their best clothes and were standing in a row, right next to their tent. I stood on the hill, looking down at them. I didn't like the camera angle. "Please," I said, "come closer so that I can see you better." They protested indignantly: *laa; maaḥnaa ṭaali'iin fi ish-shaari'* ("No; we're not going out into the *street!*"). Of course there was no street there. What they meant was that they would not permit me to photograph them standing in the open desert, in men's space, where women should not go unescorted. Men's space was where people could be attacked, where men from other "tribes" might try to rape or seduce our women, and where men from our "tribe" (*gabiilatnaa*) should be ready to confront (*yugaabil*) them.

I came across this association between men's social roles and open, unenclosed spaces many times. My friend Muḥammad ibin Mujalli reminded me of it once when I was with him in Kassala. Poor Muḥammad had contracted tuberculosis and had steadily lost weight. After trying a series of folk remedies that did him more harm than good, he finally decided to go to a doctor and asked me to accompany him. As we walked down the street to the clinic, Muḥammad reflected anxiously about his weakness. "Where has my manhood gone? (*weyn rujuulati?*)," he asked. I thought he was talking about his loss of weight, something which was clearly on his mind. But no, he said he was anxious about not having any *weapons* with him. He had no pistol, no sword, not even a herding stick with him, because he was too weak to carry these things around. "If someone attacked us in the street now, the only thing that I could use to defend myself would be my sandals!" "Your sandals?" I thought to myself, too surprised by the suggestion that sandals could be weapons to come up with a reply. Simply walking down the street had brought these thoughts to his mind.

I did not know any of these things during my first migratory season, of course. At the time I simply made a note of the division of our group into a team of men and a team of women and children. A few days later I would discover that this division was not just visible but was also verbal. After we reached our camp, we set up our tent and watched new groups of households arriving. I went out to photograph them and shot a picture of the women and children on camelback. When I returned to our tent, Suluum asked me whether I had photographed *aḍ-ḍu'uun* ("the migrating women and children"). She used a different term for a team of men traveling together on camelback; this she called a *zimaala* ("group of companions").

As I learned more about this distinction, I saw that it was motivated by both technical and social considerations. On the one hand, the men had to manage the milch camels and small stock while the women had to transport the household furnishings and shelters; these tasks were a necessary part of pastoral production. On the other hand, the entire household had to be able to back up its claim to pasture, water, and territory, if necessary by force of arms. In neo-Marxist terms, one could say that it was based on the Rashaayda's mode of production and their social relations of production. Yet the opposition between "men riding (*zimaala*)" and "women and children migrating (*ḍu'uun*)" had implications that went beyond the domains of production and inter-"tribal" hostilities. The men on camelback were described as *khafiif* ("lightweight, fast"), while the women were said to be *thagiil* ("heavy, slow"), and this secondary opposition was actually realized in movement. Women ordinarily did walk slowly and were not supposed to run, while men were always urged to be quick.

I had already seen the same opposition between fast and slow in Rashiidi weddings. On the first day of the wedding, when animals are slaughtered and butchered to provide meat for the guests, the men of the host's household compete with each other, each trying to finish butchering first. On the second day of the wedding the men race each other on camelback. But the bride is slow. At night, when she is led from the tent where she has been secluded to the groom's tent, she walks very slowly. As Pierre Bourdieu, an anthropologist who has studied peasant societies in northern Algeria, puts it: "Through the division between the sexes of labour that is inseparably technical and ritual, the structure of ritual practice and representations is articulated with the structure of production" (Bourdieu, 1990, p. 218). So, although the different paces adopted by men and women were partly grounded in the technology and social relations of pastoral production, they were also part of the Rashaayda's concepts of gender. And like gender identity everywhere, this was not just an expression of economic forces.

I could not possibly have known about these distinctions and oppositions (ahead/behind :: fast/slow :: *zimaala/ḍu'uun* :: men/women and children :: armed/unarmed) at this early stage in my fieldwork. They were implicit in the order which surrounded me and in which I unknowingly played a part, but neither I nor my companions could have made them explicit. I was simply ignorant of them, while Ḥaamid's family had no practical reason to pause in their work and analyze their actions and motives. All that they wanted to do was reach our dry season camp without incident.

We moved on. The air was now hot and dry and the sun was far above the horizon. We measured the passage of time by referring to the sun—more exactly, by glancing at our shadows on the ground below; they grew shorter as the sun rose. When I had gotten up early in the morning it had been during *al-ghubaysha* ("the little dawn"), when there was hardly enough light for us to see. The adults had prayed during *al-ghubsha* ("dawn"), and we had been sipping our morning tea at daybreak (*al-fajr*). Now it was well past *aḍ-ḍuḥaa* ("mid-morning"), and noon (*aḍ-ḍuhur*) was approaching. We wanted to reach the mid-way point between our old camp and our new camp by noon, so that we could dismount and nap (*nugayyil*) during the hottest hours of the day (*il-gayla*). 'Abdallah had not returned to us, however, so we were not sure where our temporary campsite would be nor how much farther ahead it was. The heat and the slow, monotonous gait of my mount were making me drowsy, and I was no longer following the conversation. Faḍiyya, always quiet at any event, was silent. Even 'Aabda, who liked to talk and did not have the taciturn habits of her mother- and sister-in-law, had little to say to Suluum. We scanned the horizon for signs of our herd and our scout.

It was noon before we saw a rider approaching. I hoped it was 'Abdallah, so that we could make camp for the day and rest, but as the rider came closer I could see that it was only Naafi', coming back to check on us again. 'Aabda called out to him in her high-pitched voice: *maa 'ayyantu ḥaṭab?* ("Haven't you spotted any firewood?"). Naafi' nodded, a thin-lipped, ironic smile on his face. "I saw a dead tree and dismounted to take a look. But when I touched it with my herding stick, it went like this—" (here he raised his hands, wiggling his fingers). "It was crawling with scorpions!" "May our fate and yours be safety! (*faalnaa wa faalk as-salaama*)," Suluum exclaimed. "I hope you weren't stung." "No," Naafi' said, he was all right. He turned his mount around so he could ride with us, side-by-side. We kept our eyes open for firewood and eventually came across a bunch of dead scrub that Suluum and 'Aabda could use for kindling. I knew this wasn't enough. Once they had started their fires, I thought, they would have to use goat dung to keep them burning. Fortunately dung was never in short supply. The spaces in front of our tents, where the goats were tethered, were always littered with small, dry turds, half undigested grass that burned well without odor or smoke. So we would have plenty of fuel.

I was getting hungry and remembered the piece of bread in my pocket. I took it out and tried it. It tasted good. Sorghum bread was coarser and heavier than the wheat bread that I ate in Kassala but it was still fresh and moist. The only flaws were the tiny fragments of charcoal that had stuck to the dough while it was baking. I could hear them crunch while I chewed. Apparently Suluum had already eaten her bread; I hadn't noticed. Whenever she ate in the company of men, she would loosen the lower part of her mask and slip small handfuls of food into her mouth underneath it, taking care not to expose her mouth and face. She did this so discreetly that it was no surprise that I had not seen her eat. 'Aabda's little girl, 'Uweybda, had also eaten earlier, sitting by her mother on the rocking platform formed by her father's bed. 'Aabda's other child, a six-month-old boy, was too young to eat solid food. 'Aabda would nurse him when he cried, covering him entirely under her clothing to give him the breast.

Finally 'Abdallah showed up. He was tired and sweaty but still in a good mood. He had crossed a lot of ground looking for pasture, and once he had found some he had gone back to the herd to tell Ḥaamid and the boys where to go. Then he had come looking for us. It took us half an hour to follow him to our temporary campsite. The pasture there was thin, hardly more than a few large patches of grass and leafy vegetation. The milch camels were already there, grazing, when we reached it, and so were Ḥaamid and 'Abd al-Ḥamiid. I could see that they were both exhausted but did not know exactly what they had been doing that was so tiring. I had never herded camels with them because Ḥaamid doubted that I could keep up and had not asked me to join them. At any rate, they were both ready for a nap. Ḥamiid, who was still on his way with the small stock, would also be tired.

We couched our camels, saying *ikhkh* in a loud voice so they would kneel and then sit. I unhooked my right leg from the saddle pommel and turned my legs around to the left so that I could slide off the saddle onto the ground. I kept the reins in my hand, however, to make sure that Friday would not stray before we took off my saddle. My legs were stiff from the five-hour ride and it seemed momentarily odd to be walking on solid ground again.

Our first task was to unload the baggage. I was not sure what to unload first and looked around to see what the others were doing. No one seemed to be in charge. Suluum and Faḍiyya were taking the bed off the back of Suluum's camel, and 'Abdallah and Ḥaamid were busy unloading Faḍiyya's baggage. So like everyone else I just did what I thought appropriate. I unbuckled the cinch of my saddle and tried to pull the cinch out from under Friday, but his huge rib cage was squarely on top of it. 'Abd al-Ḥamiid saw me struggling with it and came over to help. He somehow persuaded Friday to shift his weight and I managed to free the cinch. Then we took the saddle and saddle pad off his back, took off his harness and reins, and let him go. He went off to graze.

Ḥaamid was walking around, inspecting the animals' backs for sores. He spotted a wound on Suluum's mount and got out a tin of homemade medicine, *guṭraan,* from his saddle bag. He dressed the wound with a small amount of this black, tarry salve, which he had made himself by cooking down the bitter fruit of the *ḥanḍal* plant. Ḥaamid was an expert veterinarian. He could diagnose the various illnesses that afflicted camels by inspecting their urine and feces. Whenever a camel died Ḥaamid would carry out a simple autopsy, examining its intestines, kidneys, lungs, and liver for signs of parasites. No one knew more about these things than Ḥaamid. He seemed satisfied that the camels were all healthy, and we relaxed.

Once the camels had been taken care of we started thinking about our own comforts. Suluum and Faḍiyya brought two of the beds close to each other and set them up on one end. Then they threw a canvas tent-liner over them, forming a small, low shelter. ʿAabda did the same, using the remaining bed and a pile of baggage to build a framework for a second temporary shelter. They spread quilts on the ground underneath them and we all stretched out to take a nap. I slept in the larger shelter, with the men, while the women and children slept in the second shelter.

It had taken us five hours to cover a distance of about sixteen miles. We were about five miles southwest of the wells at al-ʿUdeyd, about twenty miles west of the Gash River, some twenty-five miles north of the wells at Khor Marmadeyb, and twenty-five miles east of the ʿAṭbara River (cf. maps pp. 30–32). We had been getting our water from some rain-filled pits that had been dug out by a road construction crew near Malawiyya, about twenty miles to the south. These pits had filled up with water at the beginning of the rainy season. Months had passed since then, however, and the water was now so foul that the camels refused to drink it. We had enough water in our water skins to last us for two days, but the goats and sheep would need to drink by tomorrow evening at the latest. If there had been rainfall, we could have found pools of rainwater for the animals, but these would not appear for at least another six months. So we would have to move onwards the very next day.

We slept for about two hours. When I woke I saw ʿAbdallah getting ready to pray the noon prayer. We did not have enough water with us for making ablutions each time we prayed, so instead we would *nityammam,* "resort to the clean earth" (Qur'an, suurat al-maa'ida [the chapter entitled "The Table"], verse 6), that is, cleanse ourselves symbolically. This was what he was doing. He took off his sandals and crouched near a bare patch of ground. Then he stretched out his hands and hit the ground once with his palms so that a little sand would adhere to them. After tapping his hands together to rid them of any excess sand, he rubbed his right hand and forearm with his left hand and his left hand and forearm with his right; then he passed his hands lightly over his face and head. The sand, not water, was understood as the purifying agent. Now that he was ritually clean (*mitwaḍḍi*) he was ready to pray. He would repeat this cleansing for the afternoon (*ʿaṣr*), sunset (*maghrib*), and evening (*ʿishaa*) prayers, and would not wash with water again until the following morning, to conserve water.

I was thirsty and went to get a drink from one of the water skins. I could see it hanging from a wooden tripod near the women's shelter that Suluum had set up. It was the small kind, called a *ǧirba,* and was made of a tanned goat skin. Suluum had another, larger one (a *rayy*) made of a sheep skin, but it was empty; it would have been too heavy to take with us during migration if we had filled it. I tried to untie the *ǧirba*'s neck carefully and pour myself a cupful of water, but before I had opened it Suluum was there to do it for me. She was afraid that I would not close it again properly and would allow our water to dribble away. The water was colored a purplish-brown by the tanning agents that Suluum had used when making the *ǧirba.* It also had an acid taste, but it was cool. This was due to the *ğirba;* the water slowly percolated through the skin and evaporated, cooling what was left inside.

I asked where Faḍiyya was and Suluum told me she had gone to look for firewood. "What for?" I asked. We had already collected kindling along the way, and I thought that she would use dung for cooking, as usual. She smiled behind her mask and explained, *'andanaa dhabiiḥa* ("We have an animal to be slaughtered, cooked, and eaten").

I was very surprised. "But we have no guest (*bass maa 'andanaa ḍeyf*)," I said, puzzled.

I had never seen any Rashaayda slaughter an animal unless they needed to provide meat for a guest. When an important guest arrived it was obligatory to slaughter for him (or her), and even families that had no extra animals would buy a goat from neighbors so that they could honor their guests. The nearest neighbors all had to be invited. As I learned later, a host who did not invite neighbors to share the meal with a guest was despised and almost feared. Such a host was said to be *ḥaasid,* "envious." He envied the good fortune of others and wanted to keep all of his wealth for himself. His envy might even be strong enough to harm others magically. He might have a "red eye" (*'eyn ḥamraa*) which could strike (*yaz'ar*) the people whom he envied and harm them. These beliefs were powerful sanctions against stinginess; anyone who wanted to be a member of Rashiidi society had to be generous when he slaughtered.

All of this meant that slaughtering an animal when there was no guest present made little sense. It would create no relationship of obligation between host and guest and would not add much to the diet of the host's household. Only a small amount of meat would be divided among ten to fifteen people; the hosts would get no more meat than the neighbors. The best strategy was to keep as many small livestock alive as possible, holding a few in reserve for hospitality and milking the rest.

Suluum could see my surprise and was amused. She admitted that, this time, we were not trying to demonstrate our generosity (*karam*); all we wanted to do was get a taste of meat. "Everybody does it during migration," she said, a little embarrassed. "But don't tell anyone." Still a little shocked, I walked back to the men's shelter, where I saw Naafi' sitting up and sharpening his knife on a smooth stone. "We're going to eat meat! (*naba nitlaḥḥam*)," he exclaimed.

Ḥaamid had already picked out a goat and was leading it toward us, pulling it by one ear. Before killing the goat he gave it a drink of water and made sure that the knife was razor-sharp; it was *ḥaraam* (forbidden by Islam) to make the animal suffer unnecessarily. Then he threw it on one side, facing it towards Mecca, and cut its throat in one swift, firm stroke, saying *bism illaah, allaahu akbar* ("In the name of God; God surpasses [the world of natural forces and human understanding]") as he did so. Its blood gushed out onto the sand and it kicked and thrashed in its death throes. We watched it die without touching it; it was *ḥaraam* to try to hasten the process in any way.

Once it was still Ḥaamid picked it up by its back legs and held it head down, letting all the blood drain out. Then he carried it over to another tripod that 'Aabda had set up. While Naafi' held the carcass for him, Ḥaamid carefully undercut the skin on one back leg, making an opening. Then he pursed his lips and blew through this opening, hard, to inflate the skin and separate it from the flesh and fat underneath it.

Suluum and Faḍiyya would make the skin into a *ğirba* later by removing the hair and tanning it with a solution containing acacia bark. For the time being, however, the men's task was to take the skin off the carcass without puncturing it in too many places. Then they could proceed with the butchering.

Ḥaamid broke one of the hind legs and located a thick tendon that had been exposed. He opened up a space with his thumbs between the bone and the tendon, making them into a natural "hanger" that he could hook around the top part of 'Aabda's tripod. Once the carcass was suspended from this, he could remove the guts and cut up the meat. Ḥaamid and 'Abdallah systematically detached the limbs and ribs from the carcass, handing them to Naafi' and 'Abd al-Ḥamiid. They in turn cut the meat into smaller pieces. While they were doing this Suluum started a fire (even she had to use matches this time) and Faḍiyya rolled up the goatskin and packed it away. She and Suluum would tan it later. 'Aabda poured water and a little salt into a cooking pot and put it on the fire. After the water had begun to boil Naafi' tossed the meat into the pot. We all sat in the shade near the larger shelter and waited for it to cook.

We had nothing to do in the meantime, so 'Aabda decided to entertain us by telling us our fortunes. Fortune-telling was a woman's specialty and 'Aabda enjoyed it. She took out a little cloth bag that contained some small white shells, old buttons of various colors, and chunks of white and green glass that she had found somewhere. She dumped them out and picked them up again with both hands, shaking them to rearrange them. Then she let them fall, one by one, onto the ground in front of her, so that she could read them. Each piece stood for something—or, indeed, could stand for any number of things. 'Aabda declared that this time the green glass represented a letter, that one of the white shells represented an older woman and that a small red button was a child. She read Suluum's fortune: "You're going to get a letter from Umbaarak. See the shell and the green glass? They're touching, and they are both close to the red button; that's Umbaarak."

Umbaarak was Naafi''s fraternal twin brother. He was not with us today because he was working in Saudi Arabia. Suluum was worried about him, of course, since he had never been away from home before. Umbaarak was not the first of Suluum's children to look for work there. 'Abdallah had gone to Saudi Arabia two years earlier and had stayed there for a year. He had found it hard to live in unfamiliar surroundings among strangers but was glad that he had gone; he had earned enough money to buy extra livestock when he returned. Now Umbaarak had followed in his footsteps. Another of Suluum's sons, Muḥammad, was also absent, but he was not nearly so far away. He was living at a public boarding school in Khashm al-Girba, where he was enrolled in the sixth grade. 'Aabda searched for some sign of Muḥammad in the pattern before her but nothing attracted her attention.

Next it was my turn. 'Aabda picked up the "magical" objects, shook them again, and let them fall. "Your mother is going to visit your brother. Here they are; they're touching. Does your brother have children? Here is his son. They're going to answer your letters." 'Aabda had often seen me taking notes. I had tried to explain to her what I was doing but she had not been able to understand. Like Suluum and Ḥaamid, she was illiterate. For her, "reading" meant reciting the Qur'an, which was the only book that she had heard of, and "writing" meant either writing verses of the Qur'an for use as medicinal charms or writing letters. So she thought that my family certainly owed me a reply, considering the large number of "letters" which I apparently had written them.

In the meantime Suluum kept her eye on the cooking pot, checking every now and then to see whether the meat was ready. "It's done," she finally declared, and transferred a good many handfuls of meat to one of her large, enameled tin bowls. She took it over to the other shelter, where the women and children would eat, and left the rest of the meat for us in the cooking pot. We gathered around it eagerly. Naafi' grabbed a large piece, without standing on ceremony, and 'Abdallah laughed sarcastically and tried to take it away from him. They traded insults, using words that had not yet become part of my vocabulary—but I got the basic idea! Ḥaamid sat watching them, smiling, too busy with his own piece of meat to comment.

The entire scene, with its "greedy" snatching of food and complete lack of decorum, was the reverse of the very formal performance that took place whenever we served meat to guests. Formal hospitality was ritualized. There were special formulae that both guest and host had to recite at the appropriate moments, the servings of tea, coffee, meat, and rice had to be offered according to a strict sequence, and the guests and other people invited felt constrained not to eat very much. Tonight, by contrast, we were all by ourselves; no neighbors, no guests, no wider society. We were relaxed, but even in our relaxation we reproduced, by reversing them, the formal patterns of behavior that the Rashaayda strove to perfect in other contexts.

By the time we had finished eating it was late afternoon. I wanted to write up my notes for the day; I had brought notebooks and pens with me for that purpose. First, however, I had to clean the grease from our meal off my hands. This was not an easy task without soap or water. I began by wiping some of the grease on the soles of my feet. We often did this after eating meat. Since we went barefoot often and only wore sandals otherwise, the skin on our soles tended to dry and crack. Cracks could develop into painful wounds, and to prevent this we often greased our soles.

Although this step improved the condition of my feet it did not completely clean my hands. I tried rubbing them together but this did not get me very far. What to do? I considered using the tent cloth that lay in piles around us as a towel but knew that this would not make Suluum very happy. She had woven the tent cloth herself and wanted it to look clean for as long as possible; its appearance affected her reputation. I sat there, perplexed, and could feel 'Aabda looking at me impatiently. "Wipe your hands on your clothes," she said. This had never occurred to me. "But they'll get dirty," I protested. "Well, you can wash them, can't you? We'll have water at the next camp." And so I did. Like all other men, I learned to wash the clothes that I wore (and got dirty) by myself, without relying on a wife or a sister to do it for me. Among the Rashaayda, those who care about their appearance have to expend the effort to enhance it; men wash their own clothes.

I sat for an hour working on my notes. I tried not to do this often, because I knew that the others thought it was odd and unsociable for me to withdraw from contact with them. Why should I prefer to sit and write when I could talk to human beings instead? On the other hand, they realized that I still could not follow their conversation very well, and perhaps this excused my rude behavior to some extent. Most of the notes that I took at that stage consisted of vocabulary items and fragments of half-understood phrases. After an hour, however, 'Abdallah called me back to the hearth, where Suluum was making coffee.

I know that we spent the remainder of the afternoon talking, but I can no longer remember what we talked about. The sun gradually sank in the west, casting long shadows on the ground and reminding us that the time for the sunset prayer was approaching. It seemed a little odd to be sitting out of doors at nightfall; I was accustomed to the shelter of the Rashaayda's tents. There was no reason for Suluum to set up her tent now, however. We did not expect it to rain, and we would be moving again tomorrow, anyway; so why go to all that trouble? The women could rest, for once, while the men and boys went out to collect the livestock and bring them back to our campsite. Ḥamiid brought in the goats and tethered them, while 'Abd al-Ḥamiid brought in the sheep and Naafi', Ḥaamid, and 'Abdallah brought in the camels.

As usual, they separated the male camels from the females so that none of the males would attempt to mate during the night. This was necessary to regulate breeding. We did not want all of the females to be pregnant at the same time, because then they would all drop their calves and start lactating at the same time. It was better for us to have some females dry while others were in milk, so that we would have a plentiful supply of milk for as long as the rainy season lasted. Ḥaamid and 'Abdallah brought the bulls to the "sleeping area" (*imraaḥ*) in front of our camp and hobbled them. After each bull had kneeled and sat, 'Abdallah slipped a loop of thick rope, an *'agaal,* over the knee of its front leg, working the rope past the knee joint towards the body until the lower leg was tied to the thigh. If the camel got up again, it would have to stand on three legs and could not run away. Ḥaamid and Naafi' did the same with the females, which were couched behind our campsite. (Note that, like human males and females during migration, the male camels were "in front" and the females "behind." The Rashaayda never pointed out this parallel to me, and I did not notice it until after I had left the field. So I cannot be sure that they deliberately treated male and female camels like male and female human beings.)

Ḥaamid always worried that one of the camels might take fright for some reason while grazing and start to run. A camel could run for miles and would soon be out of sight if it bolted. That was one reason why he branded them. If a stranger saw a stray camel with his brand on it, he would know at once that the camel belonged to a Rashiidi, since Ḥaamid's distinctive brand was different from the brands of all the other "tribesmen" in the region. Strangers from friendly "tribes"—such as the Arab Laḥaawiin or the *'ijimi* (non-Arabic speaking) Bani 'Aamir "tribe"—would catch hold of lost camels and try to return them to us.

Once night fell it was too dark to see. We could not burn up our firewood just to provide light and had no electricity or even kerosene lanterns. It was just as well. If we wanted to get up before dawn tomorrow, we would have to go to sleep early tonight. So we did. I lay down on a quilt and covered myself from head to toe with my unrolled turban; this would provide some protection from the mosquitoes. As I dropped off to sleep, I could hear the camels grumbling and shifting their weight as they settled down for the night. I wondered what our dry-season camp would be like, and who I would meet there.

DAY TWO: BUILDING A NEW CAMP

When I woke up the next morning it was already daylight; Suluum had let me sleep in. I got up and joined the others around the hearth. While I drank my tea I watched her cook griddle-cakes. She could not bake bread today because she had not ground any sorghum yesterday. Instead, she was making a batter with some machine-milled wheat flour that ‘Abdallah had brought from Kassala. She had a small iron griddle that she used for this when we were migrating. After mixing the batter, she greased the griddle, poured some batter on it, and watched it cook (cf. p. 7).

As usual, we were in a hurry to get moving, so Suluum did not waste much time on breakfast. After cooking a few cakes she broke them into large pieces and handed me one. *Fichch ar-riiǧ,* she said. How can I translate this? Literally it meant "do something to release the saliva," but I had learned to understand it differently: "This is not a full breakfast, but at least put something in your stomach; wet your whistle." I never heard anyone in Sudan other than the Rashaayda say this, and for me it has become a token of Rashiidi Arabic, exemplifying in two words many of the distinctive features of their dialect. But I did not pause to mull over this at the time. I ate the cake quickly and went back to my bed; I still had to repack my clothes and notebooks.

We set off today as we had yesterday but this time ‘Abdallah did not go off in search of pasture. We knew where we would be camping and did not need his guidance. Instead, he rode off in the direction of a small grocery store on the edge of the savanna that was owned by a Bani ‘Aamir man whom he knew. This merchant was keeping extra pieces of tent cloth for us. ‘Abdallah had brought him this tent cloth last June, at the beginning of the rainy season, when the family had been preparing to move south to meet the early summer rains. ‘Abdallah was a regular customer. He bought matches, cigarettes, soap, cloth, salt, coffee, and sesame oil at the merchant's little store, which was hardly more than a shack built of reeds.

‘Abdallah and Ḥaamid had not needed the extra cloth during October and November, when they were living in lightweight (but cramped) rainy-season tents (sing. *ḥajiira*), but now that we were relocating to a dry-season camp we wanted to expand the tents. Each one would be converted into a more spacious *baṭiiḥa* ("dry-season tent"). We also had stored some of our grain at his store, after we had harvested it last October, and now we needed it. ‘Abdallah would pick up the grain and the extra tent cloth and would meet us at the camp later.

We moved steadily northwards, keeping an eye out for firewood, as we had the day before. So far there was nothing to distinguish this day from the previous one. The landscape here looked a little more barren, but that was all. For me the only significant acts were those that repeated yesterday's activities: the division of the families into a team of men and a team of women and children, each using different types of saddles and each having its own responsibilities. This repetition confirmed my observations of the previous days, giving me confidence that I had recorded a culturally (as well as technically and economically) significant pattern.

I got another lesson about the sexual division of labor when we arrived at our dry-season camp, about three hours later. I caught my first glimpse of the camp when we were still about 500 yards away; it consisted of about 20 tents grouped in five clusters, each cluster at least 75 yards from the others. As we approached we could see ‘Abdallah riding toward us on his white *bishaari* camel, which Suluum recognized immediately. He had the extra tent cloth with him, wound in a loose roll around his saddle and secured with rope. Ḥaamid and the boys had taken the herd to water in the center of the camp and would join us later. In the meantime the women had to put up their tents.

After my camel was couched I offered to help them, but they waved me away. “Go say hello to Aḥmad in Mujalli’s camping cluster, over there,” Suluum said. “They’ll give you coffee.” In fact, there was nothing else for me to do, because as a man I should not concern myself with their work. None of the men in the family, for example, would ever help Suluum take her tent down or put it up; they would not even touch the tent cloth unless it was rolled up, tied, and ready to be loaded on a camel’s back. It was *‘eyb* (“shameful”) for a man to have anything to do with tent cloth. Whenever a man came into the tent he would always sit down some distance away from the household loom, where Suluum wove the cloth.

The women, on the other hand, would never carve any of the wooden poles or tent stakes that were needed for the tent; carving was a man’s work (*ṣin‘at ar-rijjaal*). I thought at first that it was the material, wood, which was associated with men, but this guess was mistaken. Women were often in contact with wood. They went out collecting firewood frequently, stacking it in piles when they found some and bringing it back to camp balanced on their heads. I had seen Faḍiyya return with a heavy load many times. She would throw it crashing to the ground and then break it into pieces with an axe. But she never carved it. Once, when Suluum needed some new wooden skewers (*akhilla*) for the tent, so that she could pin the tops of two pieces of tent cloth together, she asked Ḥaamid to carve them for her. These were hardly more than large splinters, and she could easily have carved them herself. But this was not her job.

I was pleased that today’s new data fit my earlier observations; a pattern was beginning to emerge! I walked over to Aḥmad’s tent. He was not there but Ṣaaliḥ, his brother-in-law (his wife’s sister’s husband), was camped close to him. Ṣaaliḥ greeted me and ushered me into his tent. As Suluum had predicted, he did offer me coffee.

He asked me how the migration had gone and I gave him my impressions of it. As we talked Naafi‘ arrived. I asked him where he had left the herd and he pointed toward the horizon. But then I saw something unexpected: a line of low mounds, stretching from east to west. “What’s that?” I asked Naafi‘. “It’s the pipe,” he replied, “didn’t you know about it? We’ll be drinking from it.” I could not see any pipe but Naafi‘ explained that most of it was buried under the heaps of dirt that I was looking at.

It turned out that an Italian road construction company—one of three foreign firms that had a contract with the Sudanese government to build a road from Khartoum to the Red Sea—had laid a pipe from the Nile River to their central construction site north of Kassala. They needed a reliable supply of water and were pumping it from the Nile daily. I had already heard about the construction company—and had seen the pits that they had dug, near our earlier camp—but still did not understand how we could use their water. Naafi‘ explained.

"When the foreigners (*al-khawaajaat,* approximately: "Western Christians") laid this pipe through Rashiidi territory (*diirat ar-Rashaayda*), we guessed that there was water in it. We could hear the water running through it when they turned on their pump. Last year the animals (*al-ḥalaal,* literally, "the good things made lawful by God for human beings") needed water, so we broke open the pipe." "*You* broke open the pipe?" I interrupted. "No, not our family (*'arabnaa*), other Rashaayda," he replied. "So much water spilled out that it flooded the place. Good, clean water. People from all over brought their animals there to drink." He smiled at the memory. "The foreigners came to repair it, but this didn't last; after that everyone was breaking it open. The foreigners were furious, and they said they would send the police, that they would put guards on the pipe, and that they would put everyone in prison. But how could they? Instead, they stopped pumping the water and refused to work on the road. We wanted the water, and they wanted us to stop breaking the pipe, so the company and the Rashaayda came to an agreement."

"The people from the company visited *al-'umda* ("the tribal leader") Naafi' Barakaat, and he slaughtered sheep for them and hosted them generously (*akramhuu*). Then they agreed to open up three faucets for the nomads (*il-'arab*) along the length of the pipeline. They paid a salary for each guard, gave him a key, and told him when he should open the faucet and for how long. So now we can drink from the faucet and use the water for our animals."

At first this story struck me as so outrageous that I laughed; what vandalism! "But the pipe doesn't belong to the Rashaayda," I remonstrated. "It's in our territory, isn't it?" Naafi' replied. "Why should they have water when we are thirsty (*ḍamyaaniin*)?" Later I decided that the Rashaayda's efforts at self-help were not exactly criminal. After all, the road construction project was designed to develop the national economy. Although the Rashaayda did not at that time consider themselves Sudanese, they were Sudanese citizens and had a right to be included in any development project that affected the area where they lived. The government administrators, of course, expected that the road would benefit the people in the area in the long run and were angry that the Rashaayda had interrupted the work. The Rashaayda, however, were not prepared to wait for long-term benefits when immediate benefits were within their reach. Why should they cooperate when they were not consulted about the road and were not included in development planning? This collision between the government and the Rashaayda had made both sides regard each other in a new light. Perhaps it would lead to better coordination in the future. Although the government had to bear the cost of extra fuel for pumping water to the Rashaayda, they also had given the Rashaayda a stake in the development project and would not have to worry about any more damage to the pipe.

Naafi''s story brought out two other points. The first was that the pastoralism practiced by the Rashaayda was not a moribund, inflexible, "traditional way of life." It was an adaptation to a particular geographical and social environment that could instantly be adjusted to any change in that environment. I had already seen how the Rashaayda had quickly taken advantage of the pits that had been dug to the south by the construction company, and now I was going to see how they had integrated the new pipeline into their pattern of pastoral migration. I knew that some Rashaayda (among them Suluum's daughter) had modified their pastoral adaptation when the government agricultural scheme in Khashm al-Girba had been opened, and I suspected that they would continue to fine tune it as other innovations were introduced into the region. As long as pastoralism provided them with economic security, and did not lead the Rashaayda into serious conflicts with the government (or with the other nomads who were competing with the Rashaayda for pastures and water), they would continue to practice it. It was a rational choice, not a mode of life unthinkingly clung to by a people in the thrall of a dead tradition.

The second point was that the Rashaayda did not say they were a "tribe" solely because they wanted to identify themselves as such. Outsiders (especially the Sudanese government) also viewed them as a "tribe" and dealt with them through their "tribal leaders." They found it more convenient to negotiate with one or two "tribal leaders" than to meet with all of the Rashiidi families who were constantly moving through the region. So the "Rashaayda tribe," and even the local concepts of "tribe," were at least partly the products of the political and economic relations in Sudan, both among local groups and between local groups and the central government in Khartoum.

As I discovered during my conversation with Naafi', the same thing could be said about the Rashaayda's "tribal territory" (*diira*). I told him how surprised I was to find our camp near a faucet rather than a well. Where had the family camped during the dry season before the pipeline was laid? "We used to go to al-'Udeyd and Marmadeyb for water," he explained. "But we don't own the wells there; the *'ujmaan* (non-Arabic speakers) own them. We had to pay them three piastres for every jerry can of water. It's much better to use the faucet." Although he was too proud to admit it, none of the wells in the area were owned by Rashaayda. All had been claimed by other non-Arab "tribes" long before the Rashaayda had arrived in the area.

In fact, even the notion that the Rashaayda had their own territory was subject to interpretation. Some non-Rashaayda in Kassala told me later that the Rashaayda lived in areas that no one else wanted to exploit, because the other "tribes" raised cattle which could not survive in the arid interior savannas. These other nomads had to control and maintain wells because their cattle needed to drink almost every day. The Rashaayda, they said, had only managed to carve out a niche for themselves by specializing in camel breeding. But, according to the people of Kassala, the Rashaayda did not have a "territory" since they did not own any wells.

Obviously the question of whether the Rashaayda were a "tribe" with a "tribal territory" and "tribal leaders" was a complex one. Ḥaamid's family gave me their answer, while other people in the region gave me other answers. To clarify my thinking about the matter, I set about collecting more information about the Rashaayda's history and role in the regional division of labor. I will present the results of this research in Chapter Two, which discusses pastoral production and territory, and in Chapter Four, where I describe the Rashaayda history.

2 / Pastoralism and the Social Organization of the Rashaayda

This chapter describes the pastoralist economy of the Rashaayda. Unlike the previous chapter, it is written in the present tense. This is partly because much of the information it includes is just as valid today as it was when I carried out my fieldwork, from January 1978 to December 1980. Not all of the information given here is current, however. The Rashaayda have changed since I last saw them, responding to the economic and political developments that have affected both Sudan and the neighboring countries of Egypt, Eritrea, and Ethiopia. Rather than trying to bring everything up to date (a hopeless task, since like all societies the Rashaayda "tribe" is constantly changing), I have adopted the anthropologist's "ethnographic present." The reader should keep in mind that my portrayal of the Rashaayda here is like a snapshot, freezing them in time and place. Although this is highly artificial, it does allow us to see them more clearly than if we try to follow them in motion, from one year to the next.

I will begin by explaining how the Rashaayda distinguish themselves (and are distinguished by others) from their neighbors. I have addressed this issue first for purely tactical reasons. I could not answer any general questions about the Rashaayda (e.g., "How many of them are there?" "Where do they live?") without explaining how I know that any particular individual is a Rashiidi. Next I will point out the places where they live, indicating whether or not they have a "tribal territory." Then I will describe how the Rashaayda exploit these places, combining subsistence pastoralism, subsistence agriculture, commerce, and wage labor in their effort to earn a living. Finally, I will show how pastoral production tends to affect their social organization in two ways. On the one hand, the instability of pastoral production mitigates against extreme or enduring economic differentials among households. On the other hand, because pastoral production makes it necessary for the Rashaayda to live in dry-season camps, it requires them to adopt a particular kind of normative ranking for men. My argument is that these consequences of pastoral production permeate Rashiidi social life in various unpredictable ways.

HOW DO OUTSIDERS IDENTIFY THE RASHAAYDA?

One way to answer this question would be to draw up a list of essential criteria for being a Rashiidi. For example, we could say that a Rashiidi must speak a particular dialect of Arabic, must wear a particular set of clothes, must cook a particular kind of food, and so on. The problem with this approach is that it leaves no room for the individual to choose and reconstruct his identity. In fact, people may learn new dialects, change their clothing styles, discover new types of food, and yet insist that they still have the same identity. Do we take them at their word in such cases? What if they have some, but not all, of the traits we have singled out; how are we to categorize them? Furthermore, people may have multiple identities, stressing one identity in certain contexts and other identities in other contexts.

Rather than adopt a "trait-list" approach, I will just point out two markers of socio-cultural identity which in most contexts distinguish most Rashaayda from their neighbors: their clothing and their dialect of Arabic. These markers are "traditional," in the sense that they have been transmitted from parent to child in the course of daily life, but are also "up-to-date" since they are not regarded as old-fashioned or outmoded. The Rashaayda do not reproduce these cultural markers unthinkingly, without periodically asking whether they are still worth preserving. Quite the opposite; they deliberately hold on to them in order to perpetuate the distinction between "Rashaayda" and "non-Rashaayda." Such cultural markers are not so much essential elements of identity as they are contrastive. They could not be used as flags of cultural identity in other social environments. When Rashaayda go to Saudi Arabia, for example, their clothing and dialect do not set them apart from Saudi citizens with nearly the same clarity as they distinguish them from other Sudanese.

Distinctive costume: Turbans and veils. The Rashaayda's most visible signs of cultural identity are their clothes—in particular, the men's turban (*'imaama*) and the married women's mask (*ǧinaa'*). Wearing a turban is not by itself distinctive, since most men in the northern, Arabic-speaking part of Sudan wear turbans, especially on formal occasions. Rashiidi turbans, however, are much longer than those of other men in Sudan; mine was three meters long, which was not exceptional. Photographs of Rashiidi men from the 1920s prove that this style is of long standing. In recent years most Rashaayda have added to the distinctiveness of their turbans by wrapping them around colored felt caps that they import from Saudi Arabia. Other men in Sudan do not use these caps. Finally, I should point out that in northeastern Sudan (but not elsewhere) the turban is viewed as an "Arab" style that contrasts with the Hadendowa's tradition. Hadendowa men oil their hair and comb it straight up, using long-toothed combs. So the large turban distinguishes Rashiidi men at two levels of contrast: (1) Arab/Hadendowa and (2) Sudanese Arabs/Rashiidi Arabs.

The married woman's mask, which I mentioned at the beginning of Chapter One, consists of a tube of black cloth which is flared at the lower end, to cover the shoulders, chest, and back, and is narrowed at the upper end, to fit snugly around the face. The lower opening is so much larger than the upper opening that the garment resembles a hollow cone with the top end cut off. After slipping this conical tube over her head, the woman who wears it lays the posterior edge of its uppermost opening over the crown of her head. Then she pulls the opposite edge of this opening down across her face until it is almost taut against her chin. Some of the loose cloth below her chin can be pulled through the opening, resulting in a semicircle of cloth being stretched tightly across her nose and mouth (see p. 7, 46). Once put in place, the mask is so tight that the wearer cannot open her mouth widely. Almost all Rashiidi women wear both plain and decorated versions of this mask. The decorated version is covered with hundreds of tiny lead beads that frame the wearer's face. To my knowledge, this garment is unique to the Rashaayda; no other Arab women wear it, neither in Sudan nor in other Arab countries.

Arabic language: Distinctive features of the Arabic dialect of the Rashaayda; dialect variation within the Rashaayda "tribe." The Rashaayda speak a dialect of Arabic that has many features in common with the Arabic spoken in northwest Arabia (cf. Ingham, 1982; Johnstone, 1967). Two such features contrast very conspicuously with Sudanese dialects. One is the affrication of the consonants /k/ and /g/ in the presence of high, front vowels (that is, /i/, /ii/, and /ey/) so that they are pronounced as /ch/ and /ǧ/. Thus, the Sudanese Arabic greeting *keyf ḥaalik* ("How are you?" [female singular pronoun]) becomes, in Rashiidi Arabic, *cheyf ḥaalich.* The second distinctive feature is syntactic. When the Rashaayda use the masculine plural form of a verb in the imperfect mood, for instance, they add the suffix *-uun,* whereas in Sudanese Arabic dialects this suffix is *-uu.* Compare, for example, Rashiidi Arabic *wish tuguuluun?* ("What are you [masc. pl.] saying?") with Sudanese Arabic *taguuluu shinuu?* A final distinctive feature (or rather, set of features) is lexical; many of the terms used by Rashaayda for household furnishings and pastoralist activities are not found in other varieties of Arabic. I will not attempt to list them here. However, in the pages which follow (and, indeed, in every chapter of this book), I have inserted distinctive lexical items in italics, next to their English translations and glosses. Taken as a whole, they serve to distinguish Rashiidi Arabic from other Arabic dialects.

Now that I have identified two cultural markers (costume and language) that distinguish Rashaayda from non-Rashaayda, I can describe them as a set of people who, by and large, have these markers in common. In other words, I can describe them as a population.

WHERE DO THE RASHAAYDA LIVE? AREAS IN SUDAN AND ERITREA INHABITED BY THE RASHAAYDA ARABS

A small number of completely sedentary Rashaayda live in fixed houses in al-Mugrin, a town between the cities of al-Daamir and 'Aṭbara, and al-Tukna, south of al-Daamir. Both of these towns are near the confluence of the 'Aṭbara and Nile rivers (see Figure 1). A great many fully nomadic Rashaayda live southeast of al-Tukna, camping in tents along the banks of the 'Aṭbara River. These Rashaayda keep close to the river during the dry season but move inland with their camel herds, away from the river, during the rainy season. They plant grain in well-watered areas such as aṣ-Ṣafiyya, Umm Shudeyda, and Khoor as-Sudeyra and make use of inland pastures for as long as they can, only returning to the banks of the 'Aṭbara during the driest months of the year (cf. al-'Ariifi, n.d., p. 60).

Still other Rashaayda, partly sedentary and partly nomadic, live in the Khashm al-Girba agricultural scheme, near a dam which was constructed in the 1960s at the head of the 'Aṭbara. These families still consider themselves nomadic pastoralists; other Rashaayda call them *il-'arab illi ḥaṭṭoo fi il-ḥawwaashaat* ("the people who have camped in the tenancies"). They work in the scheme as tenants for most of the

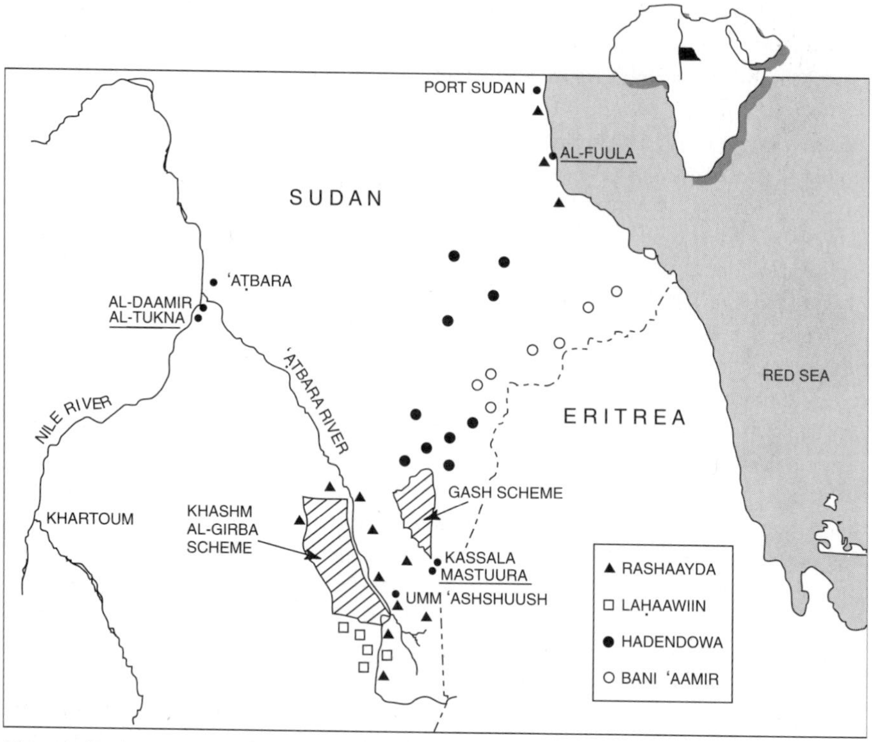

Figure 1 Territories and Villages Inhabited by the Rashaayda Bedouin of Eastern Sudan (Note: The place names which are underlined identify villages built by sedentary Rashiidi families in the 1970s.)

year, cultivating crops and raising sheep on the plots of land (tenancies) that they lease. Although many live in fixed dwellings, they have kept their tents and leave their agricultural tenancies during the peak of the rainy season to take advantage of desert pastures. These tenants return to their crops only when weeding and other agricultural tasks can no longer be postponed.

Some fully nomadic Rashaayda live to the east of the Khashm al-Girba scheme, in the area between the 'Aṭbara and Gash rivers. Most of these families (including the family with whom I lived) move south as far as the Setit River at the beginning of the rainy season and turn back towards the north, following the rains, as the season progresses. They never move south of the Setit because of the fly infestations there; these transmit microbes that cause illness and death in camels. They seldom move far beyond Gooz Rajab, in the north, because rainfall there is usually inadequate. Some 2,000 of these Rashaayda have settled permanently in Mastuura, a village southwest of Kassala that a handful of Rashiidi families established in the 1970s.

There are no Rashaayda living in the Gash River delta. This area has been utilized exclusively by the Hadendowa and Bani 'Aamir nomads since 1938, after a series of armed clashes broke out between Rashaayda and Hadendowa. These conflicts—over water and pasture—were resolved by a government-brokered agreement between the Rashaayda and their neighbors, according to which both sides recognized the Gash River as the boundary between their "territories." As a result, the Rashaayda do not move across the Gash River delta during the rainy seasons.

Other Rashaayda live some 300 kilometers northeast of the Gash on the Red Sea coast. During May (when the first rains reach the coast) they move with their herds between the city of Port Sudan and the southernmost coastal town of 'Agiig, on the border with Eritrea. After this they make the arduous journey across the Red Sea Hills, to their west, and descend to the savanna between the Gash and 'Aṭbara rivers to utilize the pastures there. When the rains in these inland pastures cease they return to their home territories along the Red Sea. To the south of these territories, in the Eritrean province of Naqfa (Turki, 1978, pp. 198–199), is another group of Rashaayda (see Perlez, 1992). They enter the Sudan only sporadically.

It is not easy to determine how many Rashaayda there are in Sudan, partly because their frequent movements within the country make census-taking difficult and partly because some of them occasionally cross the border and join relatives in Eritrea. I heard Rashiidi camp leaders tell Sudanese government officials that the Rashaayda numbered 80,000 people, but this seemed to me an exaggeration. Some of the men who represent the Rashaayda to the government tend to inflate their numbers in order to obtain more social services from Khartoum. We can safely say, however, that there are at least 40,000 members of the "Rashaayda tribe" in Sudan. It is equally difficult to ascertain how many of them are fully nomadic and how many are completely sedentarized. Except for a few well-to-do merchant families in al-Mugrin and Port Sudan, who live exclusively in concrete block and adobe housing, most Rashaayda continue to own tents. They live in tents for varying lengths of time, depending on the extent of their livestock holdings and the abundance of rain and pasture in any particular year.

In sum, the Rashaayda live in a number of noncontiguous areas. Nomadic Rashaayda do not collectively exploit a single "tribal" territory but move freely across open rangeland during the rainy seasons. During the dry seasons they congregate in their camps near dependable sources of water. Sometimes these are the banks of rivers, while at other times they are wells that are not owned by Rashaayda.

HOW DO THE RASHAAYDA EARN THEIR LIVING?

It should be clear from the preceding discussion that not all Rashaayda are nomadic pastoralists. Furthermore, even those Rashaayda who are still nomadic do not all carry out exactly the same economic activities; these vary from one location to another. It would be misleading to present a generalized picture of their economy. Hence in what follows I will concentrate on the pastoral migrations and economy of only some of the Rashaayda, those who live between the 'Aṭbara and Gash rivers. This is the area that I know best (see Figure 2).

Prior to 1965, when the Khashm al-Girba scheme was opened, almost none of the Rashaayda who lived between these two rivers were sedentary or even semi-sedentary. The overwhelming majority exploited this region by herding livestock in rainy-season pastures and cultivating small plots of grain. When the government closed off large stretches of pasture to incorporate them in the Khashm al-Girba

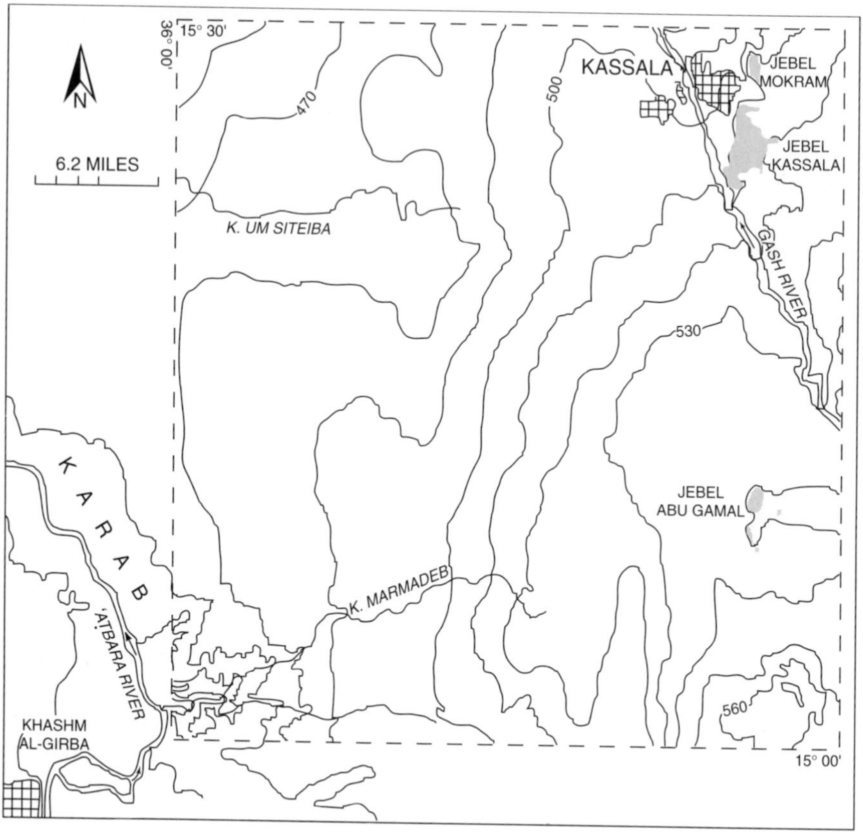

Figure 2 Agricultural and Pastoral Lands between the 'Aṭbara and Gash Rivers Utilized by Some Rashaayda (After Sadr 1991:28–29)

scheme, however, many of the region's nomads were forced out of pastoralism. Some abandoned nomadic life entirely and settled in small shanty towns on the outskirts of cities, others were granted tenancies in the scheme, and still others became seminomadic, devoting less time to livestock and more effort to agriculture than before.

Nomadic and seminomadic Rashaayda still obtain milk, meat, and hair (for weaving tent cloth) from their camels, sheep, and goats. Although they sell some of their live animals in markets, most pastoral products are not marketed as commodities but are consumed directly by their producers. But pastoral products such as meat and milk are not the primary sources of nourishment for nomadic Rashaayda; the bulk of their yearly diet consists of grain. They cultivate grain (sorghum and millet) in the beds of seasonal water courses (*khiiraan*). In other words, they combine subsistence pastoralism with subsistence agriculture.

Most Rashiidi men also work as livestock traders, and some occasionally work for wages. Those who earn part of their living in the livestock trade often buy animals from kinsmen and sell them in urban markets. Livestock traders frequently raise animals on their own as well. Those who work for wages find temporary jobs in Saudi Arabia and stay there for one or two years, bringing their wages back with them when they return (Young, 1987).

WHAT ARE THE SOCIAL RELATIONS THAT MAKE PASTORAL PRODUCTION POSSIBLE?

Nomadic pastoralists, like all human beings, depend on the cooperation and coordinated effort of relatives, neighbors, and friends for obtaining the necessities of life. Production is based on social relationships within and between groups, that is, units of production. Among most nomadic pastoralists, neither the "tribe" nor any of its genealogical segments is a unit of production. The actual work of production is carried out by *residential* units of varying scope (Cunnison, 1966; Keenan, 1977; Lancaster, 1981; Lewis, 1961), most often the household (Cribb, 1991, p. 34). The Rashaayda are no exception.

Among the Rashaayda, there are three residential units—the household, the camping cluster (or extended household), and the dry-season camp—which differ in size and in their importance for pastoral production. Each unit performs different tasks.

The household. The smallest unit of production is the household, that is, the group of people who live in a single tent (*beyt*). The members of the household consist of those people who have the right to sleep in the tent, to consume the water, milk, meat, and grain which are stored there, and to cook on its hearth. For a household to exist, it must have at least one member: an adult woman (either married, widowed, or divorced) who owns the tent. Men do not own tents, perhaps because men do not know how to maintain them; only women know how to keep tents in good repair, by weaving new tent cloth periodically. Every married woman has her own tent and is called *raa'yit il-beyt* ("the female guardian of the tent"). The people described in Chapter One—Ḥaamid, Suluum, and their unmarried children—were members of such a household.

The extended household. The household is usually part of a larger social unit, consisting of from two to as many as nine households whose tents occupy a shared campsite (*daar*). I called this a "camping cluster" in Chapter One, when I described my visit to Mujalli's tents after our arrival in our dry-season camp. I utilized this phrase to indicate how the tents used by this social unit were arranged in space and to refer to one of the activities (camping) that this unit performed. Here I will call it an "extended household." The ideal is that the members of the extended household cooperate when there is any work requiring animal labor. The animals used for this are owned by individuals but are put at the disposal of the entire extended household when necessary. My "extended household" consisted of the family living in Suluum's tent plus the family living in 'Aabda's tent. This extended household was named after its senior man, Ḥaamid, and was called *Dhuwi Ḥaamid.*

The dry-season camp. The camp (*al-fariiǧ*) is the largest residence unit recognized by nomadic Rashaayda. It consists of some fifteen to thirty extended households that congregate around a well or near a river bank in the period from February to mid-July. These households are free to choose from among a number of dry-season camp sites. They generally select the camp that is headed by a prominent man whom they respect and who they think will represent them effectively in any dealings with outsiders. This man is called "the senior man of the camp (*chibiir il-fariiğ*)." Our senior man was Naafi' Barakaat, a distant patrilineal relative of Suluum and of her deceased husband. We chose to join this camp, at least partly, because Suluum and 'Abdallah were relatives of the camp's leader.

Not all three residential and production units are active throughout the year. One of them, the dry-season camp, appears only at the beginning of the dry season and breaks up again by the middle of July. The contributions of the other two residence units to pastoral production vary according to season and according to the sex and age of their members. In short, in order to describe pastoral production among the Rashaayda I must show how it varies by season, how tasks are assigned to each of the three units of residence, and how tasks are performed by men and women.

In Chapter One I referred to only two main divisions of the year: the migratory season and the dry season. This is an outsider's view. The Rashaayda themselves divide the year into five seasons, each with its particular tasks. To describe them, I will name each season and discuss the economic roles of the men and women of the extended household. I focus on the cooperative efforts of the extended household, especially, because it is the extended household, not just single tents, which actually moves as a unit during migration. Its activities are connected very directly with the annual migratory pattern. After discussing the annual cycle and the work performed by the extended household, I will turn to the household and the dry-season camp.

The annual cycle of work for the extended household: Subsistence production. The season in which the extended household's labor is most in demand is *ar-rushshaash* ("the season of showers"), when migration begins. It starts in mid-July. As soon as the first rains fall, the extended households move away from the wells or rivers on which they have depended during the dry months. They migrate rapidly toward the area of rainfall, trying to be the first to arrive there so that they can utilize the sprouting grass.

The goal of leaving the dry-season camp takes priority over anything else; even if grass appears first near the well the camp residents do not stay there immobile. They deliberately set this area aside, since they know that once the rains have stopped, months later, they may have to return to the same well later. In that case there would still be forage left near the well for their animals. The distant desert pastures, on the other hand, can be utilized only while rain is still frequent. This is because they are so far away from water. The only source of drinking water in these pastures is scattered rain pools, and when these dry up no one can live there. So the Rashaayda's first goal is to reach these pastures while there is still enough water in them to support human life.

During *ar-rushshaash* they cover a great deal of ground and move almost daily. They are *shaaddiin* (literally, "exerting maximum effort [to move tents]," that is, continuously moving). The men of the extended household spend most of their time scouting for pasture and managing the herd. The women are preoccupied with striking

"The migrating women and children" (aḍ-ḍu'uun) *during the end of "the season of showers"* (ar-rushshaash). *In this area a great deal of pasture has already sprouted.*

their tents and setting them up again. Because rain falls frequently their families cannot do without shelter for a single day. Each married woman, assisted by her unmarried daughters, is responsible for striking her own tent and for packing its furnishings, but her load is distributed among the burden-camels that are used collectively by the extended household.

When the water and forage of a particular area are exhausted, a decision to move to a new campsite is made. The men of the extended household make this decision collectively, after having scouted for fresh pasture. The women offer their opinions but do not expect to shoulder much of the responsibility for the decision. Because they are not as mobile as the men they do not have current information about the state of the pastures nearby; their opinions are based solely on their general knowledge of the area and their experience in previous years. Hence the men decide where to go, hoping to find the kind of forage for their animals that will allow them to gain weight, make them ready to breed, and increase milk yields. If they make a bad decision the women are by no means reluctant to criticize them because this adds to the women's work unnecessarily. A campsite that lacks good pasture must be quickly abandoned, giving the women no respite from the work of taking down and putting up their tents.

The next season, *al-khariif,* is when the new pastures have sprouted and the normally parched land is covered with green. It is characterized by intermittent rain and lasts from early August to the end of September. In *al-khariif* the camels take in sufficient food and moisture simply by grazing close to the tents and need not be herded to distant pastures nor taken to wells for water. The sheep and goats, however, must be watered every two days at rivers or at rain pools if the tents are stationary; otherwise—that is, during migration—they are watered en route.

Suluum (left) and one of her married daughters striking her tent in preparation for migration. Note the decorated leather bags in front of them. They are used for storing clothing and other household goods. Ḥaamid (right) has just picked up a camel's hobble ('agaal*).*

Although the time devoted to herding during *al-khariif* is less than during other seasons, there are many other pastoral chores that must be done. Each camel must be hobbled and forced to drink quarts of highly salted water to prevent worms. The camel cows must be bred, each at the proper time, so that they do not all lactate and then go dry simultaneously. Finally, young male camels (*ği'daan*) must be broken to the saddle. To do this the trainer first ties up the animal, pierces one of its nostrils, inserts a ring into its nose, and attaches a cord to the ring. This allows him to pull on the nose-cord when he is training the camel and curb it by inflicting pain; it is forced to obey him when he mounts it. All of these tasks are dangerous and exhausting and cannot be carried out by a single man. The men of the extended household depend on each other for help.

In addition to these pastoral tasks, there is agricultural work to be done in *al-khariif.* Some of the extended household's men, who were busy herding during the previous season, now are free to plant sorghum and millet in the beds of shallow water courses. They select a site that has been well watered by runoff from the Ethiopian highlands to the east and mark off plots there, measuring them by pacing them off.

Nomadic Rashaayda do not own farmland. They claim particular desert plots informally, each year, by building or renewing low, foot-high dikes (*turuus*) on one side of each plot. These dikes trap rainwater and prevent it from flowing uselessly away. The plots of the coresident families who make up the extended household are laid out side by side. For two-day periods the migrating families leave their tents in place and their men and boys ride off to the cultivation site to prepare it for planting.

This work is not done collectively by the extended household; each family tends its own plot. But each cultivator rides one of the camels and uses the tools that are utilized by the other men of the extended household. Each of the families that make up the extended household takes its turn.

Planting is done in stages. First the cultivator clears his family's plot of heavy vegetation, using a very shallow-drought plow that is hitched to a camel. After a few days he returns to plant the seed. He opens up small holes with a foot-plow and his son or younger brother walks behind him, dropping a few seeds in each hole and then closing it. The household head and his helpers make three or four visits to the site after this, once the seeds have sprouted, to weed it and keep the wild growth from choking the domesticated grain. They coordinate these agricultural tasks with pastoral activities. The extended household moves as often as is necessary for bringing its livestock into fresh pastures, but never moves so far away from their cultivations that travel to them for work becomes impractical. Then, after weeding, the plots are abandoned. These plots are so far away from population centers and herds of domesticated animals that the Rashaayda need not stay close to them to protect the crops. They move away with their herds and let the plants grow unattended, only returning later, in early October, to harvest them.

Harvesting involves cutting the heads of sorghum off the stalks, separating the grain from the chaff, and putting it in sacks. When the harvest is over, some of the

A man and wife loading one of their burden camels. The tent cloth behind them must be rolled up before being loaded.

Two teenaged boys clearing their family's plot of vegetation in preparation for planting.

grain is sent back to the dry-season camp, but most is put in village storage pits, called *maṭaamiir.* It is kept there until after the harvest season and then is either eaten or sold (for a higher price than sellers can get during October). The *maṭaamiir* are dug and maintained by the many countryside merchants who have established small stores on the edges of the open desert (see Chapter One, p. 23). The yield of each single plot is the property of the household that planted it, but the work of harvesting the grain is done collectively by the men of the extended household.

The women and children of the extended household also help each other. When water and firewood are distant, for example, a few boys of the extended household saddle up a donkey or camel and ride off to the nearest well (to get water) or to a thicket (to get fuel). They bring back a measure of water or fuel for each of the co-resident households. When fuel and water are nearby, however, the senior woman of each household goes out to get it.

On days when the extended household does not move, the women make preparations for the coming months of stationary living, when they will live near wells. They will need fuel for cooking during the final, rapid migration to their dry-season camp. Furthermore, once they set up their tents in the camp, they will find little firewood in the over-populated vicinity of the wells. Hence, they make charcoal. Two or three coresident women go out to nearby thickets to collect firewood. They dig a pit, lower the wood into it, and after setting it on fire, bury it.

During the rainy months, when Rashiidi tents are widely scattered, people do not go far from their tents at night unless they have unusual or even illegitimate business; these are the working hours of thieves. Livestock rustlers roam the desert, trying to get close enough to nomad campsites to pick up a stray animal or two. The members of an extended household are alone in the desert and have no neighbors

The paternal cousin of the two boys in the previous photo working in an adjacent plot. He is using a foot-plow to open up the ground so that seeds can be dropped in and covered with soil.

Three little boys bringing water to their extended household on a donkey. They are living in a dry-season camp and have filled two large red plastic containers at the well in the center of this camp. The woman and child in the background are members of a household that has just finished migrating from a distant pasture. They intend to set up their tent in the camp.

who could come to their aid if they were attacked, so they stay close together. They couch their camels near their tents so they can guard them. On moonless nights it is hard to see the livestock clearly, especially after the household fires have died down. For this reason most households keep dogs, which they tether twenty feet or so away from the tents. When human eyesight fails the dogs can detect thieves with their sense of smell.

Not everyone stays at home at night, however. Occasionally some of the men go out to hunt for storks, which come to Sudan during September and October and roost in trees. A number of men cooperate, some trying to dazzle the birds with torches or flashlights while others try to shoot them while they sit paralyzed in the glare.

By the end of September there is no more rainfall and *al-khariif* is over. The nomads move farther away from their cultivated plots and spend more time herding livestock. During the period from October to December (called *ad-darat*) the desert herbs and grasses dry out and do not cover the ground as thickly as before. This means that the camels cannot graze only in the vicinity of the tents but must roam over a wider area. Each day a man from the extended household rides off to inspect the surrounding territory and spot the best foraging area (*mar'aa*). Other men or boys drive the camels to this area and let them graze. At this time the breeding season has come to an end, so the bulls and cows can be herded together. The men stay with the herd until midday and then bring it back to the tents.

At the beginning of *ad-darat* the individual households send men back to their cultivations to harvest the grain. Milk yields fall off at this time, so the grain is welcome. Their diet shifts towards a more even balance between milk and grain dishes. Tents are moved less frequently than before, once every seven to ten days. The Rashaayda say that they are just "looking for foraging areas (*mirta'iin*)" during this season; they are no longer *shaaddiin.*

By the onset of the dry, windy months which the Rashaayda call *il-bard* ("the cold season"), most of the desert rain pools have dried up and the nomads are forced to erect dry-season camps near dependable sources of water. During this season (from early January to the end of March) both men and women begin new types of work. These tasks are continued through the entire stationary phase, that is, the seasons of *il-bard* and *il-geyḍ* (the hot, arid season which lasts from April to June and is ended by the coming of the new year's rains in July). In contrast to the wet seasons, when an industrious household moves quickly to take advantage of the abundant natural resources for as long as they last, *il-bard* and *il-geyḍ* are times of slow decline in pastures, milk yields, stores of grain, and livestock, during which people try to conserve as much as they can of their animal resources.

Once the extended household has joined a dry-season camp, its camels are separated from its goats and sheep. By this time the desiccated and over-grazed pastures near wells and rivers do not have enough forage to maintain camels, so the large livestock must be moved out to distant, still untouched areas. The sheep and goats, however, can still find enough to eat nearby. Young boys take these small stock out to pasture every day and bring them back just before sunset. The older boys and young men, on the other hand, take the camels far away from the camp.

If the extended household's herd of camels is large, three or four young men work together as herders. They water the camels at a well or river and then drive them out into the open desert, where they move for five days in search of forage. If they have fewer than thirty head, only two men go "moving with the camels" (*saariḥiin fi il-bil*). They may combine their herd with that of one of their neighbors from their dry-season camp. The herders feel that there is greater safety in numbers; this is, in fact, the primary motive for combining herds.

Because neither the camels nor the herders drink water for these five days (except for the small supply that the boys take with them in leather bags), this stretch of time is called a *ḍumi* ("period of thirst"). The herders subsist almost exclusively on camel's milk for the duration of the *ḍumi* and then return to their camp to water the stock. For the day that they are "at water" (*'ala il-maa*), they can rest and eat the solid food that their mothers, sisters, and wives are quick to provide.

Their return home has meaning for them on many levels. At the sensory level, it means a departure from the "cold, windy desert" (*as-sağii'a*) where, without shelter, they are chilled by the wind at night and burned by the hot ground (*ar-ramḍaa*) during the day. At the social level, it means a reintegration of the society of men with the society of women. Not only are they able to sleep in their mothers' or wives' tents again, but they also are able to provide the women with fresh camel's milk and take in return the bread and porridge that the women cook. They also give the women some of the raw materials they need for their work. While the camels are being watered and rested in the vicinity of the well, the herders shear off their excess wool and collect it for the women in bags. The camels must be sheared to reduce mange and tick infestations; in addition, shearing yields animal fiber that can be spun into yarn by the women and used for weaving tent cloth.

The hardships of dry-season herding are not entirely imposed by the objective characteristics of the work. The herders all know how to cook and have more than enough animal power for transporting store-bought foodstuffs such as flour and dates. They do in fact take small quantities of these provisions with them. To depend on purchased goods, however, would be a poor economic strategy; it would mean that their camels' milk, which in *il-bard* is still available for free, would go to waste. The herders know that by the middle of May, when pastures all but disappear, their hungry animals will produce almost no milk and will have to be fed grain. Some of them will even die of malnutrition. It makes better sense, then, to subsist on camel's milk during *il-bard* and to eat purchased food only when this cannot be avoided.

The extended household as a unit of commodity production. It should be stressed that, even though camel's milk and meat form parts of the Rashaayda's diet, they do not raise camels only in order to subsist. They also sell livestock and use the proceeds to pay livestock taxes and to buy necessities and luxury goods, as well.

The Rashaayda have always had to buy necessities such as cloth, metal goods (such as shears, branding irons, sewing needles, knives, griddles, coffee pots, cooking utensils), containers (drinking glasses, bottles, cups), furnishings (reed mats, beds, mattresses), weapons, and other goods (soap, edible oils). Their type of camel pastoralism would be impossible without such manufactured goods; without branding irons, for example, they could not mark their camels. The grain purchased in local markets, moreover, is an important alternative resource in years of drought and helps sustain them and their animals when pastures are bad. They have also bought luxuries (especially silver rings for men and many kinds of silver jewelry for women) from urban markets ever since they arrived in Sudan. In recent years many Rashiidi men have purchased pick-up trucks and work as drivers during the dry seasons.

In short, the Rashaayda have long produced and consumed at least some market commodities. Like most Middle Eastern pastoralists, they have always had ties with urban markets and have never been purely subsistence producers; it would be a mistake to view their pastoralism as simply a strategy for survival. Even the members of the household do not really work for free, although they do not receive a salary. Boys expect, in the short run, to be compensated for their work as herders with gifts of livestock from their parents. In the long run, they hope that their labor will be rewarded by steady increases in the family herds, so that when their fathers die they will inherit a substantial amount of animal wealth or, perhaps, cash.

Girls are also compensated for their labor; they are given livestock and jewelry when they marry. Although they inherit little from their parents, girls are endowed with property before their parents die, either in the form of wedding gifts from their parents or as a transfer of animals, money, and jewelry from their husband's family to their marital family upon marriage. Every groom is required to give his bride young milking camels when he marries, and often the bride's father will also give her a male camel to ride on and some females, as well. Girls expect their parents to demand as large a payment as possible for them from their husband's family when they marry. When a woman's camels bear offspring, she often gives some of the newborn animals to her sons, so that they can start to build up herds of their own. Yet she may also keep some of them. Perhaps she will retain a set of female camels for her own use, so that in case she is divorced and leaves her husband's household she will have animals to milk. Or she may want to sell them and buy silver jewelry, which is another source of economic security.

In other words, nomadic Rashaayda are never averse to making money. But nomadic families cannot sell their livestock without regard for the needs of the other members of their extended households, because coresident families are not independent. An animal cannot be sold if a member of the extended household needs it for migration. An extended household composed of three tents needs at least five male camels, four older bulls for transporting the tents and one faster, younger male for scouting. It also needs at least ten females, both for milking and for reproducing the herd. Not all of the females will become pregnant every year, especially those with year-old calves, so some must be kept in reserve for following years even though they are not producing milk or offspring.

Surplus animals are either butchered locally (for example, to provide meat for guests at a wedding) or are sold. Extra males and old females that no longer give milk are sold in nearby markets, while young males that are strong enough to travel long distances are sent to meat markets in Egypt. Egypt has the only market for camel meat. There is little demand for camels in Sudan. Nomadic Sudanese have enough camels of their own, and urban Sudanese do not eat camel meat and use oxen, not camels, for plowing. But who decides whether or not a particular animal is "surplus"? Since the extended household migrates and uses camels for transportation as a unit, it is the extended household's senior man who decides—after consulting with the other residents, both men and women—what animals to sell and when to sell them. Camels are not collectively owned. Each member of the extended household owns his or her own animals.

Sending surplus males to Egypt is more profitable than selling them locally but is extremely difficult. It requires the cooperation of men from many extended households. The operation is begun by enterprising trail drivers, who circulate among the newly formed dry-season camps as soon as the rains have stopped. Four or five men agree to ride together to Egypt and collect a herd (*dabbuuka*) of at least 40 head. If grazing conditions have been good for the previous two years, there are likely to be many surplus male camels that their owners wish to sell. Since they have no capital at this point, the trail drivers cannot buy these camels. They simply promise the owners to get a good price for them and specify a percentage of the sale price as their compensation for the hard work. They gather the camels together to form a single herd and then set out, heading toward the town of Daraw, in southern Egypt, some 400 miles north of where most Rashaayda live.

It takes the trail drivers ten days of almost constant riding to reach the Egyptian border. They pair off into teams, two men strapping themselves into their saddles and sleeping while two other men keep the herd moving. Speed is imperative, first because of the danger of thieves and second because of the scarcity of wells in the northern deserts. If thieves get wind of the presence of a herd they will congregate and attack. Furthermore, if the camels do not move quickly enough to cover the long distance between one well and another in two or three days, some of them will start to weaken from thirst.

After arriving in Egypt, the trail drivers put their animals in quarantine for a few days, in accordance with Egyptian law, and then sell them off at auction. They use part of the proceeds to buy gifts and trade goods (cloth, cooking pots, knives) in Egypt and then return to Sudan by train. After selling their trade goods in Sudanese towns they go back to their camps.

Successful trail drivers must be exceptionally good riders and herders and must also be expert at the use of firearms. It should be borne in mind, however, that their success is not just a matter of personal skill. They also depend on the cooperation of the members of their extended households, who manage the family herd and take care of their children while they are on the trail.

The families who belong to an extended household also herd sheep during the rainy seasons. When the rain has stopped, however, sheep become a burden because they need to be watered at least once every two days. Furthermore, as the desert pastures dry up, it becomes increasingly difficult to find food for them. Often the owners decide to get rid of them. They combine their unwanted sheep with those of their neighbors and send one of their young men to town with them. Marketing the sheep, in other words, is organized by the extended household as a group.

The young herder walks to town, driving the flock in front of him. Upon his arrival he may decide to hire settled relatives or friends to care for the flock during the coming dry months. Alternately, he may sell them. During his absence in town his own camels and goats are cared for by his coresidents, who remain in the desert. The man who acts as mediator between the extended household and the townspeople during these transactions is the one who knows the market best (and can get the best possible price for the animals) and who can deliver the sheep unharmed.

Both men and women are expected to be competent in pricing, purchasing, and selling a wide variety of goods (including livestock, grain, cloth, metal appliances, medicine, perfume, and jewelry). Both sexes show great skill in bargaining, and when peddlers come to Rashiidi settlements and camps, women often buy small personal or domestic articles from them directly, using their own money. On the relatively infrequent occasions when nomadic women visit markets, they buy household necessities without hesitation. However, when a household sends one of their members to town to make expensive purchases, it chooses a man.

Rashiidi households do not choose women to make their market purchases because they believe that men are better judges of value and prices than women. Women help select their household's male go-between, tell him what prices they expect for their livestock, and instruct him how to spend their profits. They also criticize him when he makes a bad buy. Once, for instance, when I paid twenty cents too much for a packet of needles and thread, the woman who sent me sighed in exasperation: "You just don't know how to go to market (*maa ta'rif tikhaaṭir as-suug*)." Women are at a disadvantage, however, when making certain kinds of purchases, because of the sexual division of space.

As I pointed out in Chapter One, in northern Sudan space is constantly being divided into a section for men and a section for women. Among the Rashaayda, the open desert (*il-khalaa*) is thought of as a place for men. Women cannot herd sheep by themselves through uninhabited and potentially dangerous desert. No one who moves through such territories should carry large sums of money, either, without taking with him a sword or some other means of protection against thieves. While it is recognized that women can resist an attack just as courageously as men, it is also known that women are not trained in swordplay and never carry weapons. Arab Sudanese also characterize the open areas in market towns (for instance, the livestock market) as men's space. For a woman to enter such an area and linger there would be "shameful" (*'eyb*) and would elicit negative comments from the men present. Hence, when a household wishes to sell or buy animals, it sends a man to market.

In sum, the members of the extended household cooperate in herding, taking surplus livestock to market, collecting firewood, obtaining water, safeguarding their animals, and moving their shelters. For this reason, the extended household should be regarded as the basic unit of pastoral production. The other productive tasks, which do not require much animal labor, are carried out by the members of its component households or families.

The household as a unit of subsistence production, reproduction, and socialization. Just as the extended household is in charge of the production and reproduction of livestock, so the individual household (or family) takes charge of the production and reproduction of human beings. The adults of the household feed, shelter, protect, socialize, and train its children. Women begin caring for small infants as soon as they are born and continue to care for girls as they age. Girls are supervised by their mothers as they work in and near their tents. Men do not take care of children at all until the children are old enough to work, and even then look after only boys. In fact, men's child care is indistinguishable from teaching and supervision; the child works next to his father, and just as hard.

In addition to child care, there are tasks of providing food, clothing, and shelter. The two most important criteria for assigning work to household members are age and sex. Let us consider age first.

Infants and small children are not given any chores at all, but as they mature they are expected to work. In Rashiidi culture, however, maturity is not defined in terms of calendrical age. The Rashaayda do not keep track of birthdays, and many do not know (and do not care) exactly how many years have passed since they were born. Instead, they divide the human life span into a number of steps, that are marked by changes in clothing.

Infants (*bizraan,* literally "seedlings") are dressed in a loose, gownlike garment called a *thawb* for as long as they are unable to speak and walk properly and are not toilet-trained. Once they are able to keep themselves clean they are given garments that cover their legs more completely and are tied at the waist; for a girl this is a long skirt (*tichcha*), while for a boy this is a shirt and a pair of long, loose pants (*sirwaal*). The next step is marked by the addition of head coverings to their costumes. Girls lay a large piece of black or colored cloth (*garguush*) over their heads and shoulders and fasten its edges together under their chins with a pin; it covers their heads, shoulders, and chests. Boys of the same age wear a knit cap (*ṭaagiya*). Further stages of maturity are marked by the addition of still more articles of clothing. Girls first add a "virgin's veil" (*mungab*) to their wardrobe and then a black gown (*thawb*) that covers them from neck to ankle. Boys add a white *thawb* to their costume first and then follow it with a long white turban (*'imaama*), that they wrap around their knit caps.

The Rashaayda make this association between clothing and maturation explicit when they discuss aging and try to arrange the marriages of their children. When the members of a household try to find a wife for one of their young men, his mother asks other women which girls are available. She inquires about their age, not in calendar years, but in terms of the clothing that they wear. A *bint umtachchich* ("virgin wearing a skirt") is quite young, a *bint umgargash* ("virgin wearing a *garguush*") is more mature, and a *bint umnaggab* ("virgin wearing a *mungab*") is close to adolescence; her breasts have started to develop and must be covered by both the *garguush* and the lower part of the *mungab*. A *bint umthawwab* ("virgin wearing a *thawb*") is ready for marriage.

Suluum's son Aḥmad, his married sister, and his brother 'Abdallah's children. The baby boy is still too young to wear pants; the girl, two years older, wears a colored thawb.

Children of various ages. The youngest girls have very short hair and keep their heads uncovered. Older girls cover with the garguush, *and still older girls cover their faces with the "virgin's veil"* (mungab)*. One of the boys in the background is wearing the knit cap that was popular in 1978.*

As the child passes from one stage to another he or she is expected to gain increasing mastery over animals. Once the child is able to speak and walk he is assigned the job of keeping goats and sheep out of the tent. When these animals invade the tent in search of food and water the child is told to shout at them, throw clods of earth at them, and hit them to chase them out. Since the goats return to the campsite every afternoon, keeping them out of the tent is an almost constant chore.

Later in life, when children have outgrown their initial baby clothes and have been given new garments that cover their legs (such as the girl's *tichcha* or the boy's *sirwaal*), they are expected to catch and tether sheep and goats when they are close to the tent and help milk and feed them. Both boys and girls are sent to halter nearby camels, as well. Children of both sexes help to herd sheep and goats once they have started to cover their heads, although girls stay closer to their tents than do boys. By the time that a girl has donned a *mungab* ("virgin's veil") she should be able to ride a camel by herself during migration, without the assistance of adults. Boys at the same stage of maturity (who wear caps and *thiyaab*) also ride by themselves and help control the camels while the household is migrating.

Children are not formally taught how to work; they learn by observing adults and helping them. If a child is not helping an adult he is left pretty much to his own devices. Even children who are eager to join in the household's work are seldom permitted to

A married woman (left, leaning against the tent pole) and her unmarried sister. A married woman wears the "woman's mask" (ğinaa'), *while an unmarried girl wears the "virgin's veil." This particular veil is elaborately decorated, signifying that the wearer is definitely of marriageable age. The decorations on the mask clearly identify the wearer as a member of the Biraa'aṣa "tribal branch."*

do so unless they have demonstrated that they can do a good job. The parent will say, "No, you can't do this; you don't know how," quite deliberately increasing the child's frustration so that, when the time comes, the child will be highly motivated to learn and perform well. Gradually each child masters the tasks appropriate to his or her sex, taking the work of adults as models. It makes sense, then, for us to do the same; that is, to describe the household's tasks in terms of a man's work (*ṣin'at ir-rijjaal*) and a woman's work (*ṣin'at il-mara*), as the Rashaayda would.

Household tasks and the sexual division of labor. Many household tasks are broken down into a man's component and a woman's component. For example, men make the wooden portions of the tent, such as the tent poles, the tent pegs, and the small wooden skewers (*akhilla;* sing. *khilaal*) that are used to pin separate sections (*arwiğa;* sing. *ruwaag*) of tent cloth together. Women make the soft portions of the tent, such as the tent cloth (*shamla*) and the sun-screen cloth (*libbaada*). The division of labor by sex is also evident in food preparation. Only men may skin and butcher animals that have been slaughtered, and only women may grind grain by hand with a grindstone (*maṭḥana*).

Other tasks may be done by either sex, depending on the circumstances. For instance, during the summer months, when the pastures have dried out and the household must feed its livestock sorghum, one of the household members (either a man or a woman) spreads an empty burlap bag in front of each hobbled animal and pours a measure of grain onto it. He (or she) waits for the camel to finish eating, making sure that none of the goats steal the grain. Also, either a male or a female may milk the camels, sheep, and goats that belong to, or are being used by, the household. Coffee may be brewed by either men or women, and meat may be cooked by either sex once it has been removed from an animal carcass.

Some tasks, on the other hand, are done exclusively by women: grinding grain, churning milk, and weaving tent cloth. Yet even these tasks complement men's work. As we have seen, men cultivate and harvest grain, herd the female camels and milk them, and shear the camels' hair for use in weaving. This means that women's work must be synchronized with men's work.

Like men's work, a woman's household tasks vary from one season to the next. The main difference is between the tasks of the migratory seasons (*ar-rushshaash, al-khariif, ad-darat*) and between the tasks of the dry seasons (*il-bard* and *il-geyḍ*). During the first two rainy seasons women are extremely busy putting up and taking down their tents. Married women also cook for the members of their households. Cooking is never done by the women of an extended household cooperatively; each married woman provides for her own household only. During *ar-rushshaash* women make griddle cakes with machine-milled flour and are spared the hard work of grinding grain by hand. Their work load is also lightened by a change in diet. The household members drink much more milk, which is abundant during this season, than they do at other times. This reduces the time women spend in preparing meals, since it takes less time to milk animals than it does to cook.

During *al-khariif* the senior woman of each household, freed from the necessity of striking her tent daily, changes her daily routine. She returns to grinding grain once again and spends more time churning milk. Since milk is less plentiful it cannot always be drunk fresh but must sometimes be stored, even if it sours. The "female guardian of the tent" turns this sour taste to good advantage by churning the milk. She pours it into a small leather churning bag and suspends it from her tripod. Then she swings it back and forth until the milk inside it thickens and ferments enough to suit Rashiidi taste. She uses the churned milk as a sauce for dishes of sorghum porridge.

During the dry seasons women devote much more time to spinning and weaving than in the migratory season. Women spin the yarn needed for making a tent from the wool that men collect from camels and from the hair that the boys of the household shear off the goats. A great deal of fiber is needed by every household, since the entire tent is woven out of goat-and-camel-hair yarn. If a household's own animals do not yield enough fiber, the remainder must be purchased by the senior man of the household with his own money. He also buys a quantity of raw cotton, which the women incorporate into the tent cloth.

Although men provide the raw materials for the tent cloth, it is the property of the woman who makes it. She weaves most of it herself but is occasionally assisted by the other women of her extended household. The first step consists of spinning the yarn. Spinning is done with a simple spindle which is whittled by a man from a forked stick. The woman hooks a bit of hair with the fork of the spindle and holds the hair in place with the fingers of her left hand. Then she rolls the handle of the spindle between the thumb and index finger of her right hand and slowly pulls her hands apart as she does so, thus twisting the hair into yarn. Women of neighboring

A young girl churning milk in a leather churning bag.

households will often congregate to sit and chat while they spin, even though each does her own work.

Women make two types of yarn: black (consisting solely of goat's hair) and white (cotton with goat's hair to give the yarn strength). There is no technical reason to make yarn of two colors; the motive is artistic, that is, social and cultural. Women take pride in the attractive appearance of the cloth that they weave. To decorate it they make use of the particular artistic device that is their specialty: the contrast between black and white. Just as they cover their own faces with masks of black cloth covered with silvery white beads (see p. 48), so they decorate their tents with patterns of black and white yarn.

These patterns are not simply feminine, they are also "tribal." More exactly, there is a distinctive pattern for each of the three main branches of the Rashaayda "tribe": the Biraa'aṣa, the Baraaṭiikh, and the Zuneymaat. Each weaver uses the pattern appropriate for the members of the household, so that they can be identified at a glance as members of one of these "tribal" branches. Hence when women weave they express their identities as members of these "tribal" branches, as well as their identities as women.

When a woman has sufficient yarn of both colors she sets up a horizontal loom (*siduw*). The base of the loom consists of a number of stakes driven into the ground.

The weaver fastens cross-poles on top of these to hold the warp taut and passes a smooth wooden shuttle through the strands of warp to insert the strands that make up the weft. All of these implements are whittled out of durable types of wood by the men of the household.

Because weaving the tent cloth is so time-consuming it can be done only during the dry season, when it will not be interrupted by migration. But there is another reason why the dry months are more suitable for weaving. During these months the tent is set up in the form of a rectangular box, which is roomier and is easier to divide into a section for guests and a separate, screened-off section for the family. This form of tent, the *baṭiiḥa,* contrasts with the cramped, triangular form (*ḥajiira*), which is too small to keep divided constantly and which is used during migration. The section (*shigga*) that is reserved for guests is always on the eastern side of the *baṭiiḥa,* while the section on the west is reserved for household members. There is a physical barrier between the eastern and western sections that usually consists of the two large leather storage bags that hold household belongings. They are suspended from a horizontal pole that also holds up the tent cloth.

At times the western section can become the exclusive preserve of the women. This is the case, for example, when a friend or relative of the woman of the house has come to help her in the exhausting task of weaving. At such times the women close off the western section completely by hanging a cloth across the open side facing the front of the tent. Having their own screened-off place allows the women to work

A woman at her loom.

unencumbered; unseen by their brothers, sons, or other male relatives, they may remove their masks and breathe freely. Rashiidi men, who see the end of the loom protruding from the western side of the tent, do not push aside the curtain to enter without first calling to the women and giving them time to veil. This is because it is mildly "shameful" (*'aar*) for even close male relatives to see their mothers and married sisters uncovered.

Thus the sexual division of labor that underlies the weaving of tent cloth involves both an allocation of tasks (shearing and whittling for men and spinning and weaving for women) and an allocation of space. Men supply the raw materials and implements that women use and stay out of the area where women are weaving. The same can be said of another important type of activity: leather working.

Leather is obtained only from animals that have been ritually slaughtered; goats, sheep, and camels that have died naturally are never skinned. If a sick animal appears to be near death it is slaughtered immediately, because if it dies a natural death it is *ḥaraam* (prohibited) for the use of Muslims and so goes to waste. Islamic law permits only males to slaughter an animal. If a sick goat appears to be near death and there are no adult males to cut its throat, a woman cannot do the job herself but must act through one of the boys present. She puts a knife in his hand and, if he is too young to make the cut properly, guides it across the animal's throat. Before making the cut, she utters the proper Islamic formula in the boy's stead: *bism illaah, allaahu akbar* ("In the name of God; God surpasses [the profane world of human understanding]"). This makes the skin and the meat of the animal lawful (*ḥalaal*).

Animals are skinned by men and their hides are cleaned and tanned by women. Women make goatskins into small water bags (*ǧirbaan*) and turn sheepskins into prayer rugs or saddle blankets (if the wool is not removed). A sheepskin can also serve as a large water container (*rayy*). Women periodically soak water containers in tanning solution and oil them to keep them water-tight. Camel hides are used to make storage bags (*agraaf;* sing. *garaf*). Leather may be cut and shaped by both sexes (unlike wood, which only males may carve). Once the leather object has taken form, however, only females may decorate it.

The senior woman of the household usually decorates her storage bags with strips of red cloth adorned with white shells (*wida'*). Traditionally, women dyed the cloth red by steeping it in a solution of crushed acacia bark and water; in recent times women have started to buy red cloth in town markets. The shells are purchased by their husbands or male consanguines.

Women still use acacia bark for dying a sheepskin that has its wool intact; in this form it is called a *farwa.* Women dye sheepskins for the men of their households who travel frequently. The men use them as saddle blankets while riding and as prayer rugs and mattresses while resting. Because the *farwa* is used in public places, the woman who tans and dyes it red is careful to do a good job. A well-made *farwa* that is seen and admired in public can contribute significantly to her reputation. Sometimes two woolly sheepskins are sewn together and died black with a tanning solution of *garaḍ* (*Acacia etbaica Schweinf.;* see Hassan, 1974, p. 47) seedpods in water. This type of skin, called a *ṭiyeyli* ("something rather long") serves the same purposes as a *farwa.*

Men also fashion a number of articles out of leather. There is the square saddle cushion (*martaba*), that is stuffed with cotton or grass and laid on top of a riding

Two men on their mounts, displaying the long pieces of dyed, woolly sheepskin (ṭiyeyli) *that they are using as saddle blankets.*

saddle (*makhluufa*) to make the ride more comfortable. In addition, they make the two saddle pads (*ṭiyaaf;* sing. *ṭaafa*), that are placed under the *makhluufa* (one before and one behind the camel's hump) to prevent the wooden saddle from galling the animal.

It is not handling leather itself that is thought appropriate for men or for women; rather, men are associated with the initial and intermediate stages of leather working, and women are responsible for completing the job. If an entire skin is to be used, without being divided, the men do nothing more than separate it from the animal carcass, and women do the rest. If a piece of leather is to be cut into parts, women combine the parts to make "feminine" articles (such as the storage bags) and men use them for making "masculine" objects (such as the pads for riding saddles) that are never used by women. During migration, women ride with their young children on top of a pile of baggage supported by a baggage saddle (*baaṣuur*), which is sturdier. This provides a woman rider with a broad platform that infants and toddlers can ride on safely. The final step in manufacturing leather objects, decoration, is done by women.

In discussing the sexual division of labor among the Rashaayda, three points must be emphasized. First, it is the imposition of prohibitions on men and women (which prevent them from using certain utensils, altering certain materials, or completing certain operations) that is behind the division of labor into "women's work" and "men's work." When acts are not so restricted, they are categorized as neutral, that is, as neither masculine nor feminine. Neutral acts include making leather objects, brewing coffee, and stewing meat. They also include washing and mending clothes. As noted in Chapter One, all Rashaayda, both men and women, wash their own clothes. They also patch torn clothing and close seams that have opened up. Rashiidi men all know how to sew and do not think that sewing, per se, is feminine; what they refuse to do, however, is *decorate* clothing with needle and thread.

Second, the other gender-related constraints on work involve space and authority. A man may ask a woman to sew up a tear in his vest while they are in her tent, but when they are outside he repairs his clothes himself. Conversely, the same woman may ask a Rashiidi tailor to sew a dress for her when she is at his shop in the marketplace, but cannot ask him to do the same work when he is at home, even if she is his wife. People of both sexes wash their own clothes, but men wash them outside of the house, squatting near a wash basin at a well or stream, while women scrub them indoors. Men cook meat and porridge outside of the tent, when there is a wedding and large quantities of food are prepared over open-air fires, but they will not cook indoors at the women's hearth.

Third, it is not the case that all household work is performed by women; men make parts of the tent, provide leather for household furnishings, and supply weavers with their raw materials. Further, although some household tasks are sorted into men's and women's work, it would be misleading to characterize the men's work as "public" and the women's work as "private" or "domestic." In a sense, since the decorated products of women's work (tent cloth, saddle blankets, and so on) are always on display, one could say that women's work is "public," not "private." This dichotomy, however, is best avoided when describing the Rashaayda and, indeed,

A tent that has been completely opened up to catch the breeze. The men in the foreground are cooking meat for the guests at a wedding. After butchering a number of sheep, they are cutting up the meat and dropping it into pots of boiling water. The groom, who is marrying for the second time, is standing in the center.

other Arab societies. It is grounded in the history and state formations of Western Europe (for example, in the Roman *res publica,* the "public thing," i.e., the Republic) and should not be imposed on the Middle East.

The dry-season camp and production: Rationalization of access to water and defense of the herds. The dry-season camp is crucial for pastoral production. This is not because camp residents aid each other in productive tasks, narrowly defined, but rather because it is the joint action of camp members that secures for them the use of natural resources during the dry season, such as wells, pastures, and living space.

The 15 to 30 extended households that comprise the camp all send their camels out to graze for long (five-day) periods during the dry season. They bring them back to camp every sixth day and water them at the camp well. Obviously they cannot all use the well on the same day. All must agree on a campwide watering schedule, so that each of the coresident clusters can have its turn at the camp's source of water.

To work together effectively, the people of the camp obey a "senior man of the camp (*chibiir il-fariiğ*)" who regulates access to water and helps resolve any conflicts that break out among the camp residents. They determine the identity of the senior man simply by choosing to camp near him. A man who has proved to be a judicious and persuasive leader will find a large number of people camping around him by the beginning of January, when most extended households in a given region have stopped migrating and have *gaṭanoo,* "built a long-term camp near a dependable water source." His central position in the camp does not become visible immediately, however. For a short time in January the tents remain widely separated and distant from the water source, so that the various extended households can graze their goats and sheep on whatever grass remains in the vicinity. When the nearby forage is exhausted, there are no longer any pragmatic reasons to remain dispersed, and so the extended households shift their tents in the direction of the senior man's tent, located in the approximate center of the camp.

The camp senior has unquestioned authority in the organization of two things: access to water and the defense of the camp. To rationalize access to water, the senior must know when it is that each household's herd is driven out to pasture and when that herd returns. By the time large numbers of households have congregated around a well, for example, and are competing for the use of its water, the camp senior will have consulted with them all and will have allocated a specific period of time to each, during which it can bring in its camels and allow them to drink.

Since the animals cannot, of course, drink from the deep and narrow well directly, the herders build a shallow drinking pan (*ḥawḍ*) out of mud next to the well and pour water into it for the camels to drink. The camp senior organizes this, drafting camp members to form work crews who keep the well and its surroundings clean and usable. They clear away debris and repair the mud dikes around each *ḥawḍ.* The Rashaayda do not generally dig wells of their own, however, since neighboring "tribes" do not acknowledge Rashiidi ownership of land in eastern Sudan and control most of the wells there. When Rashaayda use a well that is owned by other "tribes," they must pay the Bani 'Aamir or Hadendowa owners to draw water and construct drinking pans for them. In such cases, the camp senior is responsible for maintaining peaceful relations among the camp residents themselves, and between them and the owners of the well.

If conflict arises between Rashaayda and non-Rashaayda, the camp senior should hurry to intervene and attempt to resolve it. Under such conditions the camp residents will defer to him and restrain themselves from angry actions and words until his mediation efforts either succeed or fail.

The camp senior does not only try to keep the peace; at times he must also organize the camp for war. More exactly, when a camp member has been killed in a conflict, or when a camp resident's livestock has been stolen, the camp senior "gets up a posse (*yigawwim faz'a*)." All able-bodied men in the camp are summoned to his tent and are informed of the incident, be it an offense against a human being or property. They confer briefly, each man contributing whatever relevant information he has, and then move out to either counterattack or recover the stolen animals. All of the men residing in the camp are bound to supply the posse members with whatever saddles, weapons, or riding camels that they need; even if a mount is killed in the ensuing battle, its owner cannot claim compensation from the rider who had commandeered it. During the pursuit and fighting, the camp senior leads the men of the *faz'a* and decides what strategies to follow.

The relationship between the camp senior and the other residents is not based on kinship. Any household may leave the camp at any time and move to another camp without being criticized, regardless of its consanguineal or affinal ties with the camp senior. Moreover, any Rashiidi household may join the camp, irrespective of the descent of its members. Membership in the camp is conceptualized, not in terms of kinship, but rather in terms of the members' common feeling of "propriety" (*ḥishma*) for the camp senior.

Ḥishma entails self-restraint in situations of potential conflict so that the organization of the camp will not be disrupted. In other words, even if a member of the camp has a history of quarrels and bad relations with someone else in the camp, he cannot act on his personal feelings as long as this third party is on good terms with the camp senior. The notion of *ḥishma* presupposes a set of relationships between three parties, A, B, and C, such that A is on good terms with B, B is on good terms with C, and A is indifferent to or on bad terms with C. Because of his respect (*ḥishma*) for B, A will maintain a proper decorum with C even though, left to himself, he would otherwise express his disdain for, or dislike of, C. This concept can be illustrated in another way. There is a common proverb that states: "My enemy's enemy is my friend." *Ḥishma* is based on the contrapositive of this statement: "My friend's friend is not my enemy."

Ḥishma can also be invoked to win support for the camp senior in a peaceful context. When the camp senior deals with outsiders the residents of the camp should show their solidarity with him and not detract from his dignity. When they are by themselves camp residents need not show him any special consideration, but as soon as outsiders come on the scene they must "make him senior" (*yichabbiruunah*) and behave respectfully. Thus *ḥishma* can be opposed contextually to *raaḥa* ("ease, relaxation"), as is illustrated by the following case.

Case One: *Ḥishma*

I went to visit a good friend of mine who, since he was still unmarried, was a member of his father's extended household and lived in his mother's tent. Since I was living in the same dry-season camp that he resided in, I could not be classified as a guest; rather, I was a "camp resident" (*maḥalli*). The tone of my visit was informal. My friend, who I will call Saalim, invited me into the eastern section of the tent, urged me to "relax (*irtaaḥ!*)," told me "stretch out your legs and lean on one elbow (*chawwi'*)," and gave me a saddle-pad to lean on. Soon his sister entered the eastern section, wearing her ordinary, undecorated virgin's veil, and sat down to make us tea. We began to exchange stories about people who we all knew, some of which were quite comical and made us laugh.

While we were talking, two older men rode up to our cluster of tents and went into the tent right next to ours. This tent was the one in which Saalim's father had had his breakfast that morning; it belonged to Saalim's father's other wife, a woman who was not Saalim's mother. Saalim's father was the senior man of the camp in which I was staying. He and his son 'Aamir (Saalim's half-brother) formally welcomed these guests, who had come to ask his opinion about a legal dispute. Saalim went next door briefly to see if his father needed him, but returned to us shortly afterward. We resumed our joking. Unfortunately we became so absorbed in our conversation that we forgot about the nearby guests. Our laughter grew loud enough to be heard in the other tent. After a few minutes 'Aamir came rushing into our tent angrily, picked up our teapot, and dumped its contents onto the fire. We stared at him, startled. "Are you animals? (*antuu bahaayim?*)" he whispered in disgust. "We have guests, and they can hear you laughing and shouting. Whose house do you think you are in?" He gestured in the direction of the other tent, where his father was. "This is our senior man! (*haadha chibiirnaa!*)"

Our error was not that we laughed within earshot of Saalim's father, since we had done so with impunity before the guests had arrived. The harm lay in allowing his father's guests to hear our laughter. Saalim's father had welcomed these guests and wanted to treat them with respect, while we were behaving disrespectfully and may have unintentionally hurt their feelings. They might even have thought that they were the butt of some ridicule which had caused us to burst out laughing. Even if we really had been ridiculing them among ourselves, we should not have given them cause to think so, out of consideration for Saalim's father. That is, we should have remembered his wish to honor them and should have maintained appearances for his sake, regardless of our opinion of the guests.

As can be seen from Case One, in the context of residence, *ḥishma* is the reason why the other members of a camp treat their senior man's guests and friends with respect. They do so, not necessarily because they themselves value these guests, but because they hold their senior man in high esteem. A camp resident who ignores the conventions of "propriety" causes serious trouble and is likely to be removed socially, if not physically, from the camp. The other camp residents stop speaking to him, and although the camp senior probably will not refuse him water for his livestock he will not help to resolve any quarrels in which the man becomes embroiled. If he insults or reviles the camp senior, the latter is justified in suggesting that he leave the camp. In short, those who remain in the camp observe the conventions of "propriety," while those who become enemies of the camp senior do not stay there.

PASTORALISM AND INEQUALITY

We have seen that the organization of production is based, to a certain extent, on unequal access to productive resources and on differences in authority. Children, certainly, are subject to the authority of their parents and are neither allowed to buy and sell animals nor permitted to spend any of the household's cash. The "male guardian of the tent," furthermore, has greater control over animal wealth and more direct contact with trading partners than his wife. Men inherit livestock while women generally do not; men move across open spaces and through livestock markets freely, while women who are active in commerce do not go to market but work through male intermediaries. Furthermore, the senior man of each extended household has the authority to make final decisions about where to move during migrations and which surplus animals to sell. Finally, the senior man of the camp has the authority to organize access to water and mobilize the men of the camp for combat. He also has the use of their racing camels, in that he (and the men who follow him) can commandeer any mount he needs to pursue thieves and defend the camp.

Are these inequalities characteristic of nomadic pastoralism per se, or are they "tribal"? In other words, are they the results of the Rashaayda's economic specialization (seasonal movements for the purpose of exploiting distant, wild pastures), or are they simply aspects of their "tribal" organization that would be present even if they were not pastoralists? In these final pages of Chapter Two I will examine the relationship between nomadic pastoralism and inequality, leaving the question of whether Rashiidi inequalities are "tribal." There is simply not enough space in this case study to address the latter question, primarily because the term "tribe" has been used by anthropologists in so many different and inconsistent ways. The reader who wants to know what "tribe" means to the Rashaayda and whether their "tribal" organization is stratified should refer to Chapter Four, where I discuss "tribe" in more detail.

For many years social scientists were fond of the notion that nomadic pastoralists were essentially egalitarian and that differences in authority and access to resources in a nomadic "tribe" were either not substantial or were abberations. During the 1970s three important studies of nomadic pastoralists (Asad, 1970; Asad, 1979; Black, 1972) demolished this romantic idea. Many anthropologists today accept the premise that pastoralist societies, and indeed all societies, are systems of inequality. They no longer try "to imagine a world without socially created inequalities" (Yanagisako & Collier, 1987, p. 40). For current scholars, the question is not whether, or even why, inequality is found in every society, but why inequality takes the particular form that it does in each particular case. They point out that men and women may be relatively equal in some societies that are otherwise highly stratified, while in other cases it is mainly in relations between the sexes that inequality is most marked. Inequality can take many forms: symbolic, legal, political, economic, and so forth. In the following paragraphs I will discuss primarily *political* and *economic* inequalities among the Rashaayda and ask: To what extent are they caused by the pastoral mode of production?

Pastoral production and economic inequalities among households. As ethnographers of pastoralist societies have discovered (Barth, 1961, p. 101; Dahl & Hjort, 1976, p. 17), the logic of pastoral production tends to amplify differences in wealth among pastoralist households. An initial difference between one household's herd of 50 sheep and another household's herd of 60 sheep may be multiplied severalfold over a period of years, leaving the first household with the same small herd and the second with hundreds of animals. The second, slightly larger herd can exploit that much more pasture during the rainy season, given a sufficient supply of labor and unlimited access to pastureland. This gives the larger herd a reproductive advantage, since a larger number of its females will fatten and become fertile. A larger number of offspring creates a positive feedback effect, so that after two or three years even more females will be ready to give birth. The resulting large herd can crowd out the smaller herds of competing households, monopolizing more and more pasture (Cribb, 1991, pp. 23–39).

The actual consequences of differential reproductive success between herds of different size varies greatly, however, depending on the species being herded, the breeding strategies of the herders, household size, and the social relations among livestock owners, their families, hired shepherds, and the other people involved in the production process. The basic principle—that pastoralism can lead to extremely rapid expansion of one household's herds at the expense of other households—can be counteracted by a host of environmental and political factors. If all households in a given region expand production, the local rangeland rapidly becomes overgrazed, with the result that many of the animals, weakened by hunger, fall prey to disease and die. Furthermore, the wealthy household may not have enough labor to manage its large herd, so that some of its livestock wander off or are stolen. This household's neighbors may also resent its success and deliberately steal its livestock in order to humble it. Wealthy households will of course do their best to solve these problems. When they succeed they may become the elite of a highly stratified pastoral society. When they do not succeed they either have to resign themselves to the gradual bleeding away of their wealth or sell their animals and buy agricultural land, leaving the pastoral sector altogether.

Thus the factors leading to differences in wealth among pastoralist households can be offset by factors that make it difficult for a single household to accumulate large numbers of animals. As Cribb puts it, nomadic pastoralism is a much riskier and much more unstable production system than agriculture. Pastoralists have a chance to rapidly increase their wealth but must deal with the likelihood of losing it all just as quickly.

Cribb's general statements accord well with my impressions about the accumulation of wealth among the Rashaayda. My friends told me about three men who had once owned large herds of camels (over 300 head) but who had lost most of them during a single bad year. In the camp where I lived some households had over 40 camels while others had as few as 5 or 6. I heard that two of the men in the region were extremely wealthy in livestock even though their fathers had not been wealthy when they were children. No one said that these differences in wealth were of long standing, and no entire families or lineages were described as wealthy. I was told of individual members of families who were wealthy although their brothers and cousins were not. I concluded that there is little stable economic stratification among Rashiidi households.

I should have confirmed these impressions (or proven them incorrect) by carrying out a household survey. I tried, but I found it impossible to discover how many animals people had. They had never heard of a household survey and could not imagine why I would ask such a question. If I were interested in buying a few sheep or goats, of course, it might have been reasonable, but they knew that I was not in the market for livestock. Perhaps, they thought, I wanted to classify them all according to wealth, branding one family as "poor" and another as "rich." In their view, this kind of invidious comparison could only be an expression of ill-will and envy on my part. Why should it matter to me that a particular family was "rich" unless I envied them their good fortune?

So their most common reaction was to remind me that my question was malicious. They referred obliquely to a verbal formula that they thought protected them from envy: "five in your eye" (*khums fi 'eynk*). They did not repeat this formula directly, but told me they had "five sheep" and sometimes even showed me five fingers as they spoke.

People resort to such formulas when they think that others are regarding their good luck, good health, or good looks with envy. The Rashaayda believe that envy (*ḥasad*) is a real force, a power that can jump from the eyes of an envious person (whether he wills it or not) and harm the objects of his envy. So they sometimes take precautions against it. When a Rashiidi man hears an envious statement he may shield himself by mentioning "five." When he makes a statement that could be interpreted as envious (for example, by praising someone's skill or admiring someone's attractive children) he quickly follows this by saying *maa shaa' allaah* ("What God has ordained"). The following story illustrates the Rashaayda's attitude toward economic stratification.

Myth One: Envy (*ḥasad*)

Years ago, before the region's pastures had been overgrazed, Ḥaamid (the head of my household) had a fine milch camel that always gave a lot of milk. He also had many other female camels, and so when pastures were good his family had more milk than they could drink. During the rainy season they sometimes even poured it onto the ground, there was so much. Because of this they were glad to have visitors come, and would call to passers-by and offer them milk.

One time an envious man (*rijjaal ḥaasid*), who was known to have an envious, "red eye" (*'eyn ḥamraa*), came riding past. It was in the middle of the rainy season. Ḥaamid was milking his best female camel, and called to this man to invite him to have some milk. When the man approached he stood next to the camel, watching Ḥaamid fill the milk bowl to the brim. He did not say *maa shaa' allaah* ("[See the good things] that God has ordained [for you]") like most people say when they see something nice, but just waited, staring. When Ḥaamid had finished milking he ordered the camel to sit and gave the man some milk. He drank a little, thanked Ḥaamid, and rode away.

A few minutes later, when Ḥaamid tried to make his camel get up again, he found out that she was dead. She had died on the spot. There was nothing wrong with her before, no sickness. It was just that the envious man had struck her (*za'arhaa*) with his dangerous eye, and that's why she died.

This myth shows us that even though the Rashaayda recognize that some people are wealthier than others, they view differences in wealth as an aspect of relations among isolated individuals. One man may have more livestock than another but may be poorer than a third. What matters for the Rashaayda is the individual's attitude towards those who have more wealth (or less) than he has. They do not picture their society as a set of economic strata or classes (unlike the "upper," "middle" and "lower" classes, which are central to the American view of society). They avoided talking about differences in wealth with me because they thought doing so was a sign of envy. So all I had to go on was stories about the changing fortunes of rich and poor men.

Pastoral production and economic inequality between the sexes. Having discussed economic inequality among households, what can I say about inequality between men and women? What are the factors that give men more control over property than women have? At the same time, what are the factors that tend to secure economic resources for women and limit sexual inequalities?

Probably the single most important constraint on women's economic activity and independence is a tradition which, paradoxically, has no necessary connection with the pastoral economy: the sexual division of space. If women could herd their own animals, even small stock, within a wide perimeter around their tents, they could have an independent source of wealth. Women with infant children might find herding difficult to reconcile with the demands of child care, but those with older children would have no problem, and unmarried girls could also work as herders (as is the case, in fact, among the Bedouin of the southern Sinai; see Lavie, 1990). Further, if they could drive their animals to town and sell them in town markets themselves, they could transform this perishable animal wealth into more permanent cash. But, as we have seen, women do not move through unenclosed spaces, men's spaces, by themselves; they stay largely within the confines of their tents.

This sexual division of space is not necessary for pastoral production. It seems to be a by-product of the Rashaayda's Arab—that is, cultural—traditions, on the one hand, and of the regional balance between law and order, on the other. In many Arab societies it is "shameful" (*'eyb*) for women to stay in men's space for any extended length of time (Mernissi, 1987), and in this particular Arab society, that has a history of armed conflict with its nearest neighbors, it is not always safe for unarmed women to leave the protection of their camps.

The other main constraint on women's economic position is legal: Women rarely inherit property and do not receive a share of the proceeds from livestock sales. Men own most of the livestock that the household cares for and pass most of this animal wealth on to their male children. Yet the consequences of this formal, legal inequality between men and women with regard to inheritance cannot be understood in isolation from the wider social context. To understand women's economic position one must weigh their theoretical rights against their actual, practical situation as members of a household.

It is best to picture women as members of a household "corporation." Generally, all of the members of the household, including both men and women, contribute their labor to household production and pool their wealth. They usually consume only a small amount of the household's resources (in the form of food, clothing, and shelter) and plow the rest back into livestock breeding and various trading ventures. Household wealth that is so invested can be increased; in other words, it is productive capital. Household members usually try not to waste this capital on personal (nonproductive) luxury goods, but there are certain occasions when they have the right to withdraw their shares. The most important of these occasions are births, Islamic holidays, marriages, and deaths.

Married men have the right to withdraw shares from the household's pool of wealth on three occasions: births, marriages, and deaths. When a man's wife gives birth to a son, he can give the boy animals from the household herd. When the boy grows older the animals are his, and he will use them eventually to marry and establish his own household. The boy also has the right to some of the household's cash and tent cloth when he marries. His father must give him a marriage payment (*siyaag*) so he can hand it over to his fiancée's family and complete the marriage. This payment consists of cash and livestock and ranges in value from 500 to 3,000 Sudanese pounds, depending on the relationship between the intermarrying families. He also needs at least one piece of tent cloth, so that he can build the shelter where the wedding takes place. Finally, when a man's father dies, he has the right to a share of his natal household's property. Whatever was owned by his father or by his father's household is divided equally between him and his brothers. In other words, he inherits from his father.

Women also have rights to household wealth on three occasions: Islamic holidays, marriage, and divorce. When a holiday (*'iid*) is celebrated, each member of the household has the right to *kiswat al-'iid,* "holiday clothing." The "male provider of the house" (*mu'iil il-beyt*) buys new clothing for his dependent children (*il-'iyaal*) and for his wife. When a girl is married, she also has the right to keep the bulk of the marriage payment (*siyaag*) that her family has received. Part of this payment is given to her in the form of silver and gold jewelry (*ṣiigha*), while the rest comes in the form of livestock. According to Islamic law, the girl's father is not supposed to keep any of the payment for himself, and since the payment is openly negotiated and discussed the girl knows exactly how much she should receive. This is her last share of her natal household's wealth, however; she does not inherit from her father. If she is divorced, she has the right to a single payment from her husband as compensation, and she also has the right to move to her brother's camp and take her tent with her. Her husband also must support his children.

Marriage payments ensure that almost no women are without independent resources of their own while they are married, and divorce payments give women some income after they are divorced. But unlike the household capital that men invest in livestock breeding and trading ventures, women's wealth is not productive.

Women hold on to their jewelry, milking animals, and cash as forms of security, in case their husbands divorce them, fall ill, or die. Thus, although a girl may belong to a prosperous household before she marries, and may become a member of an even more prosperous household after she marries, she cannot become wealthy in her own right. She contributes to the wealth of her household by working for it, but her rights to take her share are more limited than the rights of men.

Simply contrasting men's rights to household wealth with women's rights, in the abstract, does not tell us whether in actual practice men enjoy a real advantage. It all depends on what men can do with the resources that they withdraw from the household's wealth. Here is where pastoral production and the structure of local markets can make a difference. Even though a man may have the right, in theory, to appropriate animals whenever he wants, in practice he is limited; if his family is large and their herd fairly small, he cannot take many animals because doing so would make migration impossible. Furthermore, it does him no good to take camels unless he can market them, and even if he manages to sell them he might have little immediate use for cash. He has no reason to buy land or other real estate and can buy only luxury goods that are easily transported. So his theoretical advantage over his wife may not be an advantage in practice.

There are other factors, also, that limit sexual inequality. There is no question that subsistence production among the Rashaayda tends to improve the bargaining position of women. Men are completely dependent on their wives and mothers for shelter and largely dependent on them for food. Men cannot even move the tent cloth under which they sit, much less weave it or repair it. If a man divorces his wife she has a right to the household tent and takes it with her when she returns to her father's camp or moves to a sibling's camp. Unless he has a second wife and a second household where he can live, he is left without shelter. He must either return to his mother's tent or must live as a guest with one of his brothers. Both options can be humiliating for a man who has become accustomed to being the head of a household.

We should not ignore another legal inequality, however, before concluding that men's greater access to property is not a real advantage. Even if a man cannot sell his household's animals locally and cannot purchase real estate, he can always use animals to make a special, noncommercial transaction. That is, he can use livestock as a marriage payment and take a second wife. Islamic law permits men to marry up to four wives, with the proviso that each of a man's wives must be given exactly the same economic support that the others enjoy. The Rashaayda recognize this principle and practice polygyny. This means that a man may use the family herd to finance a second marriage, whether or not his first wife agrees.

But even here this theoretical right is limited by practical considerations. A man who uses his family's wealth to contract a second marriage is likely to face the opposition of his sons as well as that of his wife. If his sons are old enough to have worked as herders, they will have tried hard to increase the family's herd, expecting to use part of it to find wives of their own and, ultimately, to inherit portions of it. They will likely resent it if their father appropriates some of these animals to marry a second wife before they themselves have been able to marry. Furthermore, they are bound to sympathize with their mother against their father.

The first wife's reaction also cannot be ignored. The Rashaayda admit that a man's first wife may feel betrayed by her husband when he marries again and that polygynous marriage often causes jealousy between co-wives. Although a first wife cannot prevent a new marriage from taking place, she has many ways of making life miserable for her husband and his second wife once the second wife has joined her extended household. As in other Arab societies that practice polygyny (Lewando-Hundt, 1984, pp. 106–108; Eickelman, 1984, pp. 68, 110), relations between co-wives are generally tense. Quarrels between them are common, especially during the first few years after the second marriage, and their husband is always under pressure to reconcile them and treat them equally. A woman who has many young children, who brought many milking camels with her when she married, and who is still healthy and attractive, is in a strong position because she can threaten to leave her husband and take her children and livestock with her. If she is determined, and if her brothers agree that she is being maltreated and support her, she can sometimes force her husband to divorce her co-wife.

Not all women, however, can enlist the support of their natal families when their husbands take new wives. The Rashaayda do believe that if a man wants many children, can support more than one wife, and needs a large family to further his political ambitions, he has a right to more than one wife. Polygyny, they say, is especially justified when the first wife has not borne her husband any children after the first few years of marriage, but is also acceptable even if she has proven her fertility. One of my women informants suggested that if a woman is fortunate enough to have a prominent, vigorous, and successful husband, she should not be angry when he takes a second wife as long as her rights are respected. Such a woman, if she is "intelligent" and "rational" (*'aağila*), will treat her co-wife correctly. In other words, if she wants to enjoy the benefits of marriage to a prominent man, she must accept its disadvantages. In such cases the first wife must simply resign herself to the situation. I noticed that even co-wives who had lived as neighbors for years did not socialize with each other very much. It seems that one device for easing tensions is simply avoidance.

Even when the first wife accepts the polygynous marriage, this does not mean that she accepts a subordinate position. Each wife has the right to her own tent, livestock, and financial support for herself and her children. Each monitors her husband's treatment of her co-wife carefully to make sure that the new spouse is given no economic advantage. An illustration of this can be seen in the following case.

Case Two: A Co-Wife's Right (*ḥagg*) to Equal Treatment

As the September rains began to slacken, Ṣuweyliḥ, one of my friends from the Baraaṭiikh "tribal branch," decided to stop migrating with his sheep and camels and moved his tents to our camp. He had two wives, whom I will call 'Aamira and Ḥimeyda. Ḥimeyda had stayed behind in her parent's *daar* to visit them, while 'Aamira had accompanied Ṣuweyliḥ to his new camp. I and a friend went to say hello to him.

When we arrived we discovered that a guest was already there and that Ṣuweyliḥ was busy butchering a goat in his honor. Since I and my friend were fellow residents of the camp, Ṣuweyliḥ asked us to help him cut up the meat. We were in good spirits. The surrounding countryside was still green, our camels were still giving quantities of milk, and we were anticipating a fine meal. Ṣuweyliḥ paused in the midst of his work, however, to express his only regret: that Ḥimeyda was not there to share it with him.

My friend's reaction made it clear to me that this was a *faux pas*. He glanced around quickly to see if anyone else had heard the remark. Later, after he and I had left Ṣuweyliḥ's tents, he told me that he hoped that neither the guest nor 'Aamira's children found out what Ṣuweyliḥ had said. If his remark were repeated to 'Aamira or her brothers it could cause serious trouble between Ṣuweyliḥ and his affines.

The principle that a woman's co-wives (*ṭabaayin*) have a right to equal treatment by their husband is expressed in other ways also. For instance, when their husband comes home after tending to his livestock, custom demands that he tether his camel in front of the tent of one of his wives if he chooses to spend the night there. He must also store his riding saddle inside it. The presence of his saddle is a clear sign to the people of the camp that he is providing his wife with the attention and sexual services which are her rights. This guarantees for the woman a favorable public image, even if it cannot insure that her husband will treat her affectionately or fairly in private.

The husband's camel and saddle can be useful communicative resources for his wife, since she can use them as evidence of her favorable or unjust treatment when discussing her married life with her natal family. Since her tent is located right next to those of her co-wives', it is easy for an outside observer to compare her treatment with theirs just by looking for the saddle. Sometimes, to forestall such comparisons and placate a jealous wife, a man will make or buy riding saddles for all of his wives.

If a polygynously married woman finds any sign of unequal treatment she will complain to her brothers, who will also resent the slight to their family and will, consequently, back her in her quarrel with her husband and support her if she leaves him and asks for a divorce. Divorce carries no stigma, and divorced women usually remarry without any difficulty.

Sometimes a man with two wives tries to pit one against the other, making invidious comparisons and trying to spur them to compete with each other for his favor and attention. This game has its down side, however, since each wife may respond competitively by trying to extract more property (jewelry, clothing, and luxury goods) from him than the other. A man who was married to two women recited the following ditty to me when discussing this; it is supposed to have been sung by a woman to her newly arrived co-wife:

marḥabaa bich yaa ḥabiibti min yamiin wa min shimaal;
nigassim illi yijiibah, wa al-ḥamla 'ala -l-ḥimaar

("Welcome, my [*fem.*] friend, from the right and left;
"We'll divide between us whatever he brings, and the
[whole] burden will be on the [*masc.*] donkey.")

That is to say, the two women should not allow their husband to pit one of them against the other but should cooperate in sharing his income equally. This is, of course, a man's view, expressing the seldom-realized hope that his wives will be satisfied with equal shares of what he chooses to give them. Polygynous marriage can be an economic burden for men.

In practice, then, men's theoretically extensive rights to appropriate livestock are restricted by the requirements of pastoral production and the local demand for camels. Their right to use livestock for arranging polygynous marriages is also limited, in actual fact, by the attitudes and reactions of their family members. Women's actual economic position varies greatly according to the economic and social resources that they can bring to bear when negotiating with their husbands.

Pastoral production and politico-economic inequalities among men. As we have seen, economic inequalities between the sexes have no obvious connection with the technical requirements of pastoralism. The authority of the "senior man of the camp," however, is much more directly related to pastoral production. Pastoralists cannot live far away from watering sources during the summer; they must live in camps. When they choose a particular campsite they simultaneously promote the senior man (and his coresident kin) in that particular location rather than a different prominent man whose household has camped elsewhere. Simply by camping near him they tacitly acknowledge his authority. This concession makes it possible for him to rationalize access to water during the summer and protect the herds from thieves. The resulting inequality among the men of the camp is transformed into political inequality among the camp households. Since each married man represents a household, his rank in the camp determines the rank of his household.

Is the senior man's authority based solely on his reputation for skill in organizing the affairs of the camp, or is it also derived from his wealth? In other words, is the inequality among men based on economic inequality among households? I would argue that it is not. Men with large herds certainly do attract attention and, sometimes, neighbors. Poor families may decide to camp near a wealthy man because he needs extra herders to manage his livestock and might hire their sons. Furthermore, he might offer them loans in exchange for their show of respect; this gives them extra capital for livestock deals and gives him extra prestige. But a large herd alone cannot guarantee a high political position, since it can be almost wiped out in a single year by disease or drought. To become a camp senior, a man must have skill in dealing with the other men of his "tribe" and men from different "tribes," as well. What is more, he must enjoy the recognition of the government. This last asset cannot be procured overnight; it may take more than one lifetime to obtain. As we will see in Chapter Four, many camp seniors belong to families which have slowly acquired government recognition over a long period. These men owe their positions not only to wealth, persuasiveness, and skill but also to the political and cultural patrimony of their families.

In sum, I can say that pastoral production does not create stable or extreme differences in wealth among households and also does not, by itself, lead to economic inequality between the sexes. Further, it does not generate political inequalities between poor and rich men; wealthy men do not necessarily become politically prominent, and prominent men do not necessarily become wealthy. However, pastoral production does lead directly to differences in authority; pastoralists must have camp seniors, at least for a good part of each year.

In the next chapter I will be looking at the same residential units (households, extended households, and camps) that I have described as units of production. Instead of viewing them as productive groups, however, I will describe them socially and culturally. I will focus on the spaces where the members of households, extended households, and camps live and on how these spaces are structured.

3 / Culture and Structure in Rashiidi Society

HABITUS—THE STRUCTURE OF HOUSEHOLD SPACE

As we have seen in the first two chapters, when the Rashaayda make a new camp they always take ecological and geographical factors into consideration. Each household pitches its tent as close to fresh pasture and water as it can and, at the same time, keeps its distance from other tents to prevent the spread of animal diseases from one herd to another. Yet these are not the only factors that influence the shape of Rashiidi camps. Every time a household arrives at a campsite, it sets up its tent in a socially appropriate place and organizes the components of the tent itself to make a culturally appropriate pattern. By doing so it sends a visual message to outsiders about the kind of social and cultural order to which it is accustomed. Visitors to the tent decode or "read" these visual signs and discover this order. The structure of the tent thus makes it possible for people inside and outside to orient themselves and behave according to custom, if they so choose.

One way to illustrate this process of encoding and decoding is to describe my first visit to Suluum's brother. This took place during the rainy season, when he was living in an extended household consisting of three tents, standing by themselves in one of the tenancies in Khashm al-Girba (a state-sponsored agricultural project; see Chapter One). I took a bus to Khashm al-Girba and walked from the bus stop to his tenancy. When I reached it and saw the tents pitched in the middle of his plowed fields, I paused to examine them carefully; I wanted to carry out this visit properly, without making any blunders.

My first task was to determine which side of the campsite to approach. Custom and good manners required me to approach the front, rather than the back, of one of the tents. The people inside would expect visitors to come from this direction and would likely see me long before I was within hailing distance. Walking up to the front of the tent (its "face," *wajh*) would be much more polite than sneaking up behind the tent (called "the back of the head," *gufaa*) because it would give the household members time to prepare for my visit. But which side was the "face"? I had learned that it is usually the side of the tent that is open to the prevailing winds. Today, however, there was little wind and both sides of each tent had been opened to catch the breeze (see p. 54). The most reliable clue was a narrow strip of tent cloth, called *as-sinaaḥ,* which is always attached to the "face of the tent" and which hangs down from the main sections of cloth even when they are raised. Once I spotted this I knew where to go.

This was the next question: Which of the three tents should I approach? Suluum had not told me much about her brother; all I knew was that he was in his late fifties and that his parents were dead. Since his father did not live with him, he was probably the senior male member of his extended household. I guessed that he was married to one woman and that his two married sons were residing next to him, in their wives' tents, which meant that I should head toward the middle tent. I based my choice on the principle that "the senior man should not be left on the periphery" (*il-chibiir maa yusiir min ṭaraf*) and on the residential norm which states that "a man's children should stand in a circle around him" (*'iyaal ar-rijjaal yugaaṭiruunah*). If this man's family was actually implementing these norms, his wife's tent should be in the center and his sons' wives' tents on either side of it.

Once I had selected the tent of the senior man's wife, I walked towards it slowly. This allowed the men of the household time to put on their turbans and gave the girls and women a chance to replace their undecorated face coverings (veil and masks) with decorated versions. My slow pace was also a sign of polite "reluctance" (*at-taḥashshud*); it would not be seemly for me to rush up to my potential host, since this would make me appear exceedingly eager to eat and drink at his expense. Next I called out my greetings: *saloom 'aleyk!* ("Peace upon you!") It was only then, and not until then, that the residents gave me a verbal welcome: *yaa marḥab!* ("welcome!") They came out to receive me.

I walked toward the oldest man there, assuming that he must be Suluum's brother. He had heard about me, also, and was ready to welcome me warmly, as if I were a kinsman. He put his right hand on my left shoulder and drew me close to embrace me, asking me loudly, *cheyf ḥaalk? 'asaak ṭayyib* ("How are you? I hope you are well") and kissing the air over my right shoulder three or four times. I replied, *al-laah yusallim ḥaalk* ("God grant you safety") and did the same; then we drew apart briefly and switched sides, so that his head was now over my left shoulder. When we had finished the embrace we stepped apart to shake hands, continuing our verbal greetings at the same time. Meanwhile the women and girls of the household had thrown the ends of their sleeves over their heads—to show their modesty—and had come out to stand beside the senior man and his sons. After I had greeted the sons as well, the women and girls shook hands with me briefly. If Suluum had come with me, she would have embraced her brother and his wife and daughters, but this was something I could not do.

At this point I had reached the threshold of the tent, which was marked by a rush mat. I had to leave my sandals at the edge of this mat, on the uncovered ground. I first stepped out of my right sandal and planted my right foot on the mat; then I kicked off my left sandal. Removing my sandals preserved the cleanliness and purity (*ṭahaara*) of the tent's interior. The sandals and the exterior area were dirty, whereas the interior of the tent was clean, both because it was swept daily by the woman who owned it and because it had been ritually purified. Each year the "female guardian of the tent" (*raa'yit il-beyt*) burned incense inside the tent and let the fragrant smoke collect around two kinds of ritual objects which were hung there: the "flags of the tent" (*raayaat il-beyt*) and the household's copy of the Qur'an (called *al-khaṭma,* the "seal of the revelations," in Rashiidi Arabic). The small, multicolored flags symbolized the honor of the house and the Qur'an symbolized its piety; the guests who sat beneath them were under the protection of the hosts from both natural and supernatural dangers.

My host took me in hand, leading me into the eastern half of the tent. If Suluum had been there she would have been led into the tent's western half. These two parts of the tent are not ordinarily separated but when guests arrive cloths are hung up that divide it into a section for men and a section for women. The senior male guest is given a seat of honor on the bed, in the eastern section, while the senior woman guest is seated close to the hearth, in the western section, where the "female guardian of the tent" makes hot beverages.

I sat down on the bed in the eastern section, after one of the senior man's sons had furnished it with a brightly colored spread (*firaash*). The six men and boys (my host, his two married sons, and his unmarried, coresident sons) filled the tent's eastern section. They sat side-by-side, in a circle; it was considered impolite for anyone to sit in front of another. (On an earlier occasion, when I had sat down in front of 'Abdallah, he had grasped my shoulder and turned me around, saying "Don't show me the back of your head [*laa tiwarrini gufaak*]!") As soon as I was seated Suluum's

*The bed (*ga'aada*) and spread (*firaash*) on which male guests are seated when they enter the tent. In this case the bed has been taken outside the tent so that there would be enough light to photograph it; ordinarily it is inside, especially during the day. One boy is holding a herding stick (*'aṣaa*) on his lap. The other boy is wearing a written charm (*chitaab*) attached to a cord around his neck. It is supposed to protect him from envy.*

brother called to his wife: *yaa mara, sawii linaa shaahi* ("O mara ["wife"/ "woman"], make us tea"). With her sleeve still thrown over her head, she entered the eastern half of the tent, dragging the portable hearth (*chaanuun*) behind her. and proceeded to do just that. She sat down silently, to one side of the gathering, near the hearth. In the meantime I sat on the bed, talking with him. As a male guest, I could not sit near the hearth, just as a female guest could not sit on the bed. Each of these objects was symbolically linked with one sex and one sex only.

Clearly I needed a great deal of background information to find my way successfully from the area outside the tent to my proper place in its interior. Put differently: The Rashiidi tent is more than just a shelter. It is an organized living space in which a whole series of meaningful distinctions and oppositions are made visible. The ground outside is not the same as the ground inside; the right foot is not the same as the left foot; the front of the tent is opposed to its back, and many other oppositions (pure/impure, male/female, east/west, bed/hearth) are implied by peoples' behavior. Furthermore, these distinctions and oppositions are related to each other in complex ways. We can see the connection between male/female, east/west, and bed/hearth, for example; it becomes clear during the first five minutes of the visit that male visitors sit on the bed in the eastern section of the tent while female visitors sit near the hearth in the western section. Space is divided according to sex. But not all of these distinctions are immediately understandable. Why, for example, do visitors put their right feet inside the tent before their left feet? What are we to make of the left/right distinction?

To answer this question, it helps to examine the next five minutes of my visit. We left the senior woman of the house at the hearth, making tea. While the water was heating she washed the tea glasses and set them on a tray. When the tea was ready she filled the glasses and passed the tray to the men without speaking, using her right hand. Suluum's brother passed the tray on to me, offering me the first glass. I picked it up with my right hand and set it down beside me while the host passed the tray to the other men, who in turn passed it to the hostess. I already knew that the guest should be the first to take food and drink and that the host (or hostess) takes his or her share last. When passing the tray to the others, the host uses his right hand. If for some reason he has to do this with his left hand, he may excuse himself with the phrase, *salamat dhiraa'ak* . . . ("May your arm escape injury . . ."). The person taking it from him replies, *tislam* ("May you be safe").

These examples give us the impression that the left hand is associated with misfortune among the Rashaayda (as it is among many other peoples). The right hand, by contrast, is thought to more auspicious and cleaner. This is apparent during meals. When food is served, it is put in two large bowls, one for men and another for women. The men gather around their bowl and pick up the food—rice, porridge, or meat—with their right hands only. Since the left hand is reserved for dirty work, no one uses it for eating, especially when sharing a meal and eating with others from a common bowl. If one man picked up food with his left hand, the others would feel that the food was dirty and would stop eating. Little children, not knowing better, have to be trained to eat only with the right.

Generally, when one Rashiidi interacts with another, he or she tries to "put his best foot forward"—literally, in the context of entering someone's home (as we saw earlier), and figuratively, when handing someone else a glass or a tray. Here it is the human body, not the tent, which has a symbolic structure, and like the structure of the tent, this one must also be learned. Furthermore, the symbolic structure which the Rashaayda impart to the body is related to the symbolic structure of the tent. The face (the most socially significant portion of the body) is made analogous to the "face" of the tent (where visitors are greeted), just as the back of the head (the least significant part of the body socially) is made analogous to the "back" of the tent (where no social interaction takes place).

This kind of structure, which links the body, space, and numerous distinctions and oppositions, is what Pierre Bourdieu (1990) has called a *habitus.* He argues that people learn a culture-specific *habitus* unreflectingly, without explicitly asking questions about it, and that the process of learning a *habitus* has a lasting, constraining influence on thought, feeling, and behavior. Bourdieu believes that any *habitus* is a collection of countless associations and abstract images that is held together only by the common reference points of the human body; it is not a completely coherent or logical system. In the Rashaayda case, for instance, the *habitus* of the household has its impact on even the simplest movements and actions: the way the Rashaayda hold their glasses of tea, their posture when they sit, and their feelings of comfort (or discomfort) when they move from one part of the house to another.

Following Bourdieu, I will describe some aspects of the Rashaayda's *habitus* in this chapter. As we have seen, the tent is an important source of spatial structure among the Rashaayda. The senior woman of the household, especially, must know how to put the parts of the tent together correctly so that this cultural order can be encoded. But the Rashaayda's *habitus* can also be detected, and learned, by decoding other patterns. It is found in the posture of the human body during the Islamic prayer, in the imaginary spaces described in Rashiidi mythology, in the pattern of tents within the camp, and in Rashiidi costume.

THE PRAYER AND SPATIAL STRUCTURE

The patterns of movement during the prayer connect the body of the worshipper with the four cardinal directions and other features of the cosmos. Like all Muslims, when the Rashaayda perform the prayer (*aṣ-ṣalaat*) they start by turning to face Mecca, which lies to the east of Sudan. But they never confuse the east (*al-maṭili'*, "the place where the sun rises" in Rashiidi Arabic) with the proper direction for prayer, the *gibla.* The *gibla* is actually a line connecting a local place of prayer with a shrine in Mecca called the *ka'ba.* When Muslims pray, they face this sacred shrine, which the Prophet Muḥammad purified and made holy for Muslims when he led them in the establishment of the first Islamic state, some 1,400 years ago.

For a Muslim the prayer is not just a conversation between God and a believer; it is a ritual performance, an expression of humility and obedience, and must be done properly. To begin, the believer starts with a declaration of God's omnipotence, raising both hands above his shoulders, palms opened, and saying *allaahu akbar* ("God is supreme"). After this he recites a passage from the Qur'an and repeats the phrase *allaahu akbar.* This is followed by a bow and then a prostration, during which the worshipper touches the ground with his or her forehead and hands. After the first two prostrations the worshipper sits briefly, keeping both knees and lower legs on the ground and turning his left foot underneath him to serve as a seat. The inauspicious left foot is thus covered while the more auspicious right foot is exposed. Then he gets up to finish the prayer, performing between one and six more prostrations depending on the time of day.

Both the worshipper and the ground must be clean. For this reason the Rashaayda keep specially woven mats, small carpets, or sometimes just empty grain sacks in their tents. They hang these up during most of the day to keep them clean and only stand on them while praying. While they stand, bow, prostrate themselves, and sit, they recite verses from the Qur'an and the various ritual formulae that are required during each of the prayer's different phases.

Learning how to pray is an aspect of becoming an adult. Most Rashaayda begin to perform the prayer when they are about fifteen years old. At first they find it difficult, because each of the five daily prayers varies in some details from the others; one must concentrate in order to keep track of the number of prostrations that have been completed. As time passes, however, the prayer becomes a part of them. The posture that is required becomes habitual. Once they have become accustomed to the prayer, young adults orient themselves in the direction of the *gibla* almost as easily as they can find east, north, west, or south. Most develop calluses on their left ankles from the frequent contact with the ground when they sit. One man I knew had even developed a pressure mark (*sajda*) on his forehead, the result of its contact with the prayer mat during prostration (*sujuud*). In the words of Michel Foucault (1977), the Islamic prayer is "inscribed" on the body of the Muslim.

The Rashaayda's experience of the prayer is integrated with their experience of time and space. The names for the five prayers (*al-fajr, aḍ-ḍuhur, al-'aṣir, al-maghrib, al-'ishsha*) are also names for five periods in the daily cycle of time (see Chapter One, p. 16). Standing to face the *gibla* also creates an altered experience of space. The distant, unseen *ka'ba* is pictured as the center of a series of circles with worshippers standing in circular rows around it. Even when the worshipper is praying alone, he feels the presence of other worshippers to his right and his left, and when he completes the prayer he greets them ritually. He first turns his face to the right and says *as-salaamu 'aleykum wa raḥmatu -llaah* ("Peace and God's Mercy upon you") and then turns to the left to repeat this greeting. The feeling of standing on the rim of a vast circle of worshippers is especially acute during the sunset (*maghrib*) prayer, when many people are trying to complete it before the sky becomes dark. Because the time allowed is short, as soon as one starts one has the sense that someone, somewhere, has surely begun his prayer at the same time; all proclaim God's omnipotence simultaneously as members of the Muslim community of faith.

SPATIAL STRUCTURE AND THE RASHAAYDA'S BELIEF SYSTEM

Not all Rashaayda picture the Muslim community in exactly this way, however. Some do not feel the presence of other worshippers to their right and left during the prayer; others do feel it but say that these are angels, not distant human beings. There is a body of Islamic lore about angels that some Rashaayda have read or heard of, and elements of this lore have become part of their belief system. They have no idea what angels look like, however, and no one adopts any dogmatic positions regarding this subject. Some Rashaayda, especially the *mawaaliid* ("descendants of free Rashiidi men and slave women"), know pious songs about the angels, but the majority hesitate to claim any definite knowledge of them.

The Rashaayda tolerate a variety of beliefs about angels, *jinn* (invisible people who live underground), and other supernatural beings, neither trying to prove them false nor attributing much importance to them. Beliefs in supernatural beings contribute to the structure of space. For example, some Rashaayda believe in a mythical race of half-humans/half-dogs called *dhuwi machlaboo* ("the dog-people"). These people are said to live "somewhere to the west." Their women are said to have the ability to switch back and forth between human and canine form but their husbands can assume only the appearance of dogs. Some Rashaayda are said to have met the *dhuwi machlaboo* during excursions to the west. The dog-men bark to welcome guests and their wives offer them coffee.

Other supernatural beings, the were-hyenas, are also associated with the west. They are said to live among the West African immigrants to Sudan who have villages in and near the Khashm al-Girba scheme. They are human sorcerers who transform themselves into hyenas (*maraafi'*) by facing west (turning their backs to the *gibla*), squatting, and urinating into their hands. Instead of using water to wash for prayer, they wash their hands and faces with urine, and this perverse rite turns them into cannibalistic hyenas. Then they go out after sunset to hunt for human prey, trying to catch and eat people who are traveling at night.

Stories of the dog-people and were-hyenas circulate, primarily as a form of entertainment. Some Rashaayda reject them scornfully and say there is no basis in Islam for such stories; they point out that dog-people and were-hyenas are not mentioned in the Qur'an. Others delight in repeating and elaborating them. Regardless of whether these stories are thought to be true, or whether they are accepted as Islamic, they endow the west with an aura of mystery.

Another important aspect of imaginary space in Rashiidi thinking is social, not geographical. The Rashaayda divide space into inhabited territory (*diira 'umraana*), empty desert (*il-khalaa*), and haunted territory (*diira maskuuna*). Haunted territory is the domain of ghosts (*hiilaan*), ogresses (*sa'aalwa*), and *jinn*. These supernatural beings are visible only at night, when they take human form. They live far away from the camps of the Rashaayda and for this reason are encountered only by men who happen to be traveling through the empty desert at night. Aḥmad, a friend of mine, told me the following story about a man who had spent the night in haunted territory, with *hiilaan*.

Myth Two: Ghosts (*hiilaan*)

Aḥmad's friend was riding back to his family's camp from the town of 'Aṭbara. It was nighttime; the sun had set long before he could complete his trip, and he had to depend on his knowledge of the stars to find his way. He was tired and hoped that he might come across a Rashiidi camp where he could spend the night. As he rode he gradually became aware of the faint beating of a drum in the distance. He looked around and saw campfires on the horizon. Apparently a group of Rashaayda had camped there and were dancing to the beat of a drum (*ṭaar*), a customary form of entertainment. He urged his camel to head toward this camp.

When he reached it he saw a cluster of about five tents. A group of young men and girls had gathered near one of the tents to dance. He dismounted and they welcomed him, giving him water to drink and making him tea. Then they resumed their dancing, and he joined the circle of young men, keeping his sword slung over his shoulder as they did. One man knelt on the ground and held the flat, broad drum. He beat out a tune with it and one of the girls knelt opposite him. Although her mouth was covered by her veil and her head covered by a large piece of white cloth, Aḥmad's friend could see how beautiful she was. She "danced" while kneeling, in the customary way, holding the white cloth over her head with both hands, bending at the waist until her face almost touched the ground and then straightening suddenly, bobbing up and down rapidly to the beat of the drum. He watched her, fascinated, and when his turn came to take the drum he played for her. All of the young men took their turns, until the girl tired and left the circle. Another girl came to replace her, and the dance continued until the middle of the night.

After the dance was over one of the men invited Aḥmad's friend to sleep in his tent, and he gratefully accepted. As he was carrying his saddle into the tent he saw his host's wife, who was standing near the hearth. He happened to glance down at her feet and saw, with a shock, that they were not normal; her left foot was attached to her right leg, and vice versa! He realized at once that these "people" were not human beings after all, but ghosts. Seized by fear, he gripped the handle of his sword and pulled the blade out of its scabbard, saying *bismi llaahi r-raḥmaan ir-raḥiim* ("In the name of God, the Merciful and Compassionate") to protect himself. He knew that ghosts feared two things: iron and the name of God. Suddenly the entire camp disappeared, and he was left standing by himself in the middle of the desert.

This story illustrated the characteristics of haunted territory and also gave me good advice about how to protect myself from ghosts. I doubted that Aḥmad entirely believed it. Credible or not, it made it possible for him to put together a detailed picture of an imaginary landscape.

Inhabited territory, in contrast to haunted territory, is where people live. Even graveyards are classified as "inhabited" by the Rashaayda because they are dwelling places for the souls of the dead. Graveyards are usually located close to the houses of the living, in towns and villages, but there are also graveyards in the desert. If someone dies in the empty desert the Rashaayda do not bury him on the spot but take the body to a site where there are graves. They do not want the dead person to lie alone in his grave until the Day of Judgment; he needs company. Regardless of whether the people in inhabited territory dwell in tents, permanent houses, graves, or other shelters, they all seek God's blessing by invoking His name. Unlike ghosts, they do not retreat in fear from the name of God.

When people are in an inhabited territory they frequently recite *al-Faatiḥa,* the opening verse of the Qur'an. When they enter a graveyard, for instance, they read *al-Faatiḥa,* asking for God's blessing for the souls who dwell there. The preeminent inhabited space is, of course, a tent. The Rashaayda recite *al-Faatiḥa* when inside tents for a variety of reasons. For example, when a "female guardian of a tent" is serving coffee to guests, she often invokes God or the memory of one of the Muslim saints (*awliyaa' allaah*). She says:

al-faatiḥa li-llaah fii sabiil illaah
allaah yiftaḥ ilnaa al-kheyr wa abwaabah
wi yighalliǧ 'annaa ash-sharr wa nishaabah

("The Opening is for God, for the sake of God;
May God open to us the doors of goodness and plenty
And shut away from us evil and its traps.")

Alternately, she may address a saint to ask for his intercession with God, especially ash-Shaadhili, whose name is associated with coffee:

yaa ash-Shaadhili yaa Abu Ḥasan
wa al-anbiyaa wa al-mursaliin

("O ash-Shaadhili, father of Ḥasan,
And the Prophets and the Messengers [of God].")

Those who hear her raise their hands, palms upward, and silently recite the first verse of the Qur'an. Then she pours the coffee. The tent is the appropriate place to ask for God's blessing and read *al-Faatiḥa* because, according to Rashiidi beliefs, it is an inhabited location that God does not forsake. It is perhaps for this reason that most of the Rashaayda's life-crisis rituals (childbirth rites, rites for naming newborn children, circumcisions, and weddings) are held inside tents, never outside them. The tent is also the locus for all formal offerings of hospitality. Guests are always served food and drink inside a tent, never outside under the hot sun.

THE EXTENDED HOUSEHOLD AND ITS SPACE

The tent is not the only inhabited space in Rashiidi society. The campsite, or *daar,* is also inhabited; it is occupied by the members of an extended household, who set up their tents close together. The *daar* has its own spatial structure. Let us continue our exploration of the Rashaayda's *habitus* by moving outside of the tent and examining the *daar.*

In many cases the *daar* consists of three or four tents standing in a row. For example, the *daar* of Suluum's brother in Khashm al-Girba, which I visited and described at the beginning of this chapter, consisted of a row of three tents. As we saw, the senior man and woman of such an extended household set up their tent in the center of the campsite, and the other tents are set up on either side of it. If the tents are more numerous they are set up to form a cluster; the junior men of the extended household "make a circle" around the senior man.

This center/periphery opposition is explicitly mentioned in the Rashaayda's legal codes. The "male guardian of a tent" is required by customary law to stop any fighting that occurs within the *guṭr* (perimeter) of his household's space; every senior man of a household is responsible for keeping the peace. To determine where this perimeter lies (and where his legal liability ends), he stands near the tent pegs of his wife's tent and throws a herding stick as far as he can. The spot where it falls marks the boundary of his household's space. If he is the senior man of an extended household (and not just the "guardian of a tent") he is responsible for preventing conflict between strangers and any member of his extended household. The perimeter of his extended household is also defined by throwing a herding stick.

From the man's point of view, therefore, the structure of the *daar* is circular, consisting of a center and a periphery. From a woman's viewpoint, however, a large *daar* ideally consists of sets of straight lines. For coresident women the straight line is the symbol of equality. When two women are camping together and have a close social relationship—for example, when a woman is living next to her mother's tent, during her first year of marriage—they symbolize this warm, egalitarian relationship by setting up their tents close together, in a row, so that the ropes of one tent cross some of the ropes of the other tent. If the women of the two or three households do not have a close relationship—for example, if they are the three co-wives of a single man—but nevertheless are equals, their tent ropes do not cross, but the tents themselves are aligned in a straight row.

At first thought it might seem difficult to understand how men and women can perceive the same pattern of tents in two different ways—as a circle and as a set of straight lines—but a glance at the actual layout of my *daar* and the *daar* of my neighbor, Mujalli (see Chapter One, p. 24) should help. I have drawn a map of my *daar* as it was at the end of my stay with the Rashaayda, after Ḥaamid and Suluum's daughter Faḍiyya had gotten married and had set up her own household to the west of Suluum's tent (see Figure 3). Mujalli appears encircled by his married sons and sons-in-law. Mujalli's two wives, Maṭar and Ṣaaliḥa (as noted earlier, these are not their real names), appear in a medial, straight line of tents, with Ṣaaliḥa flanked by her married daughter Fawt and Maṭar flanked by her son and daughter-in-law. Suluum also appears in a straight line, flanked on one side by her married daughter Faḍiyya and on the other by her daughter-in-law 'Aabda.

THE ISLAMIC HOLIDAYS, CAMP SPACE, AND COSTUME

Some of the rituals that the members of a camp carry out also create spatial structure. Activities during the two main Islamic holidays are good examples.

These two Islamic holidays—called *'iid aḍ-ḍaḥiyya* ("the Feast of Sacrifice") and *'iid al-fiṭir* ("the Feast of Ending the Fast") by the Rashaayda—occur once every Islamic (lunar) year. The *'iid al-fiṭir* is celebrated at the end of the month of Ramaḍaan, during which all practicing Muslims refrain from eating and drinking during daylight hours. Each holiday begins with a collective prayer, for which all of the males in the camp (men, adolescents, and even little boys) assemble early in the morning. They all put on clean clothes and turbans (which is a treat for adolescents and a new experience for the small children) and walk out of the camp toward a level

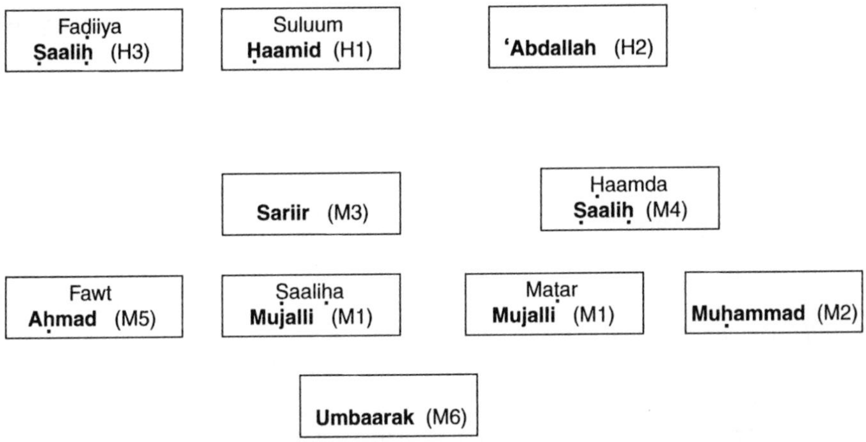

Note: Wive's names appear at the top of each rectangle, husbands' names appear in bold at the bottom of each rectangle, and the names of married men who are senior men of households are followed by a number (M1, M2, and so on).

Figure 3 The Patterning of Tents Belonging to Two Extended Households, M (dhuwi *Mujalli) and H* (dhuwi *Ḥaamid)*

stretch of ground. When they arrive they clear the ground of any vegetation that could get in the way and form two or three long rows. They stand there facing Mecca, waiting for the prayer leader, or *imaam,* to begin the ritual. He stands in front of them, also facing Mecca, and performs the bows and prostrations required for the prayer; they follow him attentively, repeating his movements. Then he turns to face them and delivers a short sermon. This ends the prayer. As soon as it is over the men in the lines turn to each other, embrace, and exchange holiday greetings.

The women and girls stay behind in their tents and perform their holiday prayers there. Then they change into their best holiday clothes and wait for the men to return.

For a woman, leaving the enclosed space of the tent and entering the open desert means that she has left Women's Space and has entered Men's Space. The boundary between these two areas is marked by an imaginary line connecting all of the wooden pegs that have been driven into the ground around the extended household's tents (including both hers and her neighbors'). These pegs anchor the ropes (*aṭnaab*) that support the tents. Even on ordinary occasions, when a woman walks beyond the tent pegs, she covers her head with her sleeve to show her modesty while in Men's Space. When she returns to her tent she lets her sleeve fall.

During the holidays women mark the boundary between Men's Space and Women's Space even more explicitly by standing right near the tent pegs. Each married woman waits in front of her tent, near the tent pegs. She covers her head with her sleeve and wears a long, richly decorated, thick veil called a *burga'* that descends

A woman covering her head with the end of her sleeve, marking her movement into Men's Space.

from her forehead to her waist, leaving only her eyes uncovered. This veil is worn only by married women and only on special occasions (such as weddings and Islamic holidays). When the men pass by on the way back to their tents they give holiday greetings to each married woman, saying *min il-'aayidiin* ("[May you be] one of the people who celebrate!") and touching her gently on one shoulder in a light embrace. She replies *kull 'aam wa anta bi kheyr* ("[May you be] prosperous and happy every year"). This brief exchange identifies the married woman as the owner of a tent and the representative of a household. It also dramatizes the contrast between Women's Space (where she stands) and Men's Space (through which the men are passing).

Another ritual activity, which takes place during the Feast of Sacrifice, emphasizes the contrast between the center of the camp and its periphery. It takes place shortly after the morning prayer, after the senior man of each household has returned to his home and has butchered a goat or a sheep in preparation for the holiday meal. After the butchering is finished, one man—the man who is also the senior man of the camp—stays in his tent, in the center of the camp. He builds a fire and puts a cut of meat from the animal he has butchered in a cooking pot. The other men leave their homes and walk to the camp senior's tent, each carrying a leg of raw mutton or goat's meat in a bowl. When they arrive they all put their cuts of meat into the pot and the camp senior puts it on the fire. After an hour or so, when the meat is well-cooked, the camp senior redistributes it. No one, not even the camp senior, receives any more than what he contributed; there is no material gain. The senior man gains symbolically, however; every household in the camp that sends a representative to his tent is giving him a gesture of respect and support.

SYMBOLISM AND PASTORAL PRODUCTION: HOW ARE THEY RELATED?

Let us pause briefly to take stock of the ethnographic information in this chapter. I have tried to show how the objects in Rashiidi tents and camps are arranged to form patterns and oppositions (front/back, center/periphery, circle/line) so that they become parts of complex spatial structures (men guests/women guests :: eastern section/western section :: bed/hearth; right foot/left foot :: exposed/covered :: auspicious/inauspicious). The dominant approach in this chapter has been to treat objects as symbols. This contrasts sharply with the approach of Chapter Two, in which objects such as pastures, tents, and hearths were treated primarily as instruments of production. At this point it may be wise to ask: What is the connection between the two? How do the Rashaayda relate—and how can we relate—instruments of production to symbols?

I do not believe that there is any simple, direct connection between the productive process and the symbolic process. For example, even though the conditions of pastoral production make it necessary for the Rashaayda to build two kinds of tent

*Two women standing in front of their reed houses with their husbands, waiting to give holiday greetings. They are wearing ritual veils (*baraaği'*) and their best, most thickly embroidered, dresses. Note how they have raised their hands to display their silver rings. This picture was taken in a new settlement where formerly nomadic Rashaayda have started to adopt a sedentary way of life.*

(one for the rainy seasons and another for the dry seasons), there is nothing in pastoral production that compels them to assign the eastern side of the tent to male guests and the western side to women guests. Symbolic thought cannot be reduced to the techniques of production.

This does not mean, on the other hand, that there is no relation whatsoever between the two. It is reasonable to suggest that the objects and acts which have the greatest importance in production in a given society are likely to have at least some symbolic significance also. As we have seen, the tents that women make in order to provide their families with physical shelter also serve as symbolic shelters that are periodically purified and blessed. The swords on which men rely to defend themselves from human enemies are also used to ward off supernatural dangers. Finally, the two cardinal directions—north and south—which are of greatest importance for pastoral production (since the Rashaayda move south in July to reach the first rainy season pastures and then move north, following the rains) also have a special place in the Rashaayda's vocabulary. Unlike the words for "east" (*maṭili'*) and "west" (*mughiib*), the nouns for "north" (*shimaal*) and "south" (*yaman*) can be made into verbs: *yitshaamil* means "to head north" and *yityaamin* means "to head south." Hence it seems that the material conditions of production influence some of the most abstract elements of Rashiidi culture: their linguistic categories. Yet material conditions do not determine the entire content of that culture.

We could debate the merits of a materialist or idealist explanation of Rashiidi behavior, thought, and culture at greater length. A Marxist might argue that the production process described in Chapter Two underlies and determines the symbolic acts described in Chapter Three. From a Boasian or Geertzian viewpoint, however, the symbolic structures come first, since without a meaningful frame of reference neither productive nor nonproductive action is possible for human beings. To take camels to pasture, for example, one must first know what "camels" are, what kinds of plants camels eat, and where these plants are likely to be found. Hence cultural knowledge precedes and guides instrumental behavior.

Which explanation is correct? It might be better to ask: How can the two explanations be reconciled? To support either a Marxist or idealist explanation of human behavior, we would have to sharply distinguish "productive" from "nonproductive" ("merely symbolic") action and decide which is the independent variable and which is the dependent variable. Unfortunately most human actions are not so easily characterized as exclusively "productive" or "symbolic"; many are both at the same time. Setting up a tent, for example, is neither purely instrumental nor purely symbolic. This is because a tent is a piece of property, closely identified with the people who make it and live in it. As property, a tent is both a symbol of the owner's identity and an object that he or she has a right to use.

In what follows, then, I will describe some kinds of property among the Rashaayda, since property has both symbolic and instrumental significance. Rather than trying to choose between a materialist and an idealist explanation of Rashiidi behavior and thinking, I will try to combine the technical/economic perspective with the symbolic perspective. I will begin with the most insubstantial yet the most important kind of property that an individual Rashiidi can have: his genealogical name. Then I will discuss households, the ways in which households are named, and the property which household members use: tents and livestock.

NAMES, SOCIAL IDENTITY, AND GENEALOGICAL STRUCTURES

There are three kinds of names among the Rashaayda: the genealogical name (*ism*), the teknonym (*kunya*), and the "teasing name" (*nibza*). Genealogical names for both men and women consist of their personal names plus the names of their male ancestors. We have already encountered many personal names: Suluum (meaning "safety and peace"), Naafi' ("beneficial, useful"), Ḥaamid ("praising [God]"), and 'Abdallah ("God's worshipper"). Each person's name is combined with his or her father's, grandfather's, and great-grandfather's personal names. For example, 'Abdallah's genealogical name was 'Abdallah ibin ("the son of") Ḥasan ibin Umbaarak ibin 'Abdallah ibin Ḥayyaan, and his mother's genealogical name was Suluum bint ("the daughter of") Muḥammad ibin Umbaarak ibin Bureych ibin Ḥayyaan.

Teknonyms have a different form. They consist of a sex-specific prefix (*abu,* "father of," for a man and *umm,* "mother of" for a woman) followed by the personal name of a child. A teknonym usually refers to one of the individual's children. Suluum, for example, was sometimes called *Umm 'Abdallah,* "mother of 'Abdallah," after her eldest son 'Abdallah. But not everyone who has a teknonym has children. For example, I was sometimes called *Abu Salma,* "father of Salma." I was of marriageable age and my friends anticipated that when I married and had children I would name my eldest daughter Salma. Men are usually given teknonyms that refer to their daughters, while women's teknonyms usually refer to their sons; each adult is identified in terms of his or her child of the opposite sex. Teknonyms are used infrequently among the Rashaayda because they are a special sign of affection. My friends only called me Abu Salma when they were especially glad to see me, for instance after a long absence; they reserved it for special occasions.

The third type of name, the *nibza* or "teasing name," is used all too often. It consists of a derisory adjective or phrase and identifies a person by singling out his ridiculous or negative characteristics. One man, for instance, was called *saafiǧ rizgah,* "squanderer of his blessings." He had more wealth than most and sometimes paid more money than he had to, without hard bargaining, when he bought livestock; he could afford to pay a little extra. His *nibza* reflected his neighbors' desire to cut him down to size. Another man was called *ar-raadi,* "the radio," because he had the bad habit of talking nonstop; he liked to sit and chat, so much that others sometimes found it hard to get a word in edgewise. Neither of these men liked their *nibzas* and would not allow anyone to use them within earshot. Other teasing names were less offensive. One woman was called *dimna,* "goat turd," because she was short and compact. She never got angry when she heard it, and people actually used it to address her.

Genealogical names as property: Names and the gift of life. For the Rashaayda the most important difference among the three kinds of names is that the *kunya* and *nibza* may be given freely while the genealogical name must be paid for. To bestow a name on the child, the parents must acknowledge their debt to God for the child's life and give away some of their animal wealth in the form of food. A child is given his name a month or so after his birth during a ritual "naming" (*ism*). His father butchers a goat and distributes the meat as *ṣiddiga* (a ritual offering for the sake of one's children or for one's parents). The child's neighbors come to share in the meal and are told what his or her name is. When the child grows up and his parents are dead, he should remember that his parents "slaughtered an animal for" his name and should reciprocate by sponsoring a meal in their memory, hoping to earn God's favor for their souls. Both men and women give *ṣiddigaat* for their deceased parents.

Genealogical names, in other words, are ratified by symbolic exchanges between the generations, living and dead. The names are publicized by concrete exchanges of food among the living. They are, in effect, a kind of property that only one particular individual has the right to use. As such, they make it possible to connect each individual with a single household and identify the more concrete kinds of property owned by that individual.

Genealogical names and the names of households. Another significant difference between the genealogical name and the *kunya* or *nibza* is that the genealogical name differentiates one individual from another in a systematic way. It is part of a system of names—a genealogy—that links a person to his or her ancestors. Although the *kunya* or *nibza* certainly can identify a person uniquely, they cannot form a system that both distinguishes individuals from each other and relates them. Only a genealogy can do that.

A *kunya* or *nibza* can become part of a genealogy if it is useful for distinguishing two different ancestors who have the same personal name. For instance, at first glance it might seem that Suluum (bint Muḥammad ibin Umbaarak) and her son 'Abdallah (ibin Ḥasan ibin Umbaarak) are descended from the same grandfather, Umbaarak. However, if we ask for their full genealogical names ('Abdallah ibin Ḥasan ibin Umbaarak ibin 'Abdallah ibin Ḥayyaan; Suluum bint Muḥammad ibin Umbaarak ibin Bureych ibin Ḥayyaan), we can see that Suluum's grandfather is not the same person as 'Abdallah's grandfather. Alternately, we can ask about the *kunyas* and *nibzas* of these two ancestors. We find that they are different: The *kunya* of 'Abdallah's grandfather is *Abu Sariir,* "the father of Sariir"), while the *nibza* of Suluum's grandfather is *as-Suweyṭiira,* "the little meat cleaver"; he was the son of Bureych *Li'baan,* "the playful." Thus 'Abdallah and Suluum have a common ancestor (Ḥayyaan) but different grandfathers (Umbaarak *as-Suweyṭiira* and Umbaarak *Abu Sariir;* see Figure 4).

Genealogical names are used to identify households. For example, my household was named after its senior man, Ḥaamid ibin 'Aayiḍ (see Chapter Two, p. 33) and 'Abdallah's household, which at the time of my fieldwork included him, his wife 'Aabda, and his infant children, was named after him: 'Abdallah ibin ("the son of") Ḥasan ibin Umbaarak. His household was called *dhuwi* 'Abdallah ("'Abdallah's people").[1] Both *dhuwi* Ḥaamid and *dhuwi* 'Abdallah were part of our extended household, which was also named after Suluum's husband Ḥaamid. When we joined the dry season camp near the water pipe we set up our tents near another extended household called *dhuwi* Mujalli. It was named after Mujalli ibin Umbaarak, the extended household's senior man (see Chapter One, p. 24).

It may seem surprising that these households were named after men even though the tents in which the household members lived were owned by women. But

[1]Note that the phrase "*dhuwi* 'Abdallah" is ambiguous; it could mean either "people living with 'Abdallah" or "people descended from 'Abdallah." I have written *dhuwi* in italics whenever it has the former meaning. When "dhuwi" names a group of descendants it appears in roman type, with a capital letter: Dhuwi.

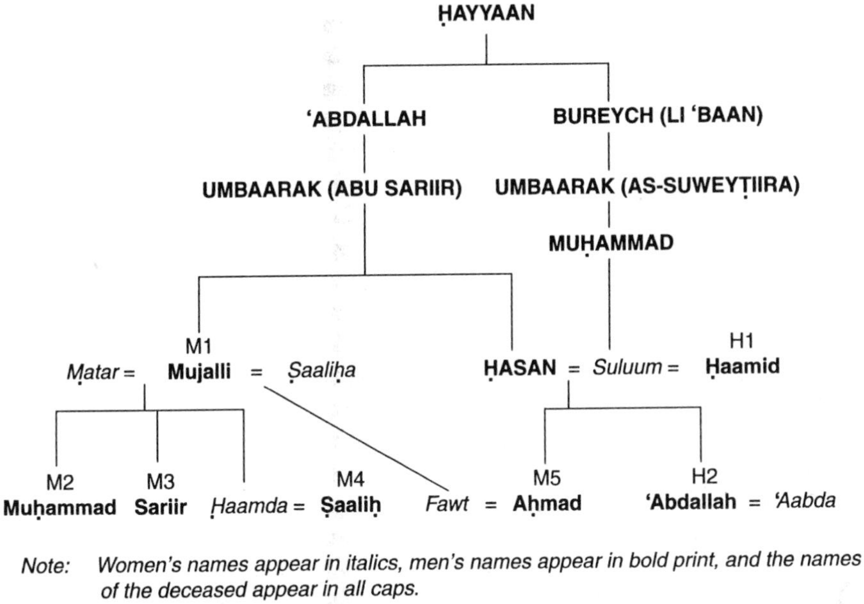

*Figure 4 Genealogical and Affinal Links among the Senior Men of Two Extended Households, M (*dhuwi *Mujalli) and H (*dhuwi *Ḥaamid)*

this makes sense in light of the Rashaayda's residence rules. Among the Rashaayda, it is customary for a newly married couple to pitch their tent near the wife's mother's tent for their first year of married life. As they say, *al-'aam il-awwil ḥagg il-mara,* "the first year after marriage belongs to the wife"; that is, the wife has the right to stay near her parents. At the end of this year, however, the couple moves to the husband's father's camp. They usually reside near the husband's father for as long as he lives. Since the husband's brothers tend to follow the same custom, the result is a cluster of married brothers living around their father's tent. So it was reasonable for them to name their extended household after their father.

This was the case for one of the two extended households mentioned above: *dhuwi* Mujalli. *Dhuwi* Mujalli consisted of seven tents. First came the tents of Mujalli's two wives, who I will again refer to as Maṭar and Ṣaaliḥa. Each of Mujalli's wives had her own tent and her own children, and so Mujalli was a member of two different households simultaneously. He spent half of his time in one tent and the rest of his time in the other. Each of his wives' households could be called *dhuwi* Mujalli, since he was the senior man of each—but whenever we needed to distinguish one from the other, we named them after their senior women: *beyt Maṭar* ("Maṭar's tent") and *beyt Ṣaaliḥa* ("Ṣaaliḥa's tent").

Of the five other tents clustered around Mujalli's wives' tents, three were inhabited by Mujalli's married sons and their wives and the other two belonged to his married daughters. All of these households were named after their senior men: Muḥammad ibin Mujalli ibin Umbaarak, Sariir ibin Mujalli ibin Umbaarak, Umbaarak ibin

Mujalli ibin Umbaarak, Ṣaaliḥ (Mujalli's eldest son-in-law), and Aḥmad ibin Ḥasan ibin Umbaarak (Suluum's recently married son and the husband of Mujalli's daughter). Once his first year of married life was over, Aḥmad was expected to move his wife's tent next to his mother's tent, in my extended household's campsite. This would leave *dhuwi* Mujalli with only one attached son-in-law; all of the other married men in his extended household would be Mujalli's sons. Thus Mujalli's extended household consisted of a core of his sons and daughters, to which was added his sons' wives and daughters' husbands. With only one exception, the extended household did truly consist of "Mujalli's people" (see Figures 3 and 4).

It is easy to see from Figure 4 that the genealogical names and the idea of patrilineal descent gave structure to the large group of people—some 35 people in all—who were members of the two extended households. On a person-to-person basis, the genealogical relationships between some of them were complex. For instance, Maṭar was the wife's father's wife (WFW) of Aḥmad, the father's father's father's brother's son's son's wife (FFFBSSW) of Suluum, and the husband's brother's wife's father's wife (HBWFW) of 'Aabda. Maṭar herself would find this genealogical description unnecessarily complicated; when the people are considered as members of households the relationships are simple. She would say that she belongs to *dhuwi* Mujalli by marriage and so does Aḥmad; hence they are related. Suluum is a "blood" relative of Maṭar's husband Mujalli, hence an affine of Maṭar. 'Aabda belongs to *dhuwi* Ḥaamid by marriage, and *dhuwi* Ḥaamid, as an extended household, is related to *dhuwi* Mujalli by marriage. So Maṭar is also related to 'Aabda by marriage; 'Aabda is one of Maṭar's husband's affinal relatives. Genealogical names make it possible to identify households and then to describe relationships between individuals belonging to different households.

Genealogical names and property marks: Symbols as instruments of production. Genealogical names are used for identifying property as well as individuals, particularly animal property (livestock). Names are used in combination with brands (*wusuum*) to mark and identify animals. As we see in Figure 5, there are three main forms for Rashiidi livestock brands, each of which pertains to a "branch" (called a *gabiila*) of the Rashaayda "tribe" (also called a *gabiila*).

The original ancestor of the Rashaayda is said to be a man named Rashiid or Rashiid az-Zool. The Rashaayda do not know how many generations have passed since this man died nor whether the next three names in the genealogy are the names of his children, great-grandchildren, or even more distant descendants. Most of them simply assume that they are somehow descended from Rashiid az-Zool and that they are the founders of the three "tribal branches": the Baraaṭiikh, the Biraa'aṣa, and the Zuneymaat. They also say that these three ancestors fathered many sons who in turn had many male children. These latter became the ancestors of the numerous small lineages that are part of each "branch." For example, Ḥayyaan, the grandson (or great-grandson?) of Burey'aṣ, became the ancestor of the Dhuwi Ḥayyaan lineage, and Mufliḥ, the descendant of Barṭiikh, became the ancestor of the Mafaaliḥa lineage.

The Rashaayda have little interest in the intervening ancestors who link the three original founders' names (Barṭiikh, Burey'aṣ, and Zuneym) to the founders of

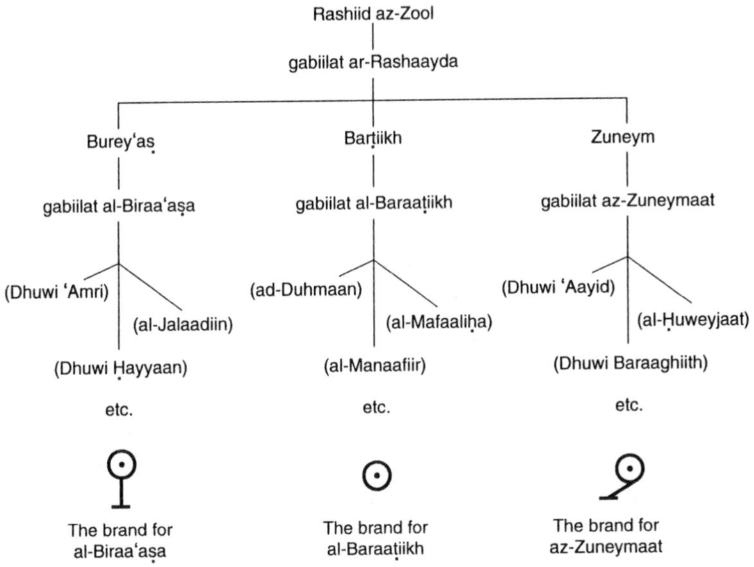

Figure 5 Brief Genealogy and Brands of the Rashaayda of Sudan

the lineages (for example, Ḥayyaan, founder of the Dhuwi Ḥayyaan and the great-great-grandfather of Suluum). What matters to them is that each lineage is part of a "tribal branch," and each "branch" has an ancestor, a name, and a distinctive brand that all the members of that branch use for marking their livestock. The best way to grasp the close connection between genealogical names, household identity, and livestock brands is to examine some brands. One man from the Dhuwi Ḥayyaan lineage had two brothers and three sons. He used brand number 1 (see Figure 6) to mark his livestock, while his brothers used brands 2 and 3. Two of his sons were still unmarried and lived with him in the same household; they used his brand (i.e., number 1) to mark their animals. His third son had married and had set up an independent household; he and his wife lived in a separate tent, next to the tent of his father and mother. After marrying he added a distinguishing mark to his father's brand to produce brand number 4. He took great care when adding this mark to make sure that his brand contrasted with all other currently used brands and not just his father's brand. He asked the other men in our camp whether they recognized it, and when he was satisfied that they did not, he used it. All of these brands contrasted with the brand used by one of their neighbors in their dry-season camp, who belonged to the Dhuwi 'Amri lineage of the Biraa'aṣa "branch." This neighbor used brand 5.

Brands are of great usefulness for nomadic Rashaayda because they allow each family to distinguish its livestock from that of its neighbors. This is vital during the dry season, when dozens of unrelated households camp around a well and must constantly keep their animals from mingling. The brands are also used for identifying and recovering stray animals, as I pointed out in Chapter One (p. 22). Because the system of "tribal brands" and "tribal branches" is so important practically and economically it is very difficult to change. Thousands of Rashiidi households use the

Figure 6 Brands Used by Members of the Biraa'aṣa "Branch"

brands, sort them into three basic types, and associate each type with a "tribal branch." Anyone who wants to challenge the notion that there are three "tribal branches" has to go against the current of public opinion and established usage, as the following case shows.

Case Three: "Branches" and Brands

I went to visit a man from the Manaafiir lineage to ask him for his genealogy. While he was giving me the names of his ancestors he said there were four "branches" (*gabaayil*) of the Rashaayda "tribe" (*gabiila*): the Biraa'aṣa, the Zuneymaat, the Baraaṭiikh, and the Manaafiir. I was surprised. "Aren't the Manaafiir part of the Baraaṭiikh 'branch'?" I asked. "No," he said, and proceeded to recite a long list of names that placed the ancestor of the Manaafiir in the same generation as the ancestors of the three "branches" which I already knew. "The founders of the four 'branches' were brothers," he said.

I knew that most other Rashaayda—and the Sudanese government, as well—recognized only three "tribal branches" and concluded that this man was making a political claim. He wanted his lineage to be recognized as equal in numbers and

Men from the Dhuwi Ḥayyaan lineage burning their brand into the hide of a camel. Note how they have hobbled the camel. To keep it from biting, one of the men is gripping it by its sensitive nostrils, thus immobilizing its head. Fifteen minutes after being branded, the camel was walking around and grazing normally.

An assortment of brands used by the Biraa'aṣa "tribal branch." This photograph was taken inside one of the houses in Kassala frequented by the Rashaayda; whenever they spend the night there, they rent a bed from the owner of the house. During their leisure hours these guests have carved their brands into the walls.

political importance to one of the three main divisions of the "tribe." At the time I had been living with the Rashaayda for two years and had never heard anyone else make such a claim. I decided to ask Suluum what she thought of it.

When I went home I told Suluum what I had heard. "Is it true that the ancestor of the Manaafiir was the brother of Burey'iṣ?" I asked. "I don't know," she said, a little impatiently. "My grandfather only said that Burey'iṣ had two brothers. But the Manaafiir use the Baraaṭiikh brand, don't they?" she asked rhetorically, tracing it in the sand in front of her with her finger. "Yes, they do," I replied. "Then how can they be a separate 'branch'?" she said triumphantly. "They must be Baraaṭiikh."

This case illustrates the gap between the genealogical names of living individuals and their families, on the one hand, and the schematic, pseudo-genealogical units known as "tribes" and "branches," on the other. Suluum did not care whether the ancestor of the Rashaayda had fathered three sons or four; what mattered to her was the system of brands. Although she knew her great-great grandfather's name she was only vaguely familiar with her more distant ancestors. Her detailed genealogy of recent ancestors was merged with a superficially "genealogical" set of names that was actually grounded in the Rashaayda's branding system. It was the use of these brands that preserved the structure of the "tribe" and its "branches," not detailed genealogical knowledge.

Property, residence rules, and household structure. Just as property marks affect the structure of genealogies, the ownership of property itself (livestock, tents) affects the structure of households. A household's composition changes as its members die, leave in order to marry, or give birth to children. Although the Rashaayda have conventions about where people should live when their parents die, when they marry, or when they become parents, these conventions are not always strictly applied. The Rashaayda take property into consideration when they decide whether or not to follow the "residence rules" described earlier.

The Rashaayda say, for example, that a man is supposed to live uxorilocally, with his wife's parents, for the first year of marriage. After that, he is expected to return to his father's camp and live near his father and married brothers. Mujalli's sons had put this ideal into practice, but Aḥmad ibin Ḥasan (Suluum's second son) had not done so. Mujalli's sons were not any more respectful of tradition than Suluum's son; they simply had different material interests.

The members of an extended household cannot be expected to have exactly the same needs and wants. As individuals, they differ in their abilities, plans, and ages, and as the married heads of households, they have different strategies for allocating their labor and material resources. They do not all own the same kinds of livestock and do not all have the same number of dependents and co-workers (wives and children). Some arguments about where to migrate, how to use the extended household's beasts of burden, and how to invest their cash in nonpastoralist ventures are bound to emerge from time to time. As long as the senior man of the extended household is still alive, however, he has the authority to suppress any serious conflicts among his sons. Moreover, even the losing party in any quarrel would retain his dignity since he would be conceding defeat to his father rather than to his brother.

Mujalli's sons all expected to inherit some of their father's livestock when he died; Islamic law specifies that a man's sons should inherit equal shares of his property. (Islamic law also grants a daughter a portion of the inheritance, equal to one-half of a son's share, but the Rashaayda do not apply this part of the law.) Because their father was still alive they all had an interest in preserving and increasing his animal wealth, and so they were willing to live with him and help him with the tasks of livestock breeding. Staying in his extended household made it possible to protect and augment their inheritance, but it also meant that they had to subordinate their personal interests and the short-term interests of their individual households for the common good. Mujalli was so successful in his role of family mediator that I never heard of any serious conflicts among his married sons. One quarrel between two of his unmarried sons did take place, however, and shed light on the structure of his household.

Case Four: Fathers and Sons

Two of Mujalli's sons, whom I will call 'Ali and 'Umar, were in their late teens and were trying to accumulate some extra cash. They needed money to get married and knew of only two ways to earn it: Either they could find a labor contract and go work in Saudi Arabia, or they could work in the livestock trade, buying and selling sheep or taking camels to Egypt. Neither of them had ever worked in Saudi

Arabia, but they were prepared to try it since the salaries there were much better than in Sudan. Thus they were delighted when one of their relatives returned from a sojourn in Riyadh and offered to sell them a labor contract, signed by a Saudi businessman.

But the problem was: They had only one contract. Which of the two boys would use it? 'Ali was especially eager to go but 'Umar was the older of the two. Mujalli decided that 'Umar should use it. He reasoned that the older son should be the first to marry and so should be the first to go abroad. 'Ali was bitterly disappointed. For two years he had dreamed of going abroad, ever since 'Abdallah had gone to Saudi Arabia. He had more initiative and intelligence than his brother and was convinced that he could succeed there. His only consolation was that his brother would work in Riyadh for one year and then return, bringing him a contract of his own.

When the time came for 'Umar to depart, however, it seemed that he might be getting cold feet. He was a skilled handler of animals, a good scout, and a swift and tireless runner; in short, an excellent herder. But he had not gone to school and had spent little time in Sudanese towns and villages. How, then, would he be able to adjust to life in an entirely different country? Afraid of failure but also afraid of being ridiculed, he kept most of his misgivings to himself. His family reassured him, and he packed his things and hitched a ride to Khartoum in a passing truck with some other Rashiidi boys, trying to think of the trip as a great adventure, like they did. We—my household and Mujalli's household—saw him off, hoping for the best.

A week later I saw a pickup truck pull up in front of Mujalli's tents and went over to see who had arrived. To my astonishment, there was 'Umar, back already. He had gone to Khartoum, had obtained a passport, and had even reserved a seat on a plane to Riyadh. But at the last moment he had "gotten sick." He had told his companions that he was too ill to leave the hotel room that he had been sharing with them and said that they should leave without him. His fear of foreign travel had gotten the better of him.

When 'Ali found out what had happened he was furious. He faced 'Umar angrily, making no effort to conceal the scorn that he felt for his brother. "If you didn't want to go, why didn't you say so? Why didn't you give *me* the contract?" he said. 'Umar just stood there, a mixture of shame and defensiveness on his face. When he didn't reply 'Ali exploded with sarcastic comments and accusations. Mujalli watched them for a few moments and then decided that things had gone too far. *Chaan,* he said firmly, "that's enough." He pulled the two boys apart, and 'Ali's full brother Umbaarak took him into their mother's tent, where he could vent his frustration in private.

It would take 'Ali a long time to forget this incident, because 'Umar's bad judgment had deprived him of his best chance to marry while still young. Now he had no job and no expectations of obtaining a labor contract in the following year. If his father had not been there to intervene he might have broken with 'Umar and left the camp entirely; he could have moved to Khashm al-Girba, for example, to look for paid employment. But he still had a partial interest in his father's livestock and had work to do as a herder. It was still worth his while to stay at home.

'Ali was not the only member of Mujalli's extended household who stayed there at least partly because of his material interests. Aḥmad, Suluum's son and the husband of Mujalli's daughter, also remained within Mujalli's perimeter, even after his first year of marriage. He had no compelling reason to move back to his mother's extended household, since his own father was dead and had passed on whatever property he had many years ago. Furthermore, Mujalli and his sons owned more livestock than Ḥaamid, Aḥmad's mother's husband. During the rainy season Mujalli's animals yielded more milk than Ḥaamid's animals, which meant that Mujalli's food supply was more secure. Hence Aḥmad ignored the Rashaayda's residence rule and stayed where he was.

One might wonder, in light of these examples, whether household composition is not determined primarily by material interests rather than residence rules. What do the "residence rules" mean if they can be so blithely ignored? The answer, I believe, is that neither rules nor material interests alone determine where people live. Co-residence offers more than the material benefits of shelter and a steady food supply; the other members of the household also provide care for the sick, psychological security, and emotional support. People consider all of these benefits when they decide to move from one house to another.

Women, especially, bear these noneconomic benefits in mind when they marry and change residence. They insist on their right to reside near their mothers during the first year of marriage because doing so gives them support during the transition from girlhood to married adulthood. A woman's mother helps her adjust to married life while she slowly becomes acquainted with her husband (who may not have known her at all before the marriage). A woman also returns to her mother's tent to give birth to her children. Her mother acts as her midwife during delivery and cares for her during the forty days after childbirth, when she is ritually confined to her mother's tents and does no work for her husband.

The quality of care and psychological security that a woman's in-laws will offer her are primary considerations when she decides who to marry. Rashiidi women hesitate to marry nonrelatives precisely because they are not sure that they can rely on nonrelated in-laws in case of need. As one woman told me, "if your in-laws regard you as a stranger, they may not take care of you when you are sick." She recited a short poem to illustrate this thought:

Wooh! Wawanti wa anti 'anda al-ajnaab
Ṭiḥti, wa maa ḥad rafa' raasich

("Ooh! you moaned, when you were living with strangers;
You fell down, sick, but no one tried to lift up your head.")

Thus Rashiidi women counsel their daughters to marry relatives, so they will not end up living with strangers.

Tents: The symbolic use of women's property. Just as residence rules are not put into practice automatically (but are weighed against the economic and psychological benefits of alternative patterns of residence), so the codes for putting up the tents of an extended household are not followed automatically. Women deliberate whether or not to set up their tents as custom requires. As I pointed out earlier, every tent is made and owned by a married woman. She has the right to move her tent where she wants as long as she can still provide shelter for her husband and children. This means that women can use their tents to encode and send messages about social relations.

Case Five: Lines as Symbols of Equality

As I pointed out in Chapter Two, when a man marries two women he is expected to treat them equally. This rule applied to "'Ubeyd" (not his real name), a politically prominent, intelligent, and wealthy man in his early thirties, who decided that he wanted a second wife during my second year of fieldwork. He was ambitious, wanted numerous children, and thought he needed another wife to help him receive guests and advance his political career. He was also known for his sexual vigor. His family had married him to his father's brother's daughter, who I will call Ṣaaliḥa, when he was only fifteen; they had seen the early signs of his interest in women and were concerned that he might try to seduce someone's wife. This would have embroiled the family in a quarrel, so to prevent this they married him off early.

'Ubeyd was particularly attracted to a friend's seventeen-year-old daughter, Salma, and proposed an exchange marriage. He himself had a fifteen-year-old daughter named al-Butuul. He suggested that she marry Salma's forty-year-old father and that he would marry Salma in exchange (see Figure 7).

Salma, it turned out, was willing, and her father was also interested in marrying a second wife. Salma's mother Umbaaraka, furthermore, was not against the marriage. Umbaaraka knew that her husband wanted a second wife and thought it would be better for her if he married by exchange than if he married by making a marriage payment. If they exchanged their daughter for a co-wife, the two intermarrying families would be closely tied and would tend to migrate and camp together frequently. This would mean that Umbaaraka would not often be separated from her daughter. What is more, she wanted her daughter to marry 'Ubeyd, because of his prominence and relative wealth.

The main opposition came from Ṣaaliḥa and her daughter al-Butuul. Ṣaaliḥa did not want to share her husband with another woman and certainly did not want her daughter to marry a man who was at least twenty years her senior. She did her best to prevent the marriage, but her bargaining position was undermined by the willingness of Umbaaraka and Salma to go along with it. The women of the camp generally felt sorry for al-Butuul because her future husband was so much older than she was, yet did not expect him to mistreat her in any way. They had little sympathy for Ṣaaliḥa, however, because they thought that any attractive, vigorous, and ambitious man would naturally seek other marriage partners and would sooner or later marry again anyway.

This marriage proposal disturbed me. I had not expected 'Ubeyd to force his daughter into a marriage she hated simply to get an attractive wife for himself. I had liked and respected him previously but now I blamed him for what seemed to me a shocking disregard for his child. My friends agreed that the disparity in ages in this case was too great, but they did not agree that exchange marriage was in

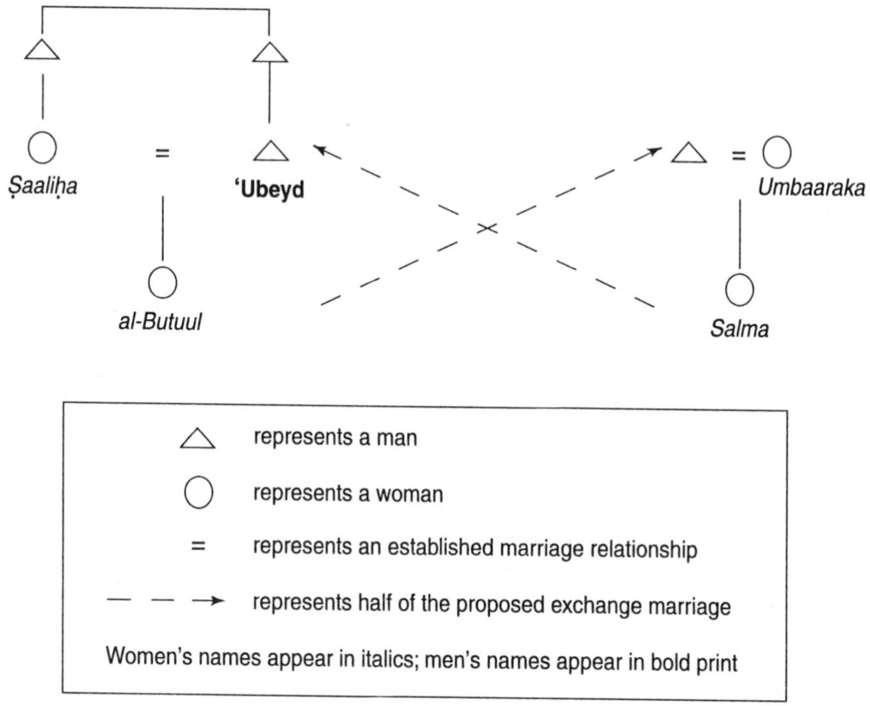

Figure 7 An Exchange Marriage

principle wrong. They pointed out that almost all marriages—especially a young person's first marriage—were arranged by the older generation; neither boys nor girls actually chose their spouses in most cases. Since that was the custom, why should it matter that this marriage involved an exchange between families? Furthermore, exchange marriage (*al-jiiza bi-il-badal*) was cheaper than marriage by means of payments (*al-jiiza bi-s-siyaag*), since it was not necessary for the groom's family to make a large payment for the marriage; they gave the bride's family a daughter rather than cash and livestock.

I continued to object. Wasn't al-Butuul too young to marry, and if so, how could her father suggest it? Wasn't he just using his daughter for his own selfish ends? No, my friends said, al-Butuul was not too young; she was clearly mature enough to have children. Furthermore, 'Ubeyd was not the only partner in this transaction; Umbaaraka also wanted to exchange her daughter for al-Butuul. Umbaaraka accepted the idea that it was normal for a man to want a second wife. She knew that if her husband married again she would lose some of his financial support and attention, so she was doing what she could to arrange a polygynous marriage that would benefit as well as harm her. Salma, also, was satisfied. If Salma and Umbaaraka had really been opposed to the deal, my friends said, they could have stopped it.

I realized that we were arguing the merits and demerits of three different aspects of the case: (1) marriage between young women and old men; (2) polygynous marriage; and (3) exchange marriage. Because the case was so complex and reflected our different values we could not reach any agreement about it. We all objected to marriage between the young and the old. I was against polygyny but had never considered the possibility of marriage by exchange, whereas my friends accepted them both as a matter of course.

The exchange marriage eventually took place, at any rate, and both Salma and al-Butuul were given tents where they could begin their married lives. Al-Butuul took every opportunity to make her unhappiness visible, refusing to wear the new clothes that her husband bought her. She constantly kept her sleeve over her head, draping it lower over her forehead than normal so that her face was half-hidden; even her bangs (which married women usually display) were covered. Her tent, however, was aligned with Salma's and Umbaaraka's tents; she felt no ill will toward them. It was her mother, Ṣaaliḥa, who refused to take her place in the line. Instead of putting up her tent next to Salma's, she moved it some twenty feet ahead of the line and remained there, in furious protest, for many months after the marriage.

As this case demonstrates, a married woman's tent is more than just a shelter; it is a communicative resource that she can use to express her opposition to her husband and call attention to her viewpoint. It does not by itself guarantee that the woman will win every dispute, however. She needs other resources as well. Another case of polygynous marriage made this clear.

Case Six: Divorce and Women's Property

A man I knew who was living in Mastuura, a village built by some newly sedentary Rashaayda, decided to marry a second wife. He and his first wife were living with their teen-aged children in a house made of adobe brick and thatch, and when his second wife joined the household he added two rooms to the house to accommodate both wives. I visited him shortly after the marriage and saw the two new rooms, each built cheaply of wooden poles and reeds. His first wife made me coffee. She said nothing to me about the marriage and gave me no indication that she was unhappy about it, but I wondered how she felt. If she had been living in a tent she could have moved it to her brother's camp, but in this sedentary village she appeared to have few choices.

My unspoken questions were answered quite dramatically two weeks later when the first wife left the household and asked for a divorce. She made no verbal declaration of her discontent, but her anger was obvious to all. She had literally taken her share of the house; she and her brothers (who also lived in Mastuura) had pulled down one of the new rooms and had taken the building materials away! This left one side of the house completely open to public view. Not only was the husband exposed to the elements; he was also exposed to public ridicule. When I visited him again I saw him trying to tough it out, sitting in the half-dismembered house and drinking tea with his new wife and children. Although he was doing his best to appear completely unperturbed, his discomfort was obvious.

I learned that his neighbors did not sympathize with him. He was in his sixties and barely had enough income to feed and clothe his first wife and children; what did he need with a second wife, at his age? Furthermore, no one thought that his first wife had done anything wrong. If the house had been a tent, she would have had every right to take it; so why not take her portion of the building?

These cases show how rules, cultural conventions, material interests, and communicative goals all contribute to the structure of extended households. The lines and circles that connect the tents in a Rashiidi camp reflect the political and affinal relationships that connect households. By "reading" the spatial patterning of tents one can pick up clues about these social relations. Tents, the genealogical names which identify them, and the property marks that are linked to them, are symbols, elements in residential structure, and instruments of production, all at the same time.

GENEALOGICAL DISTANCE AND SPATIAL DISTANCE

To complete our study of structure in Rashiidi society we should examine two more domains: (1) the structure of space between camps and (2) the genealogical structures that link spatially distant households. These structures become apparent only during times of conflict; when social life is untroubled people do not need them. To make it clear what these structures are, I will describe a variety of quarrels and more serious altercations in the next few pages. The reader should not conclude, however, that the Rashaayda are necessarily more quarrelsome than any other society. Arguments and fights were by no means weekly or even monthly events. The disagreements that I witnessed made a strong impression on me at least partly because they were so unusual.

Conflicts within the camp and its spatial solutions. As we shall see, spatial and genealogical structures are connected in practice; when conflict breaks out between people living in different camps, it becomes necessary to calculate the genealogical distance between them. To see why this is so, let us compare conflict between members of the same camp with conflict between members of different camps.

As I said in Chapter Two (p. 56), when two members of the same camp cannot resolve their differences they nevertheless try not to come into open conflict. Both respect the senior man of the camp and exercise self-restraint in observance of the norm of "propriety" (*ḥishma*). If one party can no longer bear to live in close proximity of the other it will usually move to a different camp. The reason given is always "propriety." The household that moves never says it has been driven out of the camp by its antagonists. Rather, it says that it has moved to avoid conflict, out of respect for the camp senior. This face-saving interpretation preserves the dignity of the people who leave. It is only under unusual circumstances that people who are on bad terms will reside within sight of each other.

Case Seven: Coresidence and Litigation

I heard about an antagonistic relationship between neighbors when visiting some semisedentary Rashaayda in Khashm al-Girba. They were living in tents and cheap reed houses in a village that they had recently built. They cultivated plots of land nearby and during the month of September, when they harvested their grain, they would move their tents right into their fields so that they could bring in their crops conveniently.

Two of the men had planted in adjacent plots. They had quarreled a number of times that summer over animal trespass: One man accused the other of allowing his sheep to invade his plot and damage the grain that had sprouted there. When the accused man discussed the case with a neutral third party (in an effort to resolve the conflict), it developed that the two quarreling parties had been involved in another dispute a year ago in which one man had been required to pay a fine to the other.

The neutral man asked the accused, *wish khallaak tiḥuṭṭ jamba khaṣiimk,* "What made you set up [your tents] next to your former litigant?" He replied that he had no choice, since both he and his opponent had claimed these plots of land long before their relationship had soured, and now there were no other comparable plots available. The shift from nomadic to agricultural, sedentary life had made it difficult to reside only with friends, according to custom.

Conflicts between camps and genealogical calculations. In nomadic communities, by contrast, serious conflicts seldom break out among coresidents. Antagonists usually separate long before their relationship turns into open enmity. Enemies almost always belong to different camps. Since there is no relationship of coresidence between enemies, the only other way to describe their relationship is genealogical. Lengthy genealogies become important, then, in legal contexts, when an offense has been committed and someone must take responsibility for it. Let us examine a criminal case to see when and how extended genealogies are used.

Case Eight: Assault, Battery, and Genealogical Distance

It was sunset and 'Abdallah had just returned to camp with some startling news: One of Suluum's paternal cousins (from the Dhuwi Li'baan section of the Dhuwi Ḥayyaan lineage) had stabbed an intruder in his tent last night. Rumor had it that the intruder was from the Jalaadiin (but this rumor was false, as we learned later). He had visited Suluum's cousin months before and had seen the cousin's attractive young wife. Since then he had been waiting for an opportunity to talk with her in private, hoping that she might want to have an extramarital affair with him. Last night the intruder had gotten his chance. He had heard that her husband was away and had gone to her tent under the cover of darkness, slipping past the camp watchdogs and actually going inside. No one knew how long he was there or whether she had agreed to his proposition. But it was certain that he had been caught unprepared. Her husband had shown up unexpectedly and had stabbed him in the shoulder before he could manage to escape.

Fortunately, 'Abdallah said, the intruder was still alive, although he had lost a lot of blood before morning came. Suluum's cousin had taken him to a nearby police post in a pickup truck. He was now in the hospital, Suluum's cousin was in jail, and the intruder's close relatives were angrily thinking of revenge.

"What did Suluum's cousin do to his wife?" I asked. "Did he stab her, too?"

"Why should he do that?" 'Abdallah replied. "If he stabbed her he wouldn't have a wife! He's not such a fool that he would allow her to provoke him; he would only lose if he attacked her. Anyway, she was not the trouble-maker; it was the intruder who had to be punished." "Oh," I said stupidly. I had thought that this was a case of a wife's infidelity, but from their viewpoint the main crimes were the intruder's trespass and his attempt to obtain the sexual services that lawfully belonged to the husband alone. The bloodshed, also, was a crime, and Suluum's cousin and his immediate family were responsible for it.

"So what will Suluum's cousin do now?" "First he'll send a neutral go-between to the intruder's kin," 'Abdallah answered. "He'll ask for a cooling-off period (*al-'aani*), so that the intruder's family won't try to take revenge by attacking Suluum's cousin and his brothers. Once they agree to cease hostilities, they can begin to negotiate. Eventually Suluum's cousins will have to pay them compensation. In the meantime they'll have to lay low; the intruder's kinsmen will be looking for them."

We ate our dinner and kept on discussing the case until we were ready to go to sleep. Suluum banked the embers of her fire and we all retired to our beds and mats. Some hours passed, and then we were suddenly awakened by the sound of camels trotting in the distance. I sat up in my bed, and Suluum and Naafi' got up, peering into the moonless night outside. We saw four riders approach. *Saloom 'aleyk,* one said. "*Uṣṣṣ,* don't answer," Suluum whispered to Naafi'. "*Yaa marḥab* (Welcome)," she called out to them. "We want the tents of the Dhuwi Ḥayyaan," the rider said; "who are you?" "The tents of the Dhuwi Ḥayyaan are to the west," she replied; "we are Dhuwi 'Amri." They halted briefly, hesitating, trying to see who was inside our tent. Then they turned away. When they were gone we all breathed a sigh of relief. Suluum had wanted them to think that there were only women and children in the tent, so that they would have no targets in case they were seeking revenge. "Who knows who they are or what they are looking for?" she remarked.

We later learned that the intruder's family had agreed to a reconciliation and had accepted compensation instead of revenge. Suluum's numerous male cousins and paternal uncles all had contributed to the payment, since they were genealogically close to the attacker. If the intruder had been killed the compensation fund would have been larger, and all of the Dhuwi Ḥayyaan men—including 'Abdallah—would have been asked to contribute to it.

Generally speaking, when crimes are committed the close relatives of the criminal are potentially exposed to retribution and must pay compensation if they want to settle peacefully. The closer they are genealogically to the criminal, the greater their share of the costs of reconciliation. Furthermore, the greater the seriousness of the crime, the larger the compensation demanded and the wider the circle of patrilineal kin who must help to pay this compensation.

Genealogical distance is also considered when marriages are being arranged. In theory, the *'iyaal 'amm il-bint* ("sons of the girl's paternal uncles") have the right to be consulted before a girl's family gives her away in marriage. One of them might want to marry her, and if he does, he can insist on his right and try to prevent any genealogically more distant suitor from approaching her family. He cannot force the girl to marry him but he can stop her from marrying anyone else (except for another close paternal cousin, who would have exactly the same right to her).

In actual practice, most paternal cousins do not interfere in the marriages of their female relatives. I heard of only one case while I was with the Rashaayda.

Case Nine: Marriage and Genealogical Distance

Jaabir, a young man from the Jalaadiin lineage, discovered that one of his patrilineal parallel cousins (*bint 'amm,* "paternal uncle's daughter") was engaged. Since he did not live in her camp, he had not heard about it before. He had considered asking for her in marriage but had not reached any firm decision about this. What was more disturbing, from his point of view, was his paternal uncle's decision not to inform him, even though it was his right to be consulted. He reacted by declaring publicly (at a wedding) that he would not allow the marriage to take place. He said that the successful suitor was *magruu',* "corralled." This is to say, he would act to restrict the suitor's movements, like a herder controls his livestock. If the suitor attempted to approach the girl's family's tent, he would attack him. He vowed to carry out his threat *fii sadd wajhi,* "at the cost of my honor (literally, in defense of my face)."

When the girl's father heard what had been said he went to visit the boy's father (that is, his own brother) and asked him what to do. Eventually the girl's family placated the boy by giving him gifts, and the wedding was carried out as planned.

As we can see, in most of the legal cases where genealogical distance is calculated, the disputants live in different camps. The genealogical framework of the wider society provides a convenient means for identifying families and groups who do not reside in the same camp. Genealogies also help determine what responsibilities people have when violent conflicts breaks out between people who are not neighbors.

THE REQUIREMENTS OF DAILY LIFE VERSUS THE PRESSURE TO BE "TRIBAL"

My description of pastoral production in Chapter Two made it clear that most productive tasks are carried out by relatively small groups of people (households and extended households). In Chapter Three I showed how most of the Rashaayda's other activities (offering hospitality, organizing living space, performing prayers, arranging marriages, celebrating holidays, and punishing criminals) are also carried out by small groups of coresident people. I also showed, however, that it is sometimes useful to belong to genealogical, descent units such as lineages and "tribal branches." The members of one's lineage can help resolve conflicts with outsiders and sometimes contribute to compensation funds when conflicts are resolved. The "tribe" also makes a small contribution to economic organization, in that its system of brands and genealogical branches helps people identify and recover lost livestock.

In the next chapter I will present information about the historical development of the Rashaayda's "tribal" organization. I will describe the effects of the state and the regional market economy on Rashiidi society, focusing on the emergence of various social barriers and hierarchies in eastern Sudan that have had an important impact on the Rashaayda and have forced them to become a "tribe" among "tribes." To understand why the Rashaayda have remained "tribal" we must try to discover how they got that way in the first place.

4 / History and Identity Among the Rashaayda

THE HISTORICAL REALITY OF THE RASHAAYDA'S "TRIBAL" GENEALOGY

In this chapter I will describe some of the short-term historical factors that changed the regional division of labor in northeastern Sudan and secured an economic and geographical niche for the Rashaayda. I will also indicate some of the changes in their identity that the Rashaayda have experienced since their arrival.

The Rashaayda emigrated to Sudan from Arabia in the 1860s (Turki, 1978, p. 196), long after the other Arab migrations to Sudan. It is not known precisely where they came from. My informants from the Dhuwi Ḥayyaan said that they originally lived in the Ḥijaaz (the western coastal region of Arabia), close to Mecca. There are indeed a number of small nomadic groups living in the vicinity of Mecca who today call themselves Rashaayda, but this alone is not proof of a recent historical connection. In fact there are at least a dozen small communities with the same name scattered along a huge arc that begins near Mecca, continues northwards along the Red Sea coast, curves northeast through Jordan and northern Saudi Arabia, and ends in Kuwait. In Jordan alone there are four distinct groups called Rashaayda, and they do not all claim a common historical origin or common descent. Like the Rashaayda of Sudan, however, they do claim to have originated in the Ḥijaaz.

How are we to determine which of these groups is most closely related historically to the Rashaayda of Sudan? Historical sources report that Bedouin from the Ḥijaaz did come to Sudan frequently during the nineteenth century but these reports do not identify them as Rashaayda. Perhaps the best support for the Dhuwi Ḥayyaan's claim of a Meccan origin is linguistic. Like all other Sudanese Rashaayda, the Dhuwi Ḥayyaan say they are *mitḥashshidiin* ("reluctant to accept generous gifts or hospitality") when they are guests in someone's home. This word is extremely uncommon in the Arab world and to my knowledge is used only by the Ḥarb "tribe" in the vicinity of Mecca. Other support can be found in their clothing styles. Their women's clothing, especially the *burga'*, closely resembles the clothing of Bedouin women in the northeastern Ḥijaaz (if not that of the Meccan Bedouin, specifically). Thus the same distinctive costume and the same linguistic features that distinguish the Rashaayda from the other Arab peoples of Sudan also link them to western Arabia.

One would expect that if the Sudanese Rashaayda were related to the Rashaayda of Mecca, the two "tribes" would have ancestral names in common also. Unfortunately the information available about Arabian genealogies runs counter to the evidence of a Ḥijaazi origin that is cited above. The names of the Rashaayda's three main "tribal branches"—that is, the Baraaṭiikh, Zuneymaat, and Biraa'aṣa—are not known in the Ḥijaaz. The only name that even resembles "the Zuneymaat" is a place name, not the name of a descent group; it identifies the town of Abu Zuneyma, which is on the southern coast of the Sinai peninsula, not in the Ḥijaaz. The only reference to the Biraa'aṣa comes from even farther afield; it is the name of a "tribe" in western Libya, some members of which are known to have migrated to Palestine in the eighteenth century. The names of some Rashiidi lineages—the Baraaghiith and the Ḥuweyjaat—are also found in western Libya and Palestine rather than in the Ḥijaaz. Thus most of the genealogical names used by the Rashaayda stem from places outside western Arabia. This may indicate that the Rashaayda "tribe" is a collection of groups originating in many places, including Libya and Sinai as well as the Ḥijaaz.

Perhaps the most puzzling evidence concerns the Rashaayda of Kuwait. The names of the "tribal branches" of these Rashaayda do not resemble those of the Sudanese Rashaayda, but the two groups do have one thing in common: They are both allied with a "tribe" called the 'Awaazim.

This resemblance between the Sudanese and Kuwaiti Rashaayda is not apparent to most outsiders because they assume that the Sudanese Rashaayda consist of a single "tribe." In fact, not all of the members of the Sudanese Rashaayda are believed to be descendants of Rashiid az-Zool (see Figure 5, Chapter Three). In addition to the "true" Rashaayda, there are members of "foreign tribes," such as the 'Awaazim, Gazaayiza, and 'Ureynaat, who live with the Rashaayda. These "tribes" (*gabaayil*) are said to have come to Sudan with the Rashaayda. They are now "administratively associated" with the Rashaayda "tribe" (*gabiila*). Each such "foreign" group has its own distinctive brand, quite different from those of "true" Rashaayda. Yet each is connected with one of the three main "tribal branches" (also called *gabaayil*) of the Sudanese Rashaayda. These "foreigner" Rashaayda are quite similar culturally to "true" Rashaayda and, what is more, are intermarried with the descendants of Rashiid az-Zool. They join ranks with their associated "branches" when legal or political conflicts occur and act just like "true" Rashaayda in most other contexts.

It cannot be a coincidence that the same names—Rashaayda and 'Awaazim—are found in the two different areas; they surely must have a common origin. Yet it is difficult to determine how long ago the Sudanese half of the Rashaayda/'Awaazim confederacy split from its Kuwaiti half. The only way we can explain their present distribution is to assume that the Rashaayda and 'Awaazim have been moving in tandem across the Arabian peninsula for centuries. The original birthplace of their confederation could be anywhere between Kuwait and the Red Sea.

Thus my collection of "tribal" and "branch" names gives us no straightforward clues about historical origins. If we think of a patrilineal "tribe" as a set of people descended through men from a common ancestor (like the twelve "tribes" of Israel, all descended from Jacob, that are mentioned in the Bible), then the Rashaayda are clearly not a "tribe." If anything, they are an assemblage of "tribes (*gabaayil*)," each one (Biraa'aṣa, Zuneymaat, Baraaṭiikh, 'Awaazim, Gazaayiza, 'Ureynaat) descended from a different ancestor.

The "true" Rashaayda would reject this suggestion, since they claim that at least three "tribal branches" are descended from Rashiid az-Zool. But this claim is hard to believe, given that the names of the three "tribal branches" appear to originate in the Sinai peninsula and Libya. Furthermore, even if we accept the idea that Rashiid is somehow a distant ancestor of the three "tribal branches," there is additional evidence that these "true" Rashaayda have absorbed "foreign" families, even in recent times.

Case Ten: "Refugee" Lineages

While I was living with the Rashaayda I was constantly asking for genealogies, and so when I came across a new group of people camped near Malawiyya, it was natural for me to ask them who their ancestors were. "We're Biraa'aṣa," they said. They could see that I was an outsider and did not expect me to know much about their ancestry, so they gave me an answer that was almost devoid of information. *Everyone* near Malawiyya was Biraa'aṣa! I smiled politely and explained that I, too, was a Bar'uuṣi; I was living with the Dhuwi Ḥayyaan lineage. They were pleased by this. "The Dhuwi Ḥayyaan are our close relatives!" they said. I added that I belonged to the Dhuwi Abu Sariir segment of the Dhuwi Ḥayyaan and recited "my" genealogy (or rather, 'Abdallah's genealogy). Then I asked how their ancestor was related to "my" ancestors. To my surprise they seemed embarrassed. They just asserted, "the Dhuwi Ḥayyaan's ancestor (*jadd;* literally, "grandfather") and our ancestor were brothers," without naming any names. I was mystified by their discomfort but did not press them any further.

I hitched a ride on a truck to Kassala and decided to ask for information from my good friend 'Ubeyd ibin Naafi' ibin Barakaat ibin Ghuweynim ibin Ghaanim of the Dhuwi Ḥayyaan; he was staying with his father in Kassala. I went to their house, greeted them all, and then sat down to have coffee with 'Ubeyd. I told him what had happened, and he understood immediately. "Those people are not really Dhuwi Ḥayyaan," he explained. "They are a refugee family (*'eyla umzuwiyya*). They came to the Rashaayda's territory from Egypt when my grandfather Barakaat was *'umda* (leader) of the Biraa'aṣa 'tribe.' They asked for his protection. Barakaat guessed that they had killed someone in Egypt and had fled to escape the revenge of the dead man's relatives. He did not ask them what they had done but just said they could stay as long as they wished. Later, after they had been here for a few years, we exchanged daughters. They gave us one of their girls in marriage, and we gave them one of my grandfather's sisters. Since then they have become Dhuwi Ḥayyaan. We haven't intermarried with them again, but if anyone attacks them we protect them, and if anyone attacks us they come to our defense."

To sum up: Historical research forces us to ask whether the Rashaayda were a single, unified community—a "tribe"—at all before they emigrated to Sudan. It could well be that a number of separate groups, all calling themselves Rashaayda but none claiming a close relationship with any other, all emigrated from Arabia to Sudan during approximately the same period. Once they reached the western shore of the Red Sea, they may have found it advantageous to unite under a common leader and form a new "tribal" confederation. This would have helped them penetrate the coastal territories of eastern Sudan and resist the counterattacks of the Hadendowa and Bani 'Aamir nomads. Since then, the "genealogical" identity of the

Rashaayda has probably changed continuously from one decade to the next, as new "foreign" groups have been added.

THE HISTORY OF THE RASHAAYDA'S "BEDOUIN" IDENTITY

Some Sudanese call the Rashaayda "Bedouin," thereby stressing the connection between their identity and pastoral way of life. The Rashaayda do not reject this identity, although they usually call themselves "Arabs," not "Bedouin." One might think that this is an economic or technical identity that has little connection with history. Are not "Bedouin" simply people who exploit a natural environment in a particular way, regardless of the historical period in which they do this? In fact, however, the pastoralism of the Rashaayda has been greatly affected by history. It is not an adaptation to a natural environment, because the territories the Rashaayda now inhabit are not just "natural pastures." They have been transformed by the presence of pastoralists there over millennia.

Pastoralism (based on domesticated cattle, sheep, and goats) has existed in northeastern Sudan since at least 2000 B.C. (Sadr, 1991, p. 42) and has greatly changed the landscape. As Cribb has pointed out, pastures like these are "never 'natural,' in the sense of being in a pristine condition." Continuous grazing in this area has selected against plant species favored by domesticated herbivores. Overgrazing has drastically changed their distribution, resulting in a vegetation cover unfavorable to pastoralism that is characterized by minimal plant diversity and an unusual predominance of toxic species (Cribb, 1991, pp. 27–28). The same thing can be said for the Rashaayda's ancestral homeland in Arabia, where they lived before emigrating to Sudan. Evidence of camel pastoralism in northwest Arabia dates at least as far back as 1000 B.C. (Bulliet, 1975, pp. 57–86; Finkelstein, 1988, pp. 246–247). All this means that the Rashaayda's pastoralist way of life has emerged over an extended period in two highly unnatural environments and has been shaped by a long string of historical events.

The Rashaayda say that when they came to Sudan from Arabia they brought their special breed of camels with them in small sailing boats owned by coastal merchants. This story seems credible; if they had not known how to raise camels when they arrived, they could not have succeeded as stock breeders. Yet it is not at all certain that they specialized so exclusively in camel pastoralism before they emigrated to Sudan. Did they have large herds of camels when they were living in Arabia, or did they have flocks of sheep? Did they also herd goats, or did they spend much of their time fishing (as the nomads of southern Sinai do)? We simply do not know.

We do have reason to believe that when the Rashaayda first arrived in Sudan, they tried to adopt the same combination of pastoral production and agriculture that was being practiced by the aboriginal peoples of the Red Sea coast. That is, they attempted to cultivate grain and raise cattle as well as herd sheep, camels, and goats. In order to cultivate grain, however, they needed fertile land (where they could plant sorghum), and to raise cattle they needed wells (to supply these constantly thirsty animals with water). I met a number of old men (one of whom was more than 100 years old) who recalled trying to raise cattle along the Red Sea coast.

The Hadendowa and Bani 'Aamir nomads resisted Rashiidi incursions into their coastal territories, however, and after a number of armed clashes between Rashiidi and non-Rashiidi groups many Rashaayda decided to move farther inland. This move to a more arid area made it both possible and necessary to adopt a different economic specialization. The inland Rashaayda stopped trying to raise cattle, bought more camels, and reduced the numbers of their small stock (goats and sheep). Even goats and sheep could not thrive without being watered frequently during the summer, so the Rashaayda raised them only during the rainy seasons. They kept camels year round because they needed less water.

Those Rashaayda who stayed near the sea coast combined subsistence pastoralism with trade. Crossing the Red Sea in small boats, they took various raw materials from Sudan to Arabian ports and returned with firearms, cloth, and other goods. The trade in firearms was both a source of cash income and a source of useful weapons.

It is not certain when the Rashaayda began using firearms. There is no clear evidence that they carried rifles when they first arrived in the 1860s, and the defeats that they suffered in their first skirmishes with the Hadendowa lead one to suspect that they were not heavily armed. During the early 1880s, in fact, the Hadendowa successfully prevented the Rashaayda from occupying any territory permanently and petitioned the Ottoman administrators in the coastal town of Suakin, asking that the Rashaayda be deported (Y. Ḥasan, 1975; Young, 1984). Things changed, however, when the Mahdist wars broke out, and eastern Sudan became embroiled in fighting between the Mahdist revolutionaries in central Sudan, on the one hand, and the Anglo-Egyptian garrison in Suakin, on the other.

The last quarter of the nineteenth century was marked by the Mahdist revolt (1884–1898), which plunged eastern Sudan into war. After the Mahdists expelled the Egyptian administration and its troops from Khartoum they marched toward the Red Sea and lay siege to Suakin. Mahdist troops under the command of the general Abu Qurja killed some Rashaayda on the way and asked the rest to choose sides. Either they would accept the authority of the Mahdist armies (represented locally by Hadendowa leaders, who had been the enemies of the Rashaayda for twenty years) or they would have to join forces with the Egyptian and British garrison. For most Rashaayda neither option seemed viable, and so most fled into nearby Eritrea. They remained there until about 1900, grazing their camels in the mountainous pastures of the Ethiopian highlands. After the British invaded and defeated the Mahdists, however, many Rashaayda returned to Sudan and set up camps in the arid region between the 'Aṭbara and Gash rivers (A. Ḥasan, 1974).

At that time, this region was little used by other "tribes." The Hadendowa and Bani 'Aamir "tribes," to the east, could not keep their cattle there because it was too far from reliable sources of water. Arabic-speaking "tribes," to the west, were not numerous in 1900 (having been decimated by the Mahdist wars) and tended to stay to the west and south of the 'Aṭbara. So the Rashaayda remained camel pastoralists. They prospered since they had fewer nomadic neighbors than before with whom to compete.

In short, a series of historical events (Rashiidi immigration, conflict with the Hadendowa, the Mahdist wars, the depopulation of parts of eastern Sudan, and the reestablishment of an Anglo-Egyptian administration) made camel pastoralism both viable and attractive for the Rashaayda. Their current identity as camel pastoralists has its roots in these historical—and political—events. It was not their culture per se that prompted them to specialize in camel breeding, even though the technical knowledge needed to do so was part of that culture. Camel breeding was profitable. If local economic and political relationships had been different in 1900, they may well have abandoned pastoralism years ago.

In recent times the Rashaayda's Bedouin identity and pastoral economy has been affected by economic development. Much of the rangeland they used during the 1950s was taken by the government in 1962 when it constructed the Khashm al-Girba agricultural scheme. This meant that the nomads who formerly exploited this rangeland, such as the Laḥaawiin "tribe," had to move into the pastures just outside the scheme. As a result, the pastures where the Rashaayda lived became seriously overgrazed, and some were forced to abandon pastoralism (see pp. 29–30).

Despite the decline in the quality of pastures, many Rashaayda have continued to specialize in camel pastoralism. They are able to do so because they have supplementary income from the livestock market and from wage labor in Saudi Arabia. Income from the livestock market has probably always helped to sustain pastoralism, since nomadic families who lose their herds to disease or drought during a bad year can rely on cash to tide them over until the next year.

"TRIBAL ENDOGAMY," ETHNOCENTRISM, AND HISTORY

As we have seen, most of the encounters between the Hadendowa and the Rashaayda during the first half of the twentieth century were marked by hostility and conflict. Armed clashes broke out between Rashiidi and Hadendowa groups that were competing over water and pasture. The Rashaayda were frequently victorious, despite their comparatively small numbers. One reason for their success was firepower; the Rashaayda probably could not have laid claim to any pastureland in eastern Sudan without using rifles. At the same time, they did not attract any large-scale attacks. They were both few in number and outside the customary pastures of the Hadendowa and so were not perceived as a serious threat. The Hadendowa, in turn, were not organized into large "tribes"; although numerous, they were divided into dozens of local communities. They did not unite and try to reclaim the territories where the Rashaayda lived.

In other words, during the first half of this century the nomads of eastern Sudan lived side by side, always watching for signs of trouble but never carrying out any systematic campaigns against each other. Consequently, the Rashaayda were under no pressure to ally themselves with potential supporters. They had no need to ask for help from western Arab groups, since they faced no organized threat from the Hadendowa. They also had no motive for improving their relations with the Hadendowa (for instance, by recognizing clear "tribal" boundaries or by establishing links through marriage), since they had to contend only with intermittent hostilities by small groups of Hadendowa. Thus the Rashaayda did not establish close relations with any of their nomadic neighbors. Marital or political alliances between Rashaayda and non-Rashaayda were and are still very rare; few "tribe"-exogamous marriages have taken place.

The social gap between the Rashaayda and Hadendowa was reinforced by the Rashaayda's cultural and linguistic distinctiveness; they spoke Ḥijaazi Arabic, while the Hadendowa spoke a Cushitic language (Tu Bedawie). In 1978, when the Rashaayda talked about the relations between them and the Hadendowa, they seldom spoke in terms of their "tribe" against an equal, opposing "tribe." Rather, they portrayed it as a relationship between Arabic speakers and "speakers of uncivilized languages" (*'ujmaan*). The tension and complete absence of trust between the Rashaayda and Hadendowa was vividly brought home to me by an incident that took place shortly after I began my fieldwork.

Case Eleven: Relations with Non-Arab Nomads

One day in the middle of the rainy season a Hadendowi man rode up to our campsite. It was late in the afternoon and most of our people were sleeping. 'Abdallah had been scouting for new pasture for most of the morning and Ḥaamid and his sons had been taking care of their livestock. I was still awake and so I felt obliged to welcome this potential guest. I put on my turban and walked over to the man, who remained on his mount some distance away. I greeted him with "Peace! (*saloom 'aleyk*)" and reached up to shake his hand, as Rashaayda often do to greet a rider.

Suddenly I heard 'Abdallah shout, "Leave him be!" I backed away and looked around in surprise. 'Abdallah was awake and was coming out of his tent. Tense and alert, he walked up to the Hadendowi man and politely but firmly asked him to account for his presence: "Where are you headed? Who are you looking for?" This surprised me even more, for the Rashaayda never ask such questions of visitors until after they are inside the tent and have been offered water and shelter from the hot sun.

The Hadendowi man seemed to expect this, however, and answered 'Abdallah promptly, speaking simplified Sudanese Arabic. He said that his destination was still far away and that he would like to spend the night near our campsite. 'Abdallah said he would consent to this if the visitor surrendered his sword and knife to us. The man agreed and gave 'Abdallah his weapons before dismounting.

As soon as these negotiations were over 'Abdallah took me aside and lectured me sternly. "Never shake hands with an *'ijimi* (sing. of *'ujmaan*) who is still in the saddle!" he said. "He might keep holding your hand in his grip and cut you down with his sword. Many of us have been killed in battle by the Hadendowa, and we have killed many of them."

The visitor did not enter our tents. Rather, he tethered his camel a short distance away and spread out a mat and some blankets near his camel. We offered him food and drink, but all he would accept was a few embers from our fire and a little water. He used the water to wash for prayer and for making coffee out of the coffee beans that he had brought with him. He spent the night where he was and left early the next morning, without having spoken to anyone but 'Abdallah.

The Rashaayda's distrust of the Hadendowa springs from the history of competition between the two. Their attitudes toward other Sudanese groups are less extreme but can also be ethnocentric, even racist, at times.

On the average, northern Sudanese resemble black Americans. Their African ancestry is most apparent, but Arabian and perhaps Egyptian elements in their biological makeup are manifest also in their skin color, their facial features, the curliness of their hair, and their body build. Most Rashaayda, by contrast, resemble the people of north-central Arabia, with lighter skin and straighter hair than most other Sudanese. They are much shorter than their neighbors. My northern Sudanese friends pointed out that I, at 5'9", fit in with the Rashaayda much more than with other Sudanese men, who are frequently over six feet in height. In other words, there are visible physical differences between most northern Sudanese and most Rashaayda.

For cultural anthropologists the question is: What do the Rashaayda make of these differences? It depends on the circumstances. Sometimes the Rashaayda represent the physical differences between themselves and other Sudanese as a difference in status. They refer to themselves as *aḥraar,* "free," and refer to Sudanese who have African features as *'abiid,* "slaves." This is, of course, insulting language and is intended as such. But the Rashaayda do not call all African Sudanese *'abiid,* and they are by no means the only Arab Sudanese who use this word. Before we conclude that the Rashaayda are simply racists, then, we must ask what they mean when they call someone an *'abd* and why they use this language.

The "free"/"slave" distinction is not unique to the Rashaayda; it is also found in most other Arab Sudanese communities. Although the word *'abiid* literally means "slaves" in a legal sense, it is no longer applied literally to anyone in Sudan, since slavery is illegal (and has been illegal for generations). At present it has a vague connection with very dark skin color and Central African facial features but it does not consistently equate African origin with slavery. The primary connotation of *'abd* for most Sudanese is both racial and genealogical; it refers to a person whose mother or grandmother bore her children out of wedlock, as a purchased sexual partner rather than as a legitimate wife. In other words, an *'abd* is not literally a "slave" nor necessarily African; he is the illegitimate grandchild or child of a "slave" woman and, perhaps, a "slave" man. The word is insulting because it implies illegitimacy, low status, and powerlessness. One sometimes finds that some members of a "tribe" are classified as "free" while others are classified as "descendants of slaves."

The overwhelming majority of Sudanese citizens have African features. Almost all of the shopkeepers, police, doctors, bus drivers, livestock merchants, elementary school teachers, and government employees with whom the Rashaayda deal are African, and the Rashaayda certainly do not call all of them *'abiid.* They use this insulting term among themselves—and sometimes when outsiders are present—only when they feel pressured to accept a subordinate role in their dealings with outsiders. For example, when they have to deal with politically powerful Sudanese government officials or wealthy Sudanese merchants, they may act negatively and defensively, especially if they feel they are being cheated or abused.

Case Twelve: Commerce and Ethnocentricity

In 1978 one of my friends, whom I will call Umfaḍḍi, returned from a sojourn in Saudi Arabia where he had been an assistant salesman in a car dealership. He brought a measure of pure silver with him that he intended to make into silver bracelets (*sa'af*) for his mother. His father had already given her bracelets years ago, when he married her, but these had become tarnished and broken with the passage of time and Umfaḍḍi wanted her to have new ones. He took the silver to a silversmith in Kassala and asked him to work the metal into shape. This silversmith had filled many similar orders for other Rashaayda and knew the styles that they prefer.

Months went by. Umfaḍḍi would go to ask about the jewelry whenever he was in Kassala, and each time the smith would say that he had not yet finished the work. Umfaḍḍi became increasingly suspicious. He knew that all smiths traded in precious metals and thought that this particular man (who was originally from a central Sudanese "tribe") might be speculating in silver. If this were so, he might be selling his customers' metal when its price was high and then buying what he needed to make their jewelry when its price was low; he would pocket the difference. After an entire year had passed Umfaḍḍi stopped using the smith's name when he talked about him but said, "That damned slave (*hadhaa al-'abd al-mal'uun*)," instead.

Eventually he did manage to recover his silver. After a series of fruitless visits—during which Umfaḍḍi and the smith only quarreled—Umfaḍḍi asked me if I would try to get the bracelets when I was next in Kassala. He thought that the man might be more forthcoming with me, since I was a guest in Sudan; Sudanese place great importance on hospitality and try to deal with their guests very considerately. I agreed. However, my attitudes toward the man were already strongly influenced by Umfaḍḍi's suspicions, and when I visited him I found myself quarreling with him, too, which did no good.

Fortunately, one of the people in his shop sought the intervention of the other silversmiths in Kassala. All of the smiths were members of an informal trade association that tried to maintain the good reputation of the profession among the townspeople. The senior men of the association put pressure on this particular smith to finish his work and give Umfaḍḍi the bracelets. After he received the finished goods, Umfaḍḍi resolved never to deal with him again, and the incident was closed.

Umfaḍḍi's racist remarks were directed mainly against one man who he suspected was swindling him. His racist discourse with me was both a way for him to vent his anger and a means of solidifying my support for him, just in case he needed it. To an extent he was appealing to me as one "free" man to another. Of course this made no sense to me because I was not used to categorizing people as either "free" or "slave." Worse, it reminded me of racial bigotry in the United States, and this embarrassed me, since as a European American I could not help but perceive it as an appeal for "white" solidarity against "blacks." I suspected, however, that my categories were not exactly the same as Umfaḍḍi's and would have made no sense to him.

I gradually realized that the Rashaayda's ethnocentrism or racism was not exactly what I had seen in the United States. What is more, I discovered that they themselves were sometimes victims of the ethnocentric views of other Sudanese. I became aware of northern Sudanese attitudes toward the Rashaayda when I met some high school students in Kassala. They asked me what I was doing in town, and I explained that I was carrying out research on the Rashaayda. "You mean the

Zubeydiyya," they said, using an outsider's name for the Rashaayda that apparently has a long history in eastern Sudan. I corrected them. "That's not their real name. They descend from a man named Rashiid; it's a mistake to call them 'Zubeydiyya.'" They nodded but immediately proceeded to make other prejudiced remarks. "Where are those people from? Aren't they gypsies (*ḥalab*)?" This ethnic category had no meaning for me and, as it turned out, was none too clearly defined for them either. They only knew that *ḥalab* were poor itinerant groups who had come from outside Sudan and who earned their living by begging and stealing in the larger Sudanese cities. They seemed convinced that there was a connection between the Rashaayda and these vaguely disreputable transients.

I was irritated. After many months of fieldwork I had come to identify with the Rashaayda. I later learned that this folklore about the Rashaayda's origins was widespread, and that when Rashiidi schoolboys got into fights with other students in Kassala they were sometimes called "gypsies." Of course the Rashaayda boys could give as well as they got, so that if the situation degenerated both sides would start throwing racist epithets at each other. Usually the school masters stepped in and put a stop to these exchanges.

Another year went by before a different quarrel made it clear to me that the solidarity of the "free" against "slaves" could quickly be forgotten. This quarrel pitted "Arabs" against "non-Arabs" and joined some of the Rashaayda with Arabic-speaking "tribesmen" of African origin.

Case Thirteen: Arab Solidarity

I was visiting some Baraaṭiikh friends who were camped in their cultivated fields near Malawiyya. They had sown sorghum in the bed of a wadi three months earlier and now, in late September, they had come back to harvest it. Other nomadic families, who belonged to the Arabic-speaking Laḥaawiin "tribe," had planted grain there, too.

Two of the Laḥaawiin men came to greet me while I was having coffee with my friends. They introduced themselves and said they were brothers. "Where did you spend the rainy season (*al-khariif*)?" I asked. One of them gestured vaguely toward the west and said, "Beyond Khashm al-Girba; that's where we live." He did not give me too much information; he wanted to keep the exact location of the western pastures a secret. His Arabic dialect sounded strange to me, and his facial features seemed subtlely different from the features of friends from Khartoum and western Sudan. His skin was as dark as that of a Hadendowa man, but he did not comb his hair like the Hadendowa did and his clothing seemed different. I could see his camels and tent—or rather, his shelter, made of reed mats thrown over a wooden framework—about 200 yards away. After a few minutes the two men excused themselves and went back to their work.

I stayed with my Baraaṭiikh friends for the whole day. They gave me lunch and took me to see their planted fields and the tall stalks of sorghum that they and their Laḥaawiin neighbors were harvesting. Suddenly, at around 5:00 PM, we heard shouting. It seemed to come from the south, but it was almost sunset and the light was failing; we could not see any signs of a commotion. We returned to our camp, and there we heard the news: The Laḥaawiin had been fighting with some Hadendowa.

According to a little boy who had witnessed the fight, the two Laḥaawiin men had been harvesting their grain about two hours earlier when a group of cattle appeared. The cattle were stragglers from a herd that six Hadendowa men were taking to water at a nearby well. These stragglers headed straight for the fields of sorghum and plunged into them, crushing many plants beneath their hooves and eating some grain. The two Laḥaawiin immediately drove them out. They let most of the animals go back to the herd but decided to keep one of them and hold it in a corral until its owners came to claim it. Then they would ask for compensation for the ruined grain.

An hour passed, and the six Hadendowa men did indeed show up, as anticipated. They went to the corral and identified their cow; they wanted it back. The Laḥaawiin man who was guarding it refused to hand it over, saying he would not release it unless he was compensated for his loss. The Hadendowa were angry; they said that the lost grain was surely not equal in value to the cow. They opened the corral and led the cow out. Now the Laḥaawiin man was angry. His brother, hearing him shout, ran from the fields to join him, carrying his hoe. What had begun as a quarrel was fast becoming an armed confrontation.

The Hadendowa started walking away, taking the cow with them and threatening the Laḥaawiin. The older Laḥaawiin man reacted by seizing the cow by its tail and pulling it back, hurling insults at the six Hadendowa. The latter stopped walking and turned to face their opponents. Forming a line, they gave the Laḥaawiin a silent warning. Each raised his sheathed sword above his head and pulled it out of the sheath far enough to expose the blade. This was a provocative and dangerous gesture; in eastern Sudan, men did not normally unsheathe their swords unless they intended to use them. One of the two Laḥaawiin responded to it by holding up his hoe, stepping right in front of a Hadendowi man, and staring him straight in the face. This triggered the fight. The two main combatants struck each other almost simultaneously. The Hadendowi man hit the Laḥaawiin man in the chest with his sword but was badly wounded in the shoulder by a blow from the other man's hoe. They both fell to the ground.

Shouting, the other five Hadendowa darted forward to rescue their friend. They pushed the Laḥaawiin men away from him and beat them both, but did not cut them with their swords. Leaving the wounded Laḥaawiin man on the ground, they threatened his brother and then walked away, half-carrying their seriously wounded companion.

The remaining Laḥaawiin man ran to his family's tent to get help, while the little Rashiidi boy—who had been watching from a distance the whole time—ran in the opposite direction, toward the tent of the senior man of the Baraaṭiikh encampment. This man owned a pickup truck, and when he heard the news he drove it to the scene of the fight and picked up the wounded man. He drove him to a police station, some five miles away, and reported the incident. The police took the wounded man to a hospital and sent a patrol car to look for the group of Hadendowa. They had to act quickly to prevent the inter-"tribal" fight from spreading.

After we had heard this news my friends decided to visit the Laḥaawiin, and I went with them. By now night had fallen, and when we reached the Laḥaawiin camp we could hardly see them. They had no fire burning and had grouped their camels in a dense cluster right around their shelters. After we called out our greetings a middle-aged woman replied and stepped out to take a look at us. She was clearly tense and frightened. We asked why the camels were so close to her house, and she said her sons had put them there for protection. Any intruder would have to get past the animals in order to attack the family members.

It turned out that the men of her family had gone to the Baraaṭiikh camp to ask for protection. They were afraid that the wounded Hadendowi man might die and that his relatives would seek revenge. My friends reassured the woman. "We won't leave you unprotected," he said. "If any Hadendowa come by, we'll stop them." And in fact the Baraaṭiikh did agree to defend the Laḥaawiin. As my friends said, "the Laḥaawiin are Arabs. If the Hadendowa attacked us, they would defend us; we should do the same for them."

These cases show us that the Rashaayda can distance themselves from their neighbors in a variety of ways. When they are at odds with more powerful Sudanese, they react defensively and sometimes label them as "slaves," stressing that they themselves are "free." When they quarrel with the Hadendowa, on the other hand, they seek support from other "Arabs" (regardless of their "racial" background) and portray their opponents as *'ujmaan*. When there are no conflicts between them and outsiders, the Rashaayda can invoke a number of unifying identities. All of the peoples in the region are Muslims, after all; they should deal with each other as brothers. They are also Sudanese citizens, equal under the law. These high ideals are easier to recall in times of peace, however, than in times of conflict.

These cases also help us understand why the Rashaayda have only rarely intermarried with their neighbors. They are socially distant from most urban Arab Sudanese and are in competition with non-Arabic-speaking rural Sudanese. Marriage would seem most likely with rural Arabic speakers. At the time of my fieldwork, however, the advantages of such marriages were not obvious to the Rashaayda.

SLAVERY: HISTORY AND THE INCORPORATION OF NON-RASHAAYDA INTO THE "TRIBE" BY PURCHASE

In the preceeding paragraphs I discussed the "slave"/"free" distinction in the context of inter-"tribal" relations. I must point out, however, that the same distinction does arise in the context of relations among the Rashaayda themselves. To understand this we must review the history of the "slave trade"—the trade in people—among the Rashaayda.

A number of non-Rashaayda were incorporated into the Rashaayda "tribe" as "slaves" (*'abiid*) in about 1890. This development was due to three factors: (1) the geographical location of the Rashaayda on the slave-trading route between Arabia, on the one hand, and western Ethiopia and southern Sudan, on the other; (2) the Rashaayda's long-standing involvement in commerce and their familiarity with firearms; and (3) the economic incentives for purchasing captives that stemmed from pastoral production.

The trade in people between Sudan, Egypt, and Arabia probably existed in some form long before the Rashaayda arrived in Sudan. Egyptian military forays into northern Sudan began as early as 2500 B.C., when the expanding Pharaonic state took control of trade routes along the Nile, seized large numbers of cattle (Sadr, 1991, pp. 93–104) and, probably, enslaved Sudanese captives of war. By 1500 B.C. "slaves" (along with cattle, gold, ebony, and ivory) had become a traditional part of the tribute extracted by the Egyptian state from Nubia (in northern Sudan). But the volume of the trade and the routes it took have varied considerably from one period to the next. It was not until the mid-nineteenth century that large numbers of enslaved people were being brought from the African interior to the Red Sea coast. Coincidentally, this is when the Rashaayda arrived there.

It appears that most of the enslaved people who were brought to the Red Sea had been captured by large bands of mounted raiders who had attacked small, defenseless communities in the interior. The raiders operating in southern Sudan were mostly Arabic speakers, while those in western Ethiopia were Amharic or Cushitic speakers. They took their captives to market in Suakin and other port towns and often sold them to "slave" merchants plying the trade between Arabia and Sudan (Ali, 1972, pp. 52, 94–95, 103–104; Beachey, 1976; Toledano, 1982).

The Rashaayda were in no position to carry out the initial raids but were well situated to take advantage of the resulting commerce in people. They had more commercial experience than the Hadendowa, who were primarily subsistence pastoralists and cultivators. The Hadendowa depended on the direct barter of local products for obtaining the necessities that they did not themselves produce and were not very familiar with market transactions. In contrast, the Rashaayda had been buying rifles and selling trade goods even before they arrived in Sudan. Moreover, they were well equipped to work as "slave" traders, since they had the rifles needed to could protect their illegal trade (which was banned in most parts of the Ottoman Empire in 1857) from both government inspectors and rival merchants.

Despite this, most Rashaayda never worked as "slave" merchants. Only a small number actually purchased people for resale in Arabia. Some did buy captives so that they could keep them in their homes as servants, however. Those who did this were tempted by the cheapness of coerced household labor and the economic and political rewards it could realize. They could see that there was a place for forced labor in their pastoral production system.

The logic of pastoral production is such that when herds increase in size, there is a corresponding increase in the need for pasture and labor. Conversely, when herds are depleted by drought or disease, the demand for pasture and labor also falls. A pastoralist household cannot predict exactly when its herd will increase or decrease but it can adopt strategies to protect itself. It may hedge its bets by combining pastoralism with agriculture, commerce, and wage labor outside the pastoralist sector. Alternately, it may try to prevent the depletion of its herd (caused by the overgrazing that always results from rapid herd growth during a string of good years) by acquiring extra workers. These workers can take the animals to more distant pastures; plant cultivated fodder for them; gather wild fodder from ordinarily inaccessible places; or open up neighboring pastures by forcibly expelling the people who live there (Cribb, 1991, pp. 23–24, 37–41).

At the beginning of this century some wealthy Rashiidi households did acquire extra workers. They purchased captives who had been seized in southern Sudan and Ethiopia. The Rashaayda say that all of these captives were women or young girls. They increased a household's labor supply directly, by working as servants for the "free" women who lived there, and indirectly, by bearing and raising half-Rashiidi children for the resident men. The illegitimate "offspring" *mawaaliid* (sing. *muwallad*) of these enslaved women and "free" men worked for their "free" Rashiidi genitors without receiving compensation either in cash or in the form of livestock. They were given food, shelter, clothing, and protection against hostile outsiders but were not entitled to own or inherit property. For this reason their labor was obtained cheaply in comparison with that of the household's legitimate children or hired herders.

Seventy years ago, when a man began a relationship with an enslaved woman, he would say that he had acquired a sexual partner "from the cold, windy desert." The desert was mentioned precisely because it was not the proper place for people to have sexual relations. A married man and his legitimate wife slept with each other in the privacy of their tent; only animals cohabited outside of any dwelling. If an enslaved woman joined a married couple's household, she was never permitted to set up her own, separate tent but slept in her "owner's" wife's tent. Her place was not near the hearth, where the "female guardian of the tent" stayed, but in a cramped corner of the tent on its westernmost side. Sometimes she even slept outside of the tent.

A man's relationship with an enslaved woman was not equivalent to a real marriage. No man would begin his adult life by simply cohabiting with a "non-free" woman, because this would imply that he had such a low social status that no "free" family would give him a wife. Yet the relationship could become a permanent one. Once an enslaved woman had borne children for her "owner," he was not allowed to sell her. This gave her a measure of security.

No Rashaayda have purchased captives since the early 1930s, when the trade in people was completely suppressed. Nevertheless, there are still three categories of Rashaayda: the "slaves" (*'abiid*), who became members of Rashiidi households (and so became members of the tribe) through purchase alone; the "free" (*aḥraar*), who are members by virtue of descent alone; and the *mawaaliid*, who are related to other Rashaayda by virtue of both descent and purchase.

Relations among the *'abiid, aḥraar,* and *mawaaliid* are not the same now as they were at the turn of this century. Prior to 1956 all three categories of Rashaayda were represented in every Rashiidi camp. The "slaves" and *mawaaliid* lived with "free" Rashaayda and accepted their dominance for two reasons: (1) they had no way of earning a living other than nomadic pastoralism, and (2) they depended on the "free" coresidents of their camps for protection. The small Sudanese police force could not always keep order in the region, and each "tribe" usually relied on its own armed men to protect itself from criminals.

When Sudan gained its independence in 1956, government spending for public works and police services increased. Many *mawaaliid* found employment and safe places to live outside of their nomadic camps. Since then most *mawaaliid* and *'abiid* have lived apart from the "free" Rashaayda in their own, independent agricultural settlements.

Reliable statistical data about the proportionate representation of the three categories do not exist; what is more, carrying out a statistical survey would be extremely difficult, both because Rashiidi settlements and camps are so widely dispersed and because the residents of these camps are frequently traveling and hard to question. In my opinion, only a few elderly women, who were purchased when they were young children, are called *'abiid*, and they now constitute much less than 1 percent of the total population. Their children and grandchildren, or *mawaaliid*, are more numerous; perhaps 10 percent of the Rashaayda fall into this category. The remainder are "free."

Although the *'abiid* and *mawaaliid* established separate residential communities for themselves during the 1950s, they kept the patrilineal descent model common to all Rashaayda. For example, the *mawaaliid* of the Jalaadiin lineage traced descent through their "free" Juleydi genitors. Any two *mawaaliid* from this lineage could calculate the genealogical distance between them by referring back to their common "free" ancestors. However, the *mawaaliid* of this lineage did not marry their "free" cousins. "Free" men of the Jalaadiin married only other "free" Rashaayda, while the "non-free" members of the Jalaadiin married only other "non-free" Rashaayda. By 1979 attitudes had changed somewhat. Some of the "free" Rashaayda from the Dhuwi Ḥayyaan, the Jalaadiin, and the Baraaṭiikh had exchanged daughters with *mawaaliid* families. Yet the image of "free" men having sexual relationships with "non-free" partners was still present, not in deed but in thought.

Case Fourteen: Wives and Other Sexual Partners

In 1979 marriage negotiations began between the parents of a divorced woman in her mid-twenties and a widower in his late thirties. The widower, who I will call Sariir, had two daughters. He wanted to remarry and was hopeful that the divorced woman, Ḥaamda, would accept him as a husband. He offered to give his eldest daughter in marriage to one of her five brothers.

Ḥaamda was unusually nervous about remarrying; her first marriage, to her father's brother's son, had been brief and unpleasant. Her parents were glad that Sariir was asking for her, however. They thought that Sariir, an experienced husband and father, would be a considerate and understanding husband for her. If they had any reservations they were not about him; they were more worried about his *daughters*.

The family got together to discuss the marriage, and one of the children told me about their meeting later. The question was: If Sariir gave his eldest daughter away in exchange for Ḥaamda, which of Ḥaamda's brothers would marry her? Her two elder brothers were eighteen and sixteen years old. If Sariir's daughter married Ḥimeyd, the eldest brother, he would have to wait for at least another four years, since she was only twelve. This was a long time. "And God alone knows what will happen in four years; the girls might get sick or even die," Ḥaamda's mother said. But if Ḥimeyd did not marry her, how would he find a wife? Ḥaamda was his only unmarried sister; he had no one else to exchange. What was more, his four younger brothers would also need wives.

Ḥimeyd argued that they should ask Sariir for both his daughters, not just one of them. "If we don't exchange Ḥaamda for both of Sariir's daughters, how am I supposed to get married?" They considered this. "The younger one is just a *bint umgargash* ('girl covering her head with a *garguush*,' i.e., about 10 years old)," his mother said. "Even if Sariir gave her to us, too, it would be a long time before anyone could marry her." Ḥimeyd actually began to get angry. "That doesn't mean we shouldn't ask for her," he said. The discussion was on the brink of turning into an argument when Ḥimeyd's eight-year-old brother 'Abd al-Ḥamiid broke the tension. "And where am *I* going to find a wife?" he whined comically, "from the cold, windy desert (*min as-sağii'a*)?" Everyone laughed.

I thought I understood why 'Abd al-Ḥamiid had revived this old euphemism for cohabitation with purchased women. He was suggesting that he was in truly desperate straits. Without hope of ever getting a real wife, he would have to look for sex wherever he could find it, even if this meant living with a "slave"! His joke put the situation in perspective. The other brothers, including eight-year-old 'Abd al-Ḥaamid, were really too young, after all, to be worrying about getting married now. There was no reason to involve them in this exchange, since there was plenty of time to find wives for them. As for the two oldest brothers: If they did not both marry by exchange, surely one of them could marry by *siyaag* ("making a marriage payment"). There was no need for Ḥimeyd to be so anxious.

The joke showed me that the memory of sexual partnerships with purchased women was still alive even though the trade in people had ended decades ago. It also explained why the *mawaaliid* were not eager to marry their daughters to the sons of "free" families. If they simply gave a daughter to a "free" man, they risked a loss of dignity; someone might try to misinterpret the marriage as something close to concubinage, not a legitimate union. So whenever marriages occurred between *mawaaliid* and *aḥraar,* they always took the form of an exchange. That way, neither side could ever claim that it ranked higher than the other.

In 1979 there were few *mawaaliid/aḥraar* marriages. Most *mawaaliid* lived in their own communities, apart from their "free" Rashiidi relatives. Yet relations between the "free" and "the offspring of free men and slave women" were cordial. For example, when a "free" Rashiidi was traveling to market through an area where he had no close kin, he could seek hospitality from *mawaaliid* families there. They would give him a meal and let him spend the night in their homes, with the understanding that they were equally entitled to his hospitality should the need arise. Furthermore, many "free" men were helping "non-free" relatives find employment in Saudi Arabia. "Free" Jalaadiin men had brought labor contracts with Saudi employers for the *mawaaliid* of their lineage (Young, 1987, pp. 213–215).

It seems to me likely that marriage between "free" and *mawaaliid* Rashaayda will increase. This is not only because the "free" Rashaayda want to keep their relations with the *mawaaliid* alive. The *mawaaliid* also want to forge marriage alliances with prominent families in the region. They can also choose to marry into non-Rashiidi families, but not all other Arab Sudanese are willing to establish marriage ties with them. From an outsider's viewpoint, the *mawaaliid* are the "slaves" of the

Rashaayda. This means that the "free" members of other Arab Sudanese "tribes" (such as the Laḥaawiin) do not view them as equals, despite the fact that they too are racially mixed. So a *muwallad* man who wanted to "marry up" and become the son-in-law of a "free" family had a better chance of getting a wife from his "free" relatives than from the "free" members of other "tribes."

The complexity of relations between *mawaaliid* and "free" Rashaayda was brought home to me in 1979 by a number of encounters with *mawaaliid*. They forced me to rethink my positions and led me to a clearer understanding of a kinship term, *'amm*, which the "offspring of free men" sometimes used when addressing "free" Rashaayda.

Case Fifteen: "Uncles," Patrons, and Fathers-in-Law

I was in the marketplace in Kassala looking for a ride; I wanted to visit some Rashaayda in Khashm al-Girba. I spotted a group of *mawaaliid* boys, about ten years old, standing near a tailor shop that catered to the Rashaayda. They looked like African Sudanese but were wearing large Rashiidi turbans. I hoped they might know a Rashiidi driver who was heading in my direction. When I approached them and asked them if they were waiting for a ride, however, they asked *me* for help. They had mistaken me for a "free" Rashiidi. This was a reasonable mistake; even though my freckled complexion looked strange, my brown hair was concealed by my turban and, like them, I was wearing Rashiidi clothes and spoke Rashiidi Arabic. No foreigners had ever lived with the Rashaayda before, and no matter how strange I might look the only logical conclusion to draw from my appearance was that I was a "free" Rashiidi. So one of them said, *a'ṭiini girsheyn yaa 'ammi* ("Uncle, give me a few cents").

I was a little taken aback, especially because the boy had called me *'amm* ("paternal uncle, father's brother"). I had seen *muwallad* children begging for change from "free" Rashaayda before and disapproved of it. I thought it was a sign of servile dependency, a relic of the times when people were bought and sold. I also felt uncomfortable being called *'amm* in this context. I was afraid it might mean more than just "paternal uncle"; perhaps it also meant "the patron or protector of a subordinate." This jived with the interpretion given to the term by Rashaayda working in Saudia Arabia. One man who had worked for a businessman in Riyadh, for example, had been accustomed to address him as *'amm*, even though he was certainly not his paternal uncle.

So I just replied curtly, *anaa maani 'ammak* ("I'm not your father's brother"). The boy was astonished by my answer, and I saw that I had hurt his feelings. But I still thought I had made the proper reply. I felt it was my duty to "raise his consciousness" and teach him to deal with "free" Rashaayda as his equals, not his superiors. After all, I thought, why should he call me "uncle" and ask for money rather than say *yaa rijjaal* ("Say, man . . .") like he would with a friend? So I said nothing more, and the boy walked away.

About an hour later I managed to locate a non-Rashiidi truck driver who was going to Khashm al-Girba. He said he would take me there, and I climbed into the front seat, in the cab. By coincidence his other passenger was another *muwallad*

Rashiidi, this time a man in his thirties. It developed that he lived in Khashm al-Girba and knew many Rashaayda there, both "free" and *mawaaliid.* As we rode out of Kassala I took advantage of his presence to ask for directions; I did not know exactly where my acquaintances were living. He told me how to find their houses and also talked about his relatives. He said he was living near his *'amm* and had a tenancy in the agricultural scheme.

Later, when I was writing up my notes about this trip, it occurred to me that I did not know exactly what he meant when he mentioned his *'amm*. I recalled that, as a kinship term, it had at least three distinct meanings: "father's brother," "wife's father," and "distant patrilineal relative of the older generation." My encounter with the boy in the market had alerted me to its other, political, meaning: "free patron or protector of a non-free person." Which of these meanings was the one intended by the *muwallad* man from Khashm al-Girba?

Once I recognized that the word could have so many different meanings, I began to wonder whether it was always demeaning for a *muwallad* man to call a "free" man *'amm*. In one context, surely, it was demeaning; if he asked his *'amm* for money at the same he would indeed be acting in a servile manner. But in another context it was not. For if he addressed a "free" man as *'amm* while asking for his daughter (not just money), this could not by any means be interpreted as servile. It was a polite form of address that presupposed a relationship of equality between the two, permitting the *muwallad* man to ask for a wife from a "free" family.

I decided that I had been wrong to presume to teach a Rashiidi child about his own society. He certainly must have known that it was shameful to beg for money from a stranger, but perhaps he felt that the "free" Rashaayda were not strangers. He did have a relationship with them, and although this relationship might not be as egalitarian as he could have wished, it might well become egalitarian with the passage of time. Perhaps in ten years' time he would find himself asking for a "free" man's daughter and giving his sister to that "free" man's son. Such exchanges had already occurred, and he had no reason to rule this out.

HISTORY AND GENDER IDENTITY: THE EXCLUSION OF WOMEN FROM "POLITICS"

We have seen that many aspects of the Rashaayda's identity—as members of a single "tribe," as Bedouin, or as "free Arabs"—have changed from one historical period to another. What is more, these changes in identity all have affected the kinds of marriages into which they have entered. Since history has changed marriage—the quintessential relationship between the sexes—it is a good bet that history has affected most other relations between men and women, also. It makes good sense, then, to ask how history has affected gender identity among the Rashaayda.

There are many ways of studying relationships between the sexes in any society. One can ask people about their heroes and heroines, their "role models," their ideal men and women. Alternately, one can watch people raising their children, taking note of the distinctive ways in which boys and girls are socialized. I recorded these kinds of observations during my fieldwork but found it difficult to decide how to organize them. In the end it was most useful to think in terms of three concepts: prestige, authority, and political power. I decided to look for differences in the ways in which Rashiidi women and men earn prestige, increase their authority, and accumulate political power.

Women's and men's prestige systems. Women and men generally earn prestige by excelling in the roles that their society assigns them. A woman who is an excellent worker, a generous hostess, a courageous defender of her children and her home, and a good mother is known as a *khiyyaara,* "one of the elect." The same term is applied to a man who is a good shot, a skillful rider and tracker, a dauntless protector of his family and friends, and a good judge of livestock; he is called a *khiyyaar.*

The most important sex-linked roles are those that have the most tangible impact on the material conditions of life: women's and men's roles in production. I described these roles in Chapter Two and showed how men's work and women's work complemented each other, especially among nomadic families who rely on household production for a significant part of the year. In that chapter I portrayed the products of people's labor simply as useful objects. These handmade objects are also signs of personal skill, however, and contribute to the worker's prestige.

Women often compare the work of one "female guardian of a tent" with another. They say that the tent cloth made by a skillful weaver does not leak during rainy weather and is "as smooth as silk." Properly tanned water skins, also, do not leak, and the water they contain cools quickly and does not taste too strongly of the tanning agents remaining in the leather. When women visit each other they take note of the quality of the household's food and furnishings. They recall these observations later, when choosing possible wives for their sons. Girls whose mothers are good workers are favored as marriage candidates, because women expect them to work as well as the mothers who trained them.

Men seldom comment directly on women's work, since they do not like to appear too well informed about it. If a meal is good, they eat it without remark, but if it is not to their taste they raise their hands from the common bowl and stop eating, without explaining why. There is one exception, however. When a guest is leaving his host's tent, after having been served unusually good coffee by the hostess, he will say *shakar allaah aṣ-ṣaani'* ("May God praise the maker [of the coffee]") in a loud voice. Since both men and women make coffee, the man is entitled to have an opinion about it. He speaks loudly enough for the hostess to hear him, even if she is in the western section of the tent. She comes out to thank him for his compliment.

Men also evaluate each other's work, whether it involves herding livestock, breaking camels to the saddle, carving rifle stocks and other wooden implements, or breeding racing camels. Men try hard to earn recognition for their work, partly because, like people everywhere, they want to be admired, but partly because a good reputation can bring economic rewards. A man who is known to be good at raising animals is more likely to be hired as a paid herder than a man with a poor reputation. Not all men's work has a monetary value, however. Men strive to be skillful and quick butchers, for example, even though they are never paid for this work.

Whenever a wedding is held a group of men gather to butcher the animals that have been slaughtered for the guests. They divide themselves into competing teams, each team trying to be the first to skin and dismember its camel or sheep.

Work is not the only way to earn prestige. Among the Rashaayda, both sexes are evaluated as performers as well as workers, and weddings provide the context for doing so. During weddings people are ranked according to their attractiveness, skill as athletes, artistic talents, and ability to entertain, among other things. Men compete with each other as riders and poets, and women compete as dancers and seamstresses. To illustrate this competition, I will describe part of a wedding that I attended.

Weddings: Ritual performances and prestige. The first competition, a camel race, was for men. It took place on the second day of the wedding, near the camp where the bride lived. Camel races are always held during weddings, at a stage when the bride and groom are not yet really a couple. The groom has to prove himself worthy of the bride by racing with some of the other young men. He does not have to win the race, and even if he comes in last it does not matter; the important thing is to participate.

Preparations for this particular race began early in the morning. The groom and other young men bridled their racing camels and led them off to the starting line, which was two miles away. Some of the racers had been getting ready for weeks, restricting the diets of their fastest camels and exercising them regularly to keep them in shape. I did not accompany them, but one of my friends did, and he told me later what the start of the race had been like.

The bride's brothers and uncles, who were walking with the racers, decided how far to go. After about an hour they reached what they thought should be the starting line and told the racers to mount up and face their camels toward the distant camp. The racers did without saddles, to reduce the load on their camels. They wore only their long *sirwaal* pants and close-fitting shirts; looser clothing would have increased the wind drag and would have slowed the camels down. The bride's uncle walked out in front of them and stood on one side of the race course, holding up a piece of white cloth. He checked to make sure that everyone was ready and then dropped the cloth. This was the signal for the race to begin. The riders shouted, kicked their camels, and took off.

For a few minutes they applied their thin whips vigorously, lashing the animals first on one side and then the other, but once the pace has been set they no longer needed the whips; the race itself excited the animals. The fastest camels, bred as racers for generations, soon outdistanced the ordinary mounts. They seemed to fly across the ground, almost floating, like flat stones skipping over the surface of a lake. Their broad front feet slapped the earth as they ran. The riders, tossed up and down violently by the camels' uneven gait, hugged their animals' backs with their knees and hung on for dear life.

Back at the bride's camp I and the other wedding guests were drinking tea. I sat with the men in the men's tent and the women sat with the bride's mother in the women's tent. We knew that the race had begun and kept our eyes on the horizon, trying to catch sight of the first racer. But no one appeared. We finished our tea and were served coffee, while the men from the bride's family and camp cooked the meat for our lunch in large pots outside the tent (see p. 54). Finally the first racer—a mere spot in the distance—appeared, and we all rushed out of our tent to watch him. The bride's father, also, walked outside; he would judge the race. He stood in front of the guests at the finish line. The women guests and girls stayed closer to the women's tent but were just as eager to see who the winner would be.

As the riders approached we could hear their shouts and see the clouds of dust thrown up by the camels. We all watched carefully; we wanted to be able to distinguish the first three riders from those following close behind them. When the first three racers crossed the finish line the women gave joy cries (*zaghaariiṭ*), a kind of high-pitched, ululating, wordless cheer that women make to express their happiness or to encourage and inspire others. The men singled out the winners and walked over to the finish line to congratulate them.

The momentum of the racing animals carried them far past the finish line; it took a few moments to slow them down. Once they had all been brought to a halt the three winners turned their camels around and went back to the cluster of tents. They sat on their mounts silently near the wedding tent (where the groom and bride would later take up residence) and waited to receive their congratulations and prizes. Those who had not won took their animals away from the tents and walked with them for a few minutes to cool them down.

I went over to congratulate one of the winners; I knew him and was pleased that he had won. As I reached up to shake his hand, however, I noticed a large bleeding wound above each of his ankles. I looked up at his face, shocked, suddenly unsure of what to say; should I congratulate him or commiserate with him? But he just smiled back. He had had to grip his camel's back tightly with his legs to keep his seat; the contact with the rough hide had torn his skin. Although the wounds must have been painful, he ignored them. He was enjoying his triumph in the race and, especially, the admiration of the young girls who were watching him from a distance.

It requires no great imagination to understand why the young men took part in the contest with such enthusiasm and *élan*. All were unmarried and eager for a chance to prove their courage, skill, strength, and endurance—in short, their manliness. The race was a golden opportunity to attract the attention of the opposite sex. Many girls had come with their parents from outlying camps to attend the wedding, and some of the most beautiful might be catching their first glimpses of the winners. So the race was spiced with an element of flirtation. The winners sat proudly on their camels, "stripped down (*umjarradiin*)" to their loose pants and close-fitting knit shirts, taking advantage of the race to present themselves for the girls' inspection. The only flaw, from their point of view, was that the girls were almost hidden from sight, both by the walls of the women's wedding tent and by the girls' veils.

The bride's father awarded a prize of £S20 to the first winner and gave the other two prizes of £S10 and £S5, respectively. He attached the money to the bridle of each camel, while its rider was still mounted. This money was just for display; neither the riders nor the owners of the winning camels kept it. The riders gave it to the groom later as a wedding present (*jaruura*). By giving their prize money to the groom, the riders put him in their debt and made sure that he would pay it back when their turn came to marry. He would give them equal or larger amounts when they invited him to their weddings.

When the race was over we returned to the wedding tents and had our mid-morning meal. We were served meat, as a first course, and then were given porridge. A few hours passed, while we chatted and digested our meal. When noon came most of the guests took naps, retiring to the shelter of the wedding tents or to the tents of nearby friends. It was not until afternoon that the second competition—the men's swordplay and singing—began.

The men left the wedding tent and formed two parallel lines in front of it, with the men in each line facing the men in the line opposite. A man in the center of one line started to recite poetry, composed in a distinctive meter called *az-zariibi.* He shouted out a stanza and its refrain, and the men of the opposite line, who were listening, repeated the refrain as soon as he finished it. When the men in nearby tents heard the singing they came to join in, and slowly the two lines drew farther apart until there was a wide space between them. The dancing ground—an arena for displays of swordsmanship—was ready.

The first performer, a young man in his late teens, walked into the arena and unsheathed his sword. He faced one of the lines, grasped the sword by its hilt tightly, and raised the blade in front of him. Holding it at arm's length, he swung the blade to the left and to the right in wide, flashing arcs. While he flipped the heavy sword with his right hand, he put his left hand behind his back and hopped backwards and forwards, approaching and retreating from his audience in time to their singing.

Because he was truly skillful, the two lines of singers rewarded him by allowing him a full five minutes to perform. They kept time while he danced by clapping in unison, and with every second clap they leaped, all at the same time, into the air. When they hit the ground the impact of their feet against the hard clay could be heard throughout the camp. Eventually the sword dancer grew tired, however, and his place was taken by another young man. This second dancer was not so successful; he could not swing his sword as quickly or as steadily. Passing judgment, the singers in one of the lines stopped singing after only a minute. Without accompaniment, he had to retire from the arena and give his place to a third performer.

Next came the women's competition. When the women in the women's tent heard the men start to sing and dance, they dressed themselves up (*tazachchinoo*) for dancing. They applied mascara (*kuḥil,* powdered antimony) to their eyelids and put special rings on their fingers that had long silver bangles. Those who had any extra silver necklaces or jewelry put those on, too, so that the metal would make a pleasant jingling sound as they danced. They also took out their married women's ritual veils (*baraağiʿ*), which they had brought with them for the wedding, and slipped them on over their masks.

Their change of costume complete, the women left their tents and approached the dancing ground. As soon as they arrived the swordsmen left the arena to make room for them. The two parallel lines of singing men moved closer together and everyone else crowded around them to watch the dance. Some of the young men even mounted their camels and peered down from their high perches at the dancing ground; they had the best view of the dancers.

The man in the middle of one line gave the signal for the dance to begin. He raised his right hand to silence the crowd and sang out a poem which, I was told, he had composed on the spot. He described the dance and addressed the women dancers, flirting with them in oblique, poetic language:

min il-'aṣri waağif wa adukk as-saliila
wa laa-ntuu ba'iidiin ya 'aal muu damaani

["I've been pounding the sand since the late afternoon;
you descendants of Adam were not far away."]

What he meant was: "I've been dancing at this wedding since the late afternoon, and you daughters of Adam have stayed close enough to watch me." He shouted out this stanza and its refrain and the men of the line opposite listened. They clearly liked the opening stanza and showed their approval by repeating the refrain: *wa laa-ntuu ba'iidiin ya 'aal muu damaani*. Then the first line repeated the opening stanza, and the opposite line sang out the refrain once again. One of the women responded by entering the dancing ground and starting to dance.

She did not sing or speak, but just raised her silver-laden hands and clapped them together lightly, in time with the singing. She turned around slowly, her long, colored sleeves and skirt flaring out around her body as she whirled. One of the men singers, inspired, unslung his sword from his shoulder and unsheathed it. He handed the sword to the dancer, and she took it in both hands, holding it delicately by the hilt and the blade, and rested it against her forehead. Its steel blade and the shining mother-of-pearl buttons on her *burga'* gleemed. Turning to face one row of men, she saluted them by hopping toward them as she danced. They replied by jumping still higher as they clapped and sang.

Then three other women entered the dance ground and started to turn around slowly next to her. A fourth woman took out a bottle of perfume and walked past the lines of men, splashing their white turbans and hands with it liberally. They held out their hands to receive it and wiped the excess perfume on their short beards and faces. In this way the community of men and the community of married women exchanged gestures of esteem.

After some minutes of strenuous exertion the first women to enter the dancing ground were exhausted. They paused to breathe and adjust their heavy, silver-encrusted veils. This pause gave one of the men an opportunity to enter the arena. He approached one dancer and, using a safety pin, fastened a thick wad of ten-pound notes to the right side of her *burga'*. This was not a gift; it was a prize that the woman had earned by dint of her excellence as a dancer and a seamstress.

This award was purely symbolic and had no monetary value for the woman who received it. She did not keep the money but passed it on later to the groom as a wedding gift. Gratified that she was selected as an example of an ideal woman and wife, she left the arena and made room for other women to take their turns.

Prestige, change, and history. The wedding performances and prizes represent the achievements of men and women as if they were equally rewarded and perfectly complementary. Each sex is given a chance to perform, and the best performers of each sex are given recognition. Yet we should not be misled by this image of equality

Women dancing with swords during a wedding. Note the man on the far right, who is clapping in time with the singing.

and complementarity. Taken as a whole—that is, as a system of rewards for material production and artistic performance, as well—the Rashaayda's current prestige system favors men. True, performers of both sexes are rewarded during the wedding. But many of the things produced by men—racing camels, wooden saddles, and livestock—can be sold for high prices, which means that men also gain material rewards for skillful work. Most women's products (cooked food, leather containers, tent cloth), on the other hand, are used only in the home and are seldom sold. There is no market for most women's products, so women who are good cooks, weavers, and seamstresses receive only symbolic recognition for the excellence of their work.

This imbalance is not caused by the Rashaayda's own division of labor. Rather, it originates in the market economy that surrounds Rashiidi society. If the Rashaayda were still primarily subsistence pastoralists, as they were at the beginning of this century, neither men nor women would be able to market the things they made. The goods made by all household members would be consumed by the household, and the only benefits derived from superior work would take the form of improved comfort (better housing, a better diet) and security (saftey from thieves, larger stores of food). In a subsistence economy, both men and women would receive only symbolic rewards for their accomplishments.

Changes in the balance between women's prestige and men's prestige, therefore, have depended mainly on changes in the structure of external markets. Since the 1960s there has been more and more demand for men's products and labor, while at the same time women's products are slowly being replaced by purchased goods. This means that their work is losing value.

The loss in the value of women's products can be traced by looking at a series of examples. In the 1960s, for instance, women used a cheap kind of cotton cloth, called *dammuuriyya,* to make their dresses. This cloth came in only two shades: black and white. To produce the black and red patterns preferred by the Rashaayda, the women would sew pieces of black and white cloth together and then dye the entire dress, boiling it along with pieces of acacia bark that they stripped off trees. This dyed the white cloth red. In the early 1970s they started using commercial dyes instead of acacia bark, and by 1975 they began to buy colored synthetic cloth instead of cotton. It was no longer necessary to dye the dresses at all. In 1977, after many men had gone to work in Saudi Arabia and had returned with their wages, some women stopped sewing their dresses entirely. Their husbands bought them expensive, tailor-made dresses in town, instead. By 1980 there were many Rashiidi men in Khashm al-Girba and Kassala who worked as tailors, sewing women's dresses on Singer sewing machines. The woman's role in dressmaking had almost disappeared.

The same process has begun in another domain: cooking. In the 1960s all Rashiidi women ground sorghum and millet on grindstones in their homes and used the dough for cooking. When some of them had to abandon pastoralism, however, and settled near Kassala in the village of Mastuura, they found themselves close enough to town to have their sorghum ground by machine. At first they could not afford this, but when their husbands found work in Saudi Arabia, they were given enough cash to pay a miller to grind their grain. Although none of them entirely regret this, since it has spared them the back-breaking labor of crushing the grain by hand, most of them insist that hand-ground sorghum tastes better than machine-ground sorghum. They have lost one of their traditional fields of expertise, and so far have not replaced it with a new one.

Women's and men's authority. Among the Rashaayda, authority—the legitimate right to command, condemn, or correct others—is closely linked with seniority, the sexual division of labor, and the sexual division of space. When the residents of a household are working within the men's perimeter—the line encircling the entire campsite—the senior man of that household is the ultimate authority. His wife and his sons are not supposed to countermand his orders, especially if they concern men's work. When the senior man is absent, however, and when the household members are working within the women's perimeter—the line connecting the tent pegs—the senior woman of the household has the right to give them instructions. She tells the boys to take care of the livestock and assigns other tasks to the girls. Although one of her sons may try to take over the leadership of the household when their father is absent, a strong-willed woman can quickly put a stop to this. In my household, for example, one of Suluum's sons once told her to make coffee for us. "Don't order your mother around (*laa tarsil ummak*)," she snapped back. And that was the end of it.

The extent of a senior woman's authority becomes clear when a male guest comes to visit a household and the male head of that household is absent. His wife takes on the responsibilities of hospitality. If she has sons who are at least old enough to talk, she goes into the western section of the tent and tells her sons to lay out the spread (*firaash*) for the guest and entertain him. If she has no sons she goes into the eastern section herself to greet the guest but does not stay there to chat with him. She makes him tea and coffee, serves it to him, and returns to the western side of the tent.

Since no male resident is present she cannot offer him anything else. As the Rashaayda say, *il-mara maa tigaddim* ("A woman does not [ritually] offer [food]"). The reason given for this is that no host can offer food without eating some of it; if the host does not share the meal, the guest is too "reluctant" to eat. A woman, however, may not eat with a man from the same bowl unless he is her husband; she cannot share her food with male guests.

To solve this problem, a woman host sends for a male neighbor. This neighbor, irrespective of his kinship ties to her household, slaughters one of his own animals and brings it to her tent; she will compensate him for it later. If she does not have the water necessary to cook for the guest, he also saddles up his camel and goes to a water source to fill her water bags, a duty which would ordinarily be fulfilled by her husband or sons. For the sake of the guest, her neighbor will work for her. After the guest has departed, however, these neighborly obligations are ended.

Women also have authority during marriage negotiations. Both they and their husbands can require a prospective suitor to accept their demands in order to marry their daughter. Women are always present when the marriages of their daughters are being arranged (see Case Fourteen).

The other context in which a woman can give orders to an unrelated man is when she has quarreled with her husband. She has the right to return to her father's house, in such a case, and if her husband does not agree to take her there she can ask for the help of another man. To do so she waits for any man on camelback to arrive at her camp. She quits her tent and walks over to him, in full view of the camp residents, and asks him to take her with him. He cannot refuse. He lets her ride behind him and delivers her to her father's camp. Men obey this custom, even though it restricts their authority over their wives, because it gives their sisters the ability to leave abusive husbands if they need to do so. No one can accuse a woman who is "angry with" (*chaariha,* literally "hates") her husband of any impropriety if she asks a strange man to help her in this way.

Women's authority has been equal to the authority of men in one other area: religion. For the past century, the Rashaayda have had no religious authorities of either sex. Traditionally, neither men nor women performed the prayer behind an *imaam;* both usually prayed alone. Men joined groups of worshippers to pray only during the Islamic holidays, and even then acknowledged the authority of the *imaam* only briefly (see Chapter Three, p. 79). Both men and women were illiterate. They could not read the Qur'anic passages that they recited during prayer but just learned them by listening to others (usually, their parents).

In recent years, however, religious practice among the Rashaayda has started to resemble the institutional Islam promulgated by government-supported mosques. When Rashiidi men are in towns they pray behind an *imaam* daily. Some of the young Rashiidi men who worked in Saudi Arabia returned to Sudan with the conviction that collective prayer behind an *imaam* is obligatory for men but not necessary for women. In other words, the perception is growing that men and women should worship differently, and that male religious specialists should have the authority to decide what religious practices and norms are acceptable. Thus the balance between the sexes may be disrupted.

Another force for religious change is education. The trend is for more boys to get a religious education than girls. Nomadic families typically do not send their girls to boarding schools; only boys attend these schools (see Chapter One). Hence their girls remain illiterate and do not have direct access to Qur'anic texts; they have to accept on faith the interpretations of Islamic law that they receive from men. If this trend continues Rashiidi men will acquire the kind of religious authority that stems from a knowledge of scripture, while Rashiidi women will remain uneducated and disadvantaged in religious discourse. This trend is not inevitable, however. The Rashaayda who lived in sedentary villages did send their girls to elementary schools, and a small number of girls living in al-Mugrin were actually preparing to enter the university. If girls are given equal access to schools, men will not gain a disproportionate degree of authority from their education.

In 1978 the main difference between women's authority and men's authority lay in two other domains: legal proceedings between Rashiidi litigants and official dealings between the Rashaayda and Sudanese governmental authorities. Traditionally, whenever a serious conflict broke out between two Rashiidi families, they would first arrange for a truce (working through intermediaries; see Case Eight). Then they would seek out a judge who could adjudicate the case. The judge had to be someone who was knowledgeable in Rashiidi customary law and who had some prior experience in resolving conflict. Women did not have the authority to act as customary judges. The parties involved in a case always asked men, never women, to adjudicate it. Apparently women have never been judges among the Rashaayda. They have no memory of women judges, and women judges are not mentioned in any historical or ethnographic works about the Arabian peninsula, the place of their origin. Sexual inequality in the second domain, however—the domain of "tribal"/governmental relations—dates to recent times.

In 1978 all of the Rashiidi intermediaries between the "tribe" and the Sudanese government were men. They were appointed by the governor of Kassala province to two offices: the office of *'umda* (that is, representative of one of the three main "tribal branches") and the office of *sheykh* (in essence, an administrative assistant to the *'umda*). Initially the *'umda* of each "branch" was empowered to judge murder cases, impose fines for minor violations of Sudanese law, issue export permits to livestock dealers who wanted to sell their animals in Egypt, and collect livestock taxes; later some of these powers were reduced. The *sheykh* was the link between his lineage and the *'umda* and helped him collect taxes and sort out the complications of legal cases. Neither of these offices had existed a century earlier, after the Rashaayda's arrival in Sudan.

The imposition of these government offices on Rashiidi society had three important effects: (1) it solidified the division of the "tribe" (*gabiila*) into exactly three "tribal branches" (*gabaayil*). Left on their own, the Rashaayda might have sorted themselves into four "branches" (see Case Three) or even six "branches" (see the beginning of this chapter); (2) it made lineages into clearly defined political units, each with its own *sheykh;* and (3) it increased the difference between women's authority and men's authority. Prior to government intervention, men had only two formal roles that gave them judicial authority: the role of camp senior and the role of customary judge. The government's policy of appointing men to the two new offices excluded women from these new roles, as well.

Gender and political power. Before I can describe differences in political power between men and women, I must first say what I mean by political power. In my view, political power stems from a combination of reciprocity, obligation, and outright coercion. A person who has political ambitions tries to become a leader, first of all, by attracting as broad an assortment of followers and supporters as possible. An aspiring leader plays the role of patron, rewarding his or her clients for their support with all of the material, strategic, and symbolic resources that he or she can muster. The poor are rewarded with gifts, jobs, or interest-free loans; the ambitious are given opportunities to command, make decisions, and organize; and politically marginal groups are given inside information that they would otherwise not hear.

A novice politician has to repay each gesture of support made by his or her clients, which means that he or she must have a wide array of these resources (wealth, authority, and information) that can be committed to the game. As a politician rises, however, clients value the relationship with their patron more and come to fear its loss; they become less demanding. At the same time, the politician faces increased demands from his or her peers—that is, other political figures—and must acquire additional assets from new sources. One such source might be a formal political office; this might give the politician an independent income, a police force or guard, and legally constituted authority. Another possibility is for the politician to acquire a patron of his own; this would provide extra support. Regardless of which source is acquired, it allows the successful political agent to coerce his or her supporters, who henceforth become subordinates.

This understanding of political power leads us to conclude that political inequalities between men and women stem from imbalances in the distribution of wealth and authority. As we have seen, among the Rashaayda men have greater access than women to inherited wealth and income-generating occupations. Women do not inherit livestock and do not produce many marketable commodities. Furthermore, although women do have authority over members of their households and, occasionally, neighbors, they cannot become judges nor seek political office. Men, on the other hand, can become the leaders of camps and can act as judges and office holders. They can attract followers with offers of material resources (loans and jobs), positions of responsibility (for example, peacekeeping roles in a camp or during a hearing), and information (gleaned during meetings with government officials).

This does not mean that women have no political role in Rashiidi society. It means that their political role is restricted to the one domain where they have as many, if not more, resources as men: marriage. In the context of marriage, the relevant material resource is not wealth but brides; women control access to marriageable girls. Women's control over their daughters is especially visible when marriages to strangers are proposed. A girl's mother can block such a marriage by urging her close relatives to ask for her, instead, and by insisting on an exorbitant marriage payment from the suitor. Women also control information about marriageable girls. Men cannot inquire about young girls themselves and have few opportunities to see them, much less talk to them, because of the spatial separation of the sexes. Only women have a chance to examine unmarried girls when they visit other households, and when they return to their own households they can adjust their reports about these girls to suit their own interests. This can have important political consequences for a family's relations with outsiders. As we have seen (Cases Ten and Fifteen), marriage among the Rashaayda is political.

Women's roles in marriage negotiations do not allow them to build up patronage networks, however. Although the men who marry their daughters are indebted to their mothers-in-law and must treat them with respect, they do not become clients. This is partly because brides are not like money. Marriageable girls cannot be quickly accumulated and distributed periodically to the people whose support one wants to attract. Further, a woman can have only a comparatively limited number of sons-in-law, and five or six of them do not constitute a very wide network.

Marriage can have benefits for the mother-in-law, but this is because it links two entire households, not just two persons. As such, it is constantly reinforced by a steady stream of gifts and services from the son-in-law's household. His children are sent to help their grandmother when she needs them, and his wife visits her frequently. He moves his family's tent to his mother-in-law's camp whenever his wife is pregnant and helps the members of the entire camp when they migrate. Thus the mother-in-law gains as the member of a group when her family contracts a useful marriage alliance.

In sum, the exclusion of women from most political activities (other than marriage) is the result of inequalities between the sexes with regard to their resources, kinds of authority, and material rewards for achievement. These inequalities are partly the products of the Rashaayda's value system and partly the consequences of external factors beyond their control. The kinds of prestige, authority, and political power obtainable by women have varied according to historical changes in the regional market for Rashiidi goods (such as livestock and clothing) and in the political relations between the Rashaayda and the state. They have changed significantly during the past century and can be expected to change even more as new educational and economic opportunities appear.

Epilogue

This final chapter departs from the course set by the other four. Rather than adding to the ethnographic information already presented or analyzing it, this epilogue focuses on fieldwork among the Rashaayda. It could have been written differently. I could easily have extended this case study by opening up new topics, such as the Rashaayda's poetry, medical lore, cuisine, kinship terminology, botanical and geographical knowledge, funeral practices, and so on. Alternately, I could have tried to place the material already provided in a broad, comparative context. For example, I could have compared the Rashaayda "tribe" with other social units that have also been called "tribes" in the anthropological literature to see whether or not they have anything in common. Or, I could have tried to explain why some Rashiidi practices (such as their clothing styles or their table manners) differ from the corresponding practices of other Arab or Muslim societies. But I have chosen to focus on my relationships with the Rashaayda during fieldwork, showing how my personal circumstances, acts, and attitudes affected my research.

Why have I done this? Partly to satisfy my readers' curiosity; they probably want to know how I collected my data. But my primary aim is methodological. Describing the process of fieldwork allows other anthropologists to evaluate my ethnography and see how likely it is that I could have observed the things I describe. It also makes it easier to see why I chose to study some facets of Rashiidi life rather than others. Although I have tried to make sure that this case study is a reasonably accurate representation of Rashiidi society, I am inevitably biased in my choice of topics. Because I am a man I chose not to ask women exactly how they weave tent cloth or decorate their clothing. Because I was born in a city I found it boring to ask about the different varieties of sorghum that the Rashaayda cultivate, the seasonal variations in grain prices, and the Rashaayda's livestock deals. The way in which I gained access to Rashiidi society, and my subsequent behavior in the field, also influenced my choice of topics and affected the Rashaayda's perceptions of me. This case study, with all of its gaps (and hopefully some strengths as well), is a product of my personal dealings and problems with other people. Hence some account of them should be included.

The first problem that I had to face, even before leaving for Sudan, was the issue of religion. I was interested in ritual and hoped to take part in some of the Rashaayda's religious rites (such as the fast during the month of Ramaḍaan). I imagined (accurately, as it turned out) that most Rashaayda had never met any non-Muslims and was worried that, if they classified me as a Christian, this would create a barrier between me and them. I discussed this problem with my friends and professors in Los Angeles and one of them suggested, rather casually, that I change my religion, at least for the duration. He said, "Most people aren't really that religious, after all, and once they're certain of your sympathy they'll accept you." I was, in fact, interested in Islam anyway and thought it might be fascinating to live a Muslim life. Before I arrived in Sudan I had already decided that conversion to Islam would be part of my immersion in the culture.

My fears about establishing rapport with the Rashaayda seemed to be confirmed during my first six months in the field, when I was given "housing" in a tumble-down shack in the sedentary village of Mastuura. One of the local politicians had decided that this was the best place to put me—where the Rashaayda could keep an eye on me. For those six months I was almost completely ignored. No one would tell me his name, no one would speak Rashiidi Arabic with me, and most seemed to think I was a spy for the Sudanese police.

The apparently bizarre notion that I was working for the Sudanese police made sense at the time. In early 1978 some Rashaayda were smuggling weapons from Eritrea, where battles between Eritreans and Ethiopians were occurring weekly and great numbers of automatic rifles were being sold and bartered. A small number of Rashiidi merchants bought the weapons there, took them across the border, and resold them to Rashiidi families and other Sudanese. They kept some of the weapons themselves to protect their herds against thieves. A few other merchants were exporting livestock to Saudi Arabia illegally, where meat brought a better price than in Sudan. So the Sudanese police were suspicious of the Rashaayda and occasionally searched their villages for contraband. Of course I had no inkling that this trade was going on and found myself in a tense situation when I arrived in Mastuura. The Rashaayda thought that any outsider might be trying to identify merchants who were breaking the law. Thus their "intolerance" of me had a political and economic as well as religious basis.

I soon realized that I could not make any progress by staying in Mastuura. I made efforts to contact some still-nomadic families and had the good fortune to meet Aḥmad, Suluum's son. He was one of the few Rashaayda who had graduated from high school, and he wanted to continue his studies as best he could. He suggested that I live with his family while they migrated; he would teach me Arabic and I would teach him English. I gratefully accepted his offer, and we made plans for me to join him during the summer after the rains had started.

While I waited for the migratory season to begin I resolved to eliminate at least one of the barriers between me and the Rashaayda by converting to Islam. I made a public profession of faith, saying "There is no god except God" and "Muḥammad is the Messenger of God" in the company of some people in Mastuura. They reacted cautiously. Looking back, I can see that they were surprised and a little confused; they had never met anyone who had converted to Islam. But they gave me a little advice about the proper way to pray, and I bought a Qur'an and some religious literature in Kassala.

News of my conversion spread beyond the small circle of people whom I knew, however, and it gradually became clear that I had taken a very serious step, indeed. Once, when I was in Kassala, I went into the main mosque to perform the afternoon prayer. After the prayers were over, the *imaam* of the mosque made a public announcement, informing the people present of my recent conversion. I had no idea how he had heard about it, and I certainly did not want any special attention. But a line formed immediately, and one by one people came to drop coins on the carpet in front of where I was sitting. I knew that many of these people were very poor and that they should not be giving me money. But they felt it was their duty to reward a non-Muslim who had decided to join their community. I was gratified yet felt guilty. I was not certain that I would remain committed to Islam and was not even sure what that might entail.

Some aspects of the faith did not appeal to me—especially in the form in which the Rashaayda presented it. For example, some told me that I would have to break all my relationships with my family in the United States if they refused to convert. Others were more tolerant but not much more understanding of my background. Some of the other Islamic traditions also puzzled me. For example, I was told that the Prophet Muḥammad had said that prayer at the *ḥaram al-shariif* (the sanctuary in Mecca that surrounds the ka'ba) was one thousand times better than prayer at any other mosque. I could readily grasp the idea that prayer near the ka'ba in Mecca would have a spiritual and psychological intensity unmatched anywhere else, because of the belief that the *ḥaram* was in some sense the one spot on earth touched by God and made sacred directly by Him rather than by human intentions and rites. But I could not understand how this difference could be measured. Why "one thousand times better" rather than one hundred thousand times? "Better" in what sense? In the sight of God? If so, was this a part of Judgment? Was Judgment arithmetical, literally an accounting book of sins and good works?

I found no one around me who was willing or able to discuss my questions, so I suppressed them. I found it easier and more rewarding simply to follow the Rashaayda's Islamic practices. But as long as these questions remained unanswered I was to some extent acting the Muslim without completely being one. This was what my fieldwork demanded.

During the next few months I memorized some verses from the Qur'an that I could recite during prayers. I became more adept at performing the prostrations and other movements that were required. They were more difficult to learn than I had expected but were also more interesting. During my days in Mastuura, when I was almost completely isolated socially and was struggling to understand the Rashaayda's dialect of Arabic, I turned to the prayer as a relief and a source of inspiration. No matter how much my other difficulties frustrated me, I could at least master the prayer. I was struck by the strength and beauty of the Qur'anic verses and felt relaxed during prayer by the rhythm of the prostrations.

Then the rainy season arrived. I left Mastuura and went to live with Ḥaamid and Suluum's family. They were pleased to learn of my conversion but not particularly surprised. They had never pressured me to convert but had been nervous, at the same time, about my coming to live with them. Perhaps, as a Christian, I would have some strange religious customs (eating pork? drinking wine?) that they would have had to tolerate. My conversion put them at ease. I acquired an Islamic/Rashiidi name (and a genealogy along with it) and wore Rashiidi clothing. I prayed the five daily prayers and, when the month of Ramaḍaan arrived, I fasted during daylight hours along with everyone else. Gradually my identity as a Muslim became stronger and I thought I would probably remain a Muslim even after leaving the field.

The author and Muḥammad Salaama, a Rashiidi friend, mugging for the camera. The photo was taken by Tim Keating, an American photographer who happened to be traveling in eastern Sudan in 1980.

My first months in the desert passed quickly. I enjoyed learning how to migrate (although I lost a lot of weight from malaria and drinking impure water). I made large loans to my host family, which they used to invest in livestock. In return, I depended on them for food, shelter, and data. After giving them loans I had little money to live on. My grant, which in theory was only for eighteen months, consisted of $7,000 and my airfare. Soon after arriving I could see that I would need much more time to learn the new dialect, and so I ended up subsisting on my grant for three entire years. Without extra money I could not do much for my host family. I felt guilty that I was eating their food and sharing their housing without paying for it, but they would not accept payment. They were satisfied that I had loaned them money when they could use it, and when their business deals were complete they paid me back in full. I hoped that they had made some profit, at least, from my loan, but when I asked them how they had done they would not go into detail.

During most of 1978 the Rashaayda were constantly asking me what I was doing in the desert. I kept telling them that I wanted to write a book about their customs, but they had no idea what I meant. Finally I just explained my presence by saying that I wanted to learn good Arabic and that Rashiidi Arabic was better than Sudanese Arabic. This satisfied them.

I stayed with Ḥaamid and Suluum's family for about ten months and got to know their relatives and neighbors well. Some of them became good friends of mine and introduced me to their relatives and friends. My social network expanded, and I was able to compare the many different families I know. I began to distinguish the idiosyncracies of my host family from the characteristics that seemed to be shared by all nomadic Rashaayda in the area. I thought that I could detect general patterns of behavior and thinking and also was becoming more skilled in understanding conversations and taking part in them.

At this point I felt the need to leave the Dhuwi Ḥayyaan lineage and visit other Rashaayda. I wanted to be sure that whatever generalizations I arrived at really did apply to most Rashaayda. So I went to visit Suluum's relatives in Khashm al-Girba. After a visit lasting one week I went to Kassala and met a man from the Baraaṭiikh "tribal branch" who invited me to spend some time with his family in a very small settlement known as Umm 'Ashshuush (see p. 30). I spent three months there and then went back to my host family near Kassala. After this I moved around eastern Sudan more freely, visiting some Rashaayda in the town of al-Mugrin (near the 'Aṭbara River) and taking a trip to Suwakin and Port Sudan (on the Red Sea coast), where I met still other Rashaayda. In all of these locations I was received very hospitably and managed to garner some information about how people lived there.

I made some new friends, as well, and became involved in their lives and difficulties. One of them was stricken by a tubercular infection of his foot and feared he would lose his leg. I managed to arrange for free surgical operations for him from the Red Cross, and he gradually recovered—but two years after I left the field I heard he had contracted pulmonary tuberculosis. I never found out what happened to him.

When I last saw Suluum she had just returned from making the pilgrimage to Mecca and had bought a small prayer carpet (made in Thailand, oddly enough) for me there. She gave it to me when I said goodbye to her and her family. I told her I would use it and did use it regularly for the next seven years. I noticed she had a cough but thought she was just tired from her trip (completed just a week earlier). It turned out later, however, that this was the beginning of the illness that killed her one year later.

I went back to Mastuura, where I had stored my Samsonite suitcase and portable typewriter (never used). From there I went to Khartoum to take a plane back to the States. While I was in Khartoum I was consumed by guilt and uncertainty about my religious identity. The people I had been living with believed that I was a sincere Muslim, and to a great extent I was happy with my new religious identity—but I was not completely convinced of every doctrinal point and was not sure whether I wanted to remain a Muslim after returning to the United States. All of the questions that I had suppressed came flooding back again.

During my short stay in Khartoum I found myself reading the verse from the Qur'an that begins, "He frowned and turned away. . . ." This was a description of the Prophet Muḥammad at a time when he was preoccupied with the problems facing the Muslim community; he turned away impatiently from a blind man who had come to ask for an explanation of Islam. It seemed to me that this verse was God's criticism of the Prophet for his impatience and pride. But if the Prophet had failed to set a standard for other Muslims to follow at that particular moment (and had been reprimanded for this failing by God), perhaps he had also failed at other moments in his life and thus should not be taken as a model for Muslims to follow. Yet, if I had understood this verse correctly, how could I reconcile it with the belief of many Muslims that the Prophet was infallible?

Obviously I was in a predicament. I hoped now that I could think through some of these issues in peace and perhaps discuss them with other Muslims who were better informed than I. Surely I could decide what to do once I had arrived in the United States.

I prepared for my return trip by putting on Western clothes again and taking my Rashiidi clothes to a laundry. While they were being washed I went to the airline office to have my flight reservation confirmed. I missed having a turban on my head; the bright Sudanese sunlight felt hot. I still wore sandals, however, until the last minute before my departure. I remember leaving my sandals in the airport parking lot and putting on shoes and socks for the first time in two years. Shortly after I boarded my plane.

The return flight was disorienting. I felt anxious about missing the prayer during the long flight and was worried about eating pork (which is forbidden to Muslims). I checked with the stewardess about the contents of my meals. When the meals were served, it seemed strange to eat with a knife and fork again after eating with my hands—more exactly, my right hand only—for so long. Dinner was especially odd because I was given miniature plastic implements with which to eat. I held the tiny knife and fork with my fingertips and jabbed awkwardly at the microwaved veal cutlet on my plate, laughing at my own clumsiness.

When I landed at Dulles International Airport I found myself reacting negatively to much of what I saw. It struck me as a terrible waste of money to have an expensive machine polishing the floor at the airport; what was the point of having a gleaming floor? I was disgusted by the many ads for alcoholic beverages and their photos of people in immodest, revealing clothing. The tall, modern buildings near the airport contrasted dramatically with the economic and architectural landscape of Sudan; even Khartoum had only a few high-rise buildings. I thought of the great sums of money that must have been spent to build them, and was I reminded that all of this money was contaminated by the charging of interest. It was not purified by the Islamic practice of giving alms to the needy. These Islamic attitudes stayed with me for years after my return.

When I met my brother in Washington he was shocked by my appearance—I weighed only 135 lbs. He also found my new religious practices peculiar. He let me stay with him and his wife for a week and indulged my craving for fish, fresh salads, chocolate, and ice cream—all foods that I had missed while I was with the Rashaayda. Then I headed west to visit my father and mother and, eventually, to get back to work. I had to sort out my field notes and sketch out a plan for my dissertation.

It has now (1994) been fourteen years since I last saw the Rashaayda, and I have only the most insubstantial information about how they have fared during this time. I tried at first to correspond with my Rashiidi family regularly. I would begin each letter with the standard formula that most Rashaayda use: "In the name of God, the Merciful and Compassionate, the one to whom we turn for help. I send you friendly greetings and ask God, the Lord of the glorious throne, to keep you prosperous, in a good situation, and in the very best health and happiness." Then I would greet all of the people in my household by name "from the depths of my heart" and tell them that I thought of them often. I knew that if my letter reached them—that is, if they found it at the store of a merchant in Kassala, whose shop served as an informal post office for the Rashaayda—they would open it immediately and someone (probably Aḥmad) would read it aloud while others listened. So it was important to mention everyone. Only after this did I try to explain what I was doing in Los Angeles.

Inevitably I did forget to greet one person—'Abdallah's wife—and her feelings were so badly hurt that she returned the photographs that I had taken of her and her children. I found the photos in Aḥmad's letter when he replied and reproached myself for being so thoughtless. But then I found excuses for myself, recalling how difficult it been to write them a letter in Arabic and how long it had taken. She should have understood that I had not left out her name intentionally, I thought. Upon further reflection, however, I had to admit that I was wrong. She could not write and could not be expected to understand how hard it was for me to compose an Arabic letter. What was more, she probably did not understand anything that I wrote other than the greetings. All that she knew about America was that it was somewhere west of Tunisia, the green land where an Arab folk hero, Abu Zeyd al-Hilaali, had lived centuries ago. So of course she would focus on the greeting; my other news was just too strange to grasp.

I realized that the formulas that I repeated at the beginning of my letters actually carried a huge emotional load, while the news that was important to me was probably incomprehensible to them. They wanted to know whether my father, mother, and brother were in good health and wanted me to ask them about their family members. I wanted to tell them that I had written the first draft of my dissertation and was teaching part-time. When they wrote, they just conveyed the greetings of the people in my camp, but I wanted them to tell me more about their customs. For example, while writing a description of their weddings I thought of questions that I had neglected to ask while in Sudan (Who decorates the bride's hands by dyeing them with henna? When the men celebrate by firing shots over the bride's tent, does the bride's father join them or not?) and hoped that they would answer them by mail. But they never answered these questions. Apparently they thought it bizarre for me to ask about such things in a letter; letters were for greetings, for passing on news about relatives and friends. So although we both wanted to stay in touch, we had different reasons for doing so and different understandings of what this involved.

After two years had gone by our exchanges of letters were hardly more than an exchange of greetings, gestures that we made to show that we still cared about each other. Writing did not really enable me to tell them what was happening to me, since I lived in a society that was completely outside of their experience. And they, also, could not step outside of the conventions of writing to tell me their news. I still wanted to hear from them but found I had less and less to say, especially after I learned that Suluum had died. I had felt closest to her, and once she was gone it seemed to me that my strongest link with the Rashaayda had broken. We continued to exchange letters occasionally until the shopkeeper stopped allowing my Rashiidi family (and dozens of other families) to use his address; the volume of mail had worn him out. By the end of 1984 we were no longer writing each other.

I did not hear from them again. I met Sudanese students in Los Angeles and asked them to help me contact them, but without success. Then the political situation in Sudan changed. There was a revolution and then a counterrevolution by the army, which took power. Political relations between the United States and Sudan worsened. Today Sudan is considered a "terrorist" nation by the U.S. State Department. If I wanted to visit Sudan, I would have great difficulty getting a visa. So I cannot go back and look for my host family.

I wrote most of my dissertation between 1982 and 1986. I had to portray my experiences among the Rashaayda and my personal relationships with them from an anthropological perspective. To do this I had to strike a balance between two very different sets of goals and obligations.

On the one hand I wanted to succeed as an anthropologist. This was why I had gone to Sudan in the first place, after all. During my first two years in the field I had struggled to learn the Rashaayda's language, worked at creating a place for myself in their society, and single-mindedly recorded every cultural difference that I could detect. It was difficult. I agonized about the thinness of my data, always searching for additional cultural and social differences by contrasting the Rashaayda's practices with my own. At times I thought I would have to use every incident I observed and every scrap of information that I collected.

On the other hand, I had become a member of Rashiidi society. After my second year with them had passed I reached a point where I thought I understood them fairly well, and I discovered that they were not really so different. I enjoyed being with them, identified with them, and acted like them, at times even trying (with the connivance of my friends) to make strangers believe that I was a Rashiidi. I grew more self-assured and relaxed, and my friends and family, enjoying my company more, opened up to me, telling me how they felt from one day to the next, and asking for my help when they needed it. They shared their homes and their lives with me, let me witness their family quarrels and described their problems, regrets, and setbacks. They trusted me to keep these secrets to myself and not expose them to ridicule or disgrace.

Thus when the time came to write up my notes I had to think very carefully about what to say. I could recount some of the events and actions I had observed without hesitation because they reflected well on the Rashaayda. They were generous hosts, loyal friends, and courageous fighters when they had to be. They performed the Islamic prayer without fail and faithfully observed other Islamic practices (fasting during the month of Ramaḍaan, giving alms to the poor, and so on). They would be pleased if I said so. But what about some of their other practices? Would outsiders understand exchange marriage, for example? If they read about conflict between the Rashaayda and the Hadendowa, would they blame the Rashaayda? How much should I reveal about this conflict? Would my description of the tension between the two make matters worse?

I could not betray the Rashaayda's trust. At the same time, I could not describe only the positive aspects of Rashiidi life if I wanted to make a contribution to anthropology. Every time I began to write I had to ask myself: How important is this particular detail? When deciding what to include and what to omit, I relied on my sense of what was relevant for anthropology. The anthropological perspective enabled me to view my friends as informants, at least on occasion. It gave their casual responses to my questions more than purely personal significance. It also led me to portray some of the incidents that I witnessed as cases that illustrated general patterns or practices. It was what distinguished my three years of work in Sudan from plain tourism or romantic adventurism.

Although I believe I have managed to balance my obligations to the Rashaayda against my commitment to anthropology, I have not been so successful in resolving my contradictory feelings about Islam. After I returned to the United States I thought I would be able to discuss my reservations openly. I found, however, that most of the Muslims I met were simply not interested in my questions, and some of them found them offensive. I still identified myself as a Muslim and wanted to meet Arab Muslims, especially. After struggling for so many years to learn Arabic I wanted to continue speaking the language. In a way, perhaps, I wanted to stay in the field, even though I had returned to the United States. So for social reasons, once again, I put off asking some of the questions about Islam that bothered me.

I have not stopped thinking about Islam or about the Rashaayda since my departure from Sudan. In the years since then, I have visited other Arab countries and have learned more about other pastoralist societies. Although my raw field notes have not, of course, been altered by the passage of time, my understanding of them has changed. Writing this case study has pushed me to revise many of my thoughts about the Rashaayda, and anyone who compares some of my earlier publications about them with this work will inevitably find inconsistencies.

Perhaps there is no final word to write about the Rashaayda. I certainly have more to say about them and will try to look at other aspects of their social life in future publications. For the time being, however, I do want to leave the reader with some parting thoughts.

I have portrayed the Rashaayda as if they were a unique species of human being, different from all the rest yet similar to other Arab pastoralists, at least. Since I have written an anthropological case study about them (rather than a novel, a travelogue, or an autobiography), I could not have done otherwise. But I would not want to overemphasize their differences. True, the Rashaayda are not "us" (and it is up to the reader to decide who this "us" may be). But the Rashaayda are like "us" in fundamental ways. I hope that I have conveyed their basic humanity in my descriptions of their small, unselfconscious acts: Suluum's effort to wake Naafi' in the morning, his discovery of the scorpions in the firewood, 'Abdallah's pleasure at getting an early start during migration, and so on. These acts do not require elaborate explanation or analysis to be understood. This is because, as human beings, we are all capable of understanding each other, even if differences in language, expectations, and customs do sometimes get in the way. If the case study teaches this lesson it is at least a partial success.

Glossary of Arabic Terms

Note: The terms in this Glossary are arranged in alphabetical order according to the first letter in each word. The definite article—which has a variety of forms (*al-*, *ad-*, *ar-*, *as-*, *il-*, and so on) depending on context—is not considered part of the word itself for the purpose of alphabetical arrangement.

***'aağil* (m.), *'aağila* (f.):** rational, responsible, intelligent.
al-'aani: truce or cooling-off period observed by the two parties to a violent conflict.
***'abd* (pl. *'abiid*):** slave.
'agaal: loop of thick rope used for tethering camels.
allaahu akbar: "God is supreme [and surpasses the world of natural forces and human understanding]." Said when beginning to pray and as an invocation when an animal is slaughtered.
'amm: paternal uncle; distant patrilineal relative of the older generation; wife's father; free patron or protector of a non-free person.
il-'arab: "the people," i.e., the nomads.
'arabnaa: "Our people," i.e., our family or relatives.
il-'aṣir: late afternoon; the late afternoon prayer.
awliyaa' allaah: literally, "the friends of God," i.e., the saints.
il-bard: the dry, windy months ("the cold season") when most of the desert rain pools have dried up and the nomads are forced to erect permanent camps near dependable sources of water (early January to the end of March).
***ba'iir* (pl. *ba'aariin*):** A mature male camel over six years in age.
***baṭiiḥa* (pl. *baṭaayiḥ*):** spacious, box-shaped, dry-season tent.
***bazar* (pl. *bizraan*):** infant; literally, "seedling."
***beyt* (pl. *buyuut*):** house; tent; household (i.e., the group of people living in a tent).
***bint* (pl. *banaat*):** daughter; girl; virgin.
bint 'amm: paternal uncle's daughter, i.e., "cousin."
bishaari: a white breed of camel known for its speed; named after the Bishaariin pastoralists of northern Sudan who breed them.
bismi llaahi r-raḥmaan ir-raḥiim: "In the name of God, the Merciful and Compassionate." The first sentence of almost every verse of the Qur'an and a common invocation.
***burga'* (pl. *baraağı'*):** married woman's ritual veil.
***chaanuun* (pl. *chawaaniin*):** portable hearth made of scrap metal, used by women for cooking inside the tent.
chaariha: a woman who is temporarily separated from her husband pending the resolution of an argument; the first step toward divorce. Literally, "hating."
chibiir il-fariiğ: the senior man of the camp.
chitir: a species of low bush with dark green leaves and spines.
daar: a campsite occupied by from two to nine tents; the people who live in this campsite, i.e., the "camping cluster" or "extended household."
***dabbuuka* (pl. *dabaabiich*):** a herd of male camels formed specifically to send them to market.
dammuuriyya: a cheap kind of cotton cloth.
***ḍamyaan* (pl. *ḍamyaaniin*):** thirsty.
ad-darat: season of declining rainfall (October to December).

***dhabiiḥa* (pl. *dhabaayiḥ*):** an animal ready to be slaughtered and eaten; butchering an animal in secret, just for the sake of the meat (as opposed to butchering it to offer hospitality to a guest).
dhuwi: children of; descendants of; people of.
dhuwi machlaboo: a mythical society of half-humans/half-dogs.
diira: "tribal" territory.
diira 'umraana: inhabited territory.
diira maskuuna: haunted territory.
aḍ-ḍuḥaa: mid-morning.
aḍ-ḍuhur: noon, when the sun is directly overhead and a person's shadow is pooled tightly around his feet.
ḍumi: the five-day-long "period of thirst" during which camel herders stay in the desert, far from wells, and subsist on camel's milk.
aḍ-ḍu'uun: the women and children who ride on bull camels slowly, behind the men, during migration.
'eyb: something shameful.
***'eyla* (pl. *'eylaat*):** family.
'eyn ḥamraa: red, envious eye.
al-Faatiḥa: the opening verse of the Qur'an.
al-fajar: daybreak, when the sun rises above the horizon.
fariiǧ: dry-season camp.
farwa: tanned sheepskin with the fleece still attached; used as a saddle blanket and carpet for prayer.
faz'a: posse; armed group led by the senior man of a camp to pursue livestock thieves.
fii sadd wajhi: "at the cost of my honor (literally, in defense of my face)."
firaash: the brightly colored spread that each household unfolds when guests arrive.
***gabiila* (pl. *gabaayil*):** "tribe."
gabiilatnaa: "our tribe."
garaḍ: the seed pods of a species of acacia tree (*Acacia etbaica Schweinf.*), crushed and used by women for tanning leather.
***garaf* (pl. *agraaf*):** large leather sack made of thick camel hide and used for stashing household furnishings during migration.
***garguush* (pl. *garaagiish*):** head covering worn by girls between the ages of five and ten years, approximately.
***ga'uud* (pl. *ǧi'daan*):** A young male camel between three and six years old which has not been castrated.
il-gayla: the early afternoon, when the daily temperature is highest; the early afternoon nap.
il-geyḍ: the hot, arid season (April to June).
al-ghubeysha: "the little dawn," i.e., about 4:00 AM, when the sky over the horizon is just light enough to be distinguished from the ground.
al-ghubsha: dawn, when there is just enough light to distinguish one object from another.
al-gibla: the line connecting any local place of prayer with the shrine in Mecca known as the *Ka'ba*.
***ǧinaa'* (pl. *agni'a*):** married women's mask.
***ǧirba* (pl. *ǧirbaan*):** tanned goatskin used for storing water.
gufaa: literally, "the back of the head." Figuratively, the back part of the tent.
guṭr: perimeter of the space inhabited by a household.
guṭraan: a black, tarry salve made by distilling the sap of the bitter *ḥanḍal* fruit; used for treating the skin diseases of camels.
ḥaasid: envious.
***ḥajiira* (*pl. ḥajaayir*):** small, lightweight tent used during the rainy season when tents must be moved often.
al-ḥalaal: literally, "the good things made lawful by God for human beings"; figuratively, livestock.

ḥalab: "gypsies"; non-African residents of Sudan of unidentified foreign origin (Sudanese Arabic).
ḥanḍal: a wild plant (*Citrullus colocynthis*) with an extremely bitter, gourd-shaped fruit.
ḥaraam: forbidden by Islam.
al-ḥaram al-shariif: the sanctuary in Mecca that surrounds the Ka'ba.
ḥasad: envy.
ḥaṭab: firewood.
ḥawḍ: drinking pan for camels, made of mud and filled with water near the edge of a well.
ḥawwaashaat: tenancies, plots of land in the Khashm al-Girba agricultural scheme that some Rashaayda rent from the government and use for cultivating cotton and other cash crops.
ḥishma: propriety; the exercise of respectful self-restraint in the presence of a senior man.
***hool* (pl. *hiilaan*):** ghost.
***ḥurr* (pl. *aḥraar*):** free (i.e., not a "slave").
ibriig̈: In Rashiidi and Sudanese Arabic: a container with a handle and spout used only for pouring water on the hands, feet, and other parts of the body to purify it for prayer; in other dialects: a pitcher, teapot, or jug.
'iid: Islamic holiday; two such holidays ("The Feast of Sacrifice" and "The Feast of Ending the Fast") are celebrated each year.
'iid aḍ-ḍaḥiyya: the Feast of Sacrifice.
'iid al-fiṭir: the Feast of Ending the Fast.
***'ijimi* (pl. *'ujmaan*):** non-Arabic speaker.
***imaam* (pl. *aa'ima*):** prayer leader.
***'imaama* (pl. *'amaayim*):** turban, worn by men.
imraaḥ: area outside the tent where a camel herd is tethered for the night.
il-'ishaa: evening; evening prayer.
***ism* (pl. *asmaa*):** genealogical name, e.g., Muḥammad ibin (the son of) Ḥaamid.
'iyaal: dependent children.
'iyaal 'amm il-bint: "sons of the girl's paternal uncle," i.e., the relatives who have the right to be consulted when a girl is engaged to be married.
jadd: grandfather; ancestor.
jaruura: wedding present given to the groom.
al-jiiza bi-il-badal: marriage by exchange of sisters or daughters.
al-jiiza bi-s-siyaag: marriage by means of payments.
jinn: invisible beings who are said to live in wells, caves, and other hollow places in the earth and who have the same capacity as humans for good and evil.
Ka'ba: the Muslims' most sacred shrine and the focal point of the annual Muslim pilgrimage; in Mecca.
karam: generosity.
khafiif: lightweight, fast.
il-khalaa: the open (literally, "empty") desert.
al-khariif: the season when new pastures have sprouted, characterized by intermittent rain (mid-August to the end of September).
al-khaṭma: the "seal of the revelations," i.e., the Qur'an, in Rashiidi Arabic.
khawaajaat: Western Christians (as distinct from Arab or Eastern Christians).
***khilaal* (pl. *akhilla*):** wooden skewer used for fastening two pieces of tent cloth together.
***khiyyaar* (m.), *khiyyaara* (f.):** "one of the elect"; outstanding achiever.
***khoor* (pl. *khiiraan*):** shallow gully that fills with runoff during the rainy seasons.
khums fi 'eynk: "five in your eye"; a formula said to protect the utterer from the baleful glance of an envious person.
kiswat al-'iid: holiday clothing, traditionally purchased by the head of a family for his wife and children for an Islamic holiday.
kuḥil: powdered antimony, used by women as mascara and occasionally by men as an eye medication.

kunya: teknonym, that is, a name consisting of a prefix (*abuu,* "father of" or *umm,* "mother of") and a child's personal name.
***libbaada* (pl. *labaabiid*):** sun-screen; piece of canvas pinned to the underside of a goat's hair cloth to stop sunlight from shining in through the loose weave of the material.
maa shaa' allaah: literally, "What God has ordained"; said when expressing admiration to demonstrate that the speaker is not envious.
il-maghrib: sunset; the sunset prayer.
magruu': "corralled," i.e., a man who is subject to attack by his opponent if he enters a particular territory or camp.
***makhluufa* (pl. *makhaaliif*):** camel saddle for male riders.
***mara* (pl. *niswaan*):** married woman; wife.
***mar'aa* (pl. *maraa'i*):** foraging area, pasture.
***marfa'iin* (pl. *maraafi'*):** hyena.
***martaba* (pl. *maraatib*):** square saddle cushion.
***maṭḥana* (pl. *maṭaaḥin*):** grindstone.
al-maṭili': east; literally, "the place where the sun rises" in Rashiidi Arabic.
***maṭmuura* (pl. *maṭaamiir*):** grain storage pit.
mawaaliid: see *muwallad.*
mirta'iin: literally, "looking for foraging areas," that is, migrating only intermittently rather than every day or two.
***mitḥashshid* (pl. *mitḥashshidiin*):** reluctant to accept generous gifts or hospitality.
***mitshaamil* (pl. *mitshaamiliin*):** heading north.
mitwaḍḍi: ritually clean.
***mityaamin* (pl. *mityaaminiin*):** heading south.
al-mughiib: "the place where the sun sets," i.e., the west.
***mungab* (pl. *manaağib*):** "virgin's veil" worn by girls between the ages of ten and twenty, that is, before they marry.
***muwallad* (pl. *mawaaliid*):** "offspring of a free man and a slave woman."
nibza: teasing name given to someone that recalls his or her ridiculous or amusing characteristics.
raaḥa: ease, relaxation (the opposite of *taḥashshud,* "polite reluctance, indebtedness, embarrassment").
raayaat il-beyt: the flags of the tent; small colored squares of cloth hung up inside the tent interior.
Ramaḍaan: the lunar month during which all practicing Muslims fast—i.e., refrain from eating, drinking, and smoking—during daylight hours.
ar-ramḍaa: the hot ground of the desert during the daytime.
raa'yit il-beyt: "the female guardian of the tent," i.e., the senior woman of a household.
rayy: tanned sheepskin used for storing a large volume of water.
***rijjaal* (pl. *rajaajiil*):** man.
rujuula: manhood, manliness.
ar-rushshaash: the season of showers (mid-July to mid-August).
***ruwaag* (pl. *arwiğa*):** section of tent cloth.
sa'af: silver bracelets given to a bride by the groom as part of her marriage payment.
saariḥiin fi il-bil: "moving with the camels" in the open savannah, far away from the tents (the main activity of herders during the dry seasons).
as-sağii'a: the "cold, windy desert" where herders spend the night without shelter and suffer from exposure. Figuratively: the place where illegitimate sexual relations take place, outside of the moral and ritual shelter of the home.
sajda: a grayish pressure mark on a Muslim's forehead caused by frequent and lengthy prayers and devotional exercises that require touching the forehead to the ground (*sujuud*).
as-salaama: safety.
as-salaamu 'aleykum: "Peace to you"; the proper greeting for Muslims to give to one another, in standard Arabic.

aṣ-ṣalaat: the Islamic prayer or act of worship, performed five times daily.
saloom 'aleyk!: "Peace upon you!" in Rashiidi Arabic.
shaaddiin: "exerting maximum effort [to move tents]," that is, continuously moving.
shamla: tent cloth woven of goat hair, camel hair, and cotton.
sharaf: honor.
sheykh: respected elder man; administrative assistant to a "tribal leader" (*'umda*).
ish-shimaal: left; north.
***ṣiddiga* (pl. *ṣiddigaat*):** a ritual offering for the sake of one's children or parents.
siduw: horizontal loom used for weaving tent cloth from yarn made of goat hair, camel hair, and cotton.
ṣiigha: silver and gold jewelry given by the groom to the bride as part of the payment that he makes when they marry.
***si'liyya* (pl. *sa'aalwa*):** ogress.
sinaaḥ: a strip of cloth attached to the front edge of the tent that distinguishes the front side of the tent from its back; in classical Arabic, "the good or auspicious side of a thing or person."
ṣin'at il-mara: a woman's work.
ṣin'at ir-rijjaal: a man's work.
***sirwaal* (pl. *saraawiil*):** long, wide, lightweight cotton pants worn by men and boys and tied at the waist with a cord; they are narrow at the ankles but a yard wide at the waist.
siyaag: marriage payment given by the groom's family to the bride and her family when she marries.
Suluum: a woman's personal name, meaning "safety, security."
***ṭaafa* (pl. *ṭiyaaf*):** saddle pad.
***ṭaagiya* (pl. *ṭawaaği*):** knit cap worn by boys and men; men wear it under their turbans.
ṭaar: drum; an evening of singing and dancing to the accompaniment of a drum.
***ṭabiina* (pl. *ṭabaayin*):** co-wife; one of two or three women married to the same man at the same time.
ṭahaara: purity; in the household context, the purity achieved by burning incense in the tent.
taḥashshud: polite reluctance to accept hospitality or gifts; embarrassment, indebtedness.
***ṭanb* (pl. *aṭnaab*):** tent rope.
***ṭarraash* (pl. *ṭarraashiin*):** scout who rides ahead of the women and children during migration, looking for pasture.
thagiil: heavy; slow.
***thawb* (pl. *thiyaab*):** for men: a long, loose, shirtlike garment that reaches below the knees and is usually white; for women: a long, waistless dress that reaches the ankles and is usually black with colored decorations.
***tichcha* (pl. *tichach*):** skirt worn by preadolescent girls.
ṭiyeyli: saddle blanket made of two woolly sheepskins sewn together and dyed black.
'ujmaan: non-Arabic speakers.
'umda: "tribal" leader or representative; in eastern Sudan, an administrative officer appointed by the government.
***umjarrad* (pl. *umjarradiin*):** "stripped down" to shirt and pants in preparation for riding in a camel race (men).
umzuwi: refugee.
wajh: literally, "face." Figuratively: a person's reputation; the front of a tent, where guests enter.
***wasam* (pl. *wusuum*):** livestock brand.
wida': small, white cowrie shells used by women for decorating leather and telling the future.
yaa marḥab: "Welcome!" The proper reply to *saloom 'aleyk* ("Peace upon you!") in Rashiidi Arabic.
il-yaman: right; south.
yaz'ar: to strike someone with a glance from an envious eye and harm him.
yitazachchin: to dress up in one's finest clothes.
yitlaḥḥam: to eat meat.

yityammam: "resort to the clean earth," i.e., clean one's hands and face by dusting them with sand in preparation for prayer.

yu'ayyin: to spot something, catch a glimpse of something.

yugaabil: to confront.

yugayyil: to nap during the early afternoon.

***zaghruuṭa* (pl. *zaghaariiṭ*):** joy-cry; a kind of high-pitched, ululating, wordless cheer that women make.

az-zariibi: poetry of a distinctive meter, sung during a sword dance at a wedding.

zimaala: group of male companions who ride quickly, on young male camels, during migration.

Vocabulary

affines: relatives by marriage.

belief system: the assumptions and ideas about the world that people in a society learn from each other. It includes notions about the structure of space and a classification of supernatural and natural beings. Less formalized and broader in scope than a religion.

client: anyone who offers labor and political support to a patron in exchange for the patron's services (protection, financial assistance, and so on).

commodity production: production of goods for sale in a market; the opposite of subsistence production.

ecological adaptation: the invention of practices and technologies that permit a society to survive in a particular physical environment and exploit a local ecological system.

economic stratification: the division of society into classes with varying amounts of wealth.

enculturation: the informal process by means of which children acquire a culture and learn the practices, beliefs, and values of their society.

endogamy: preference for marriage with a person who belongs to one's own kinship group, local (residential) group, political-economic class, caste, religion, or ethnic group; the pattern of marriages within such a group.

ethnocentrism: the unreflective assumption that the values and practices specific to one's own group or society should be the model for all other societies; the misunderstandings caused by such an assumption.

ethnographic description: an anthropologist's description of a particular society and its practices.

exogamy: the prohibition of marriage within one's own group, according to which in-group (endogamous) marriages are viewed as incestuous; the pattern of marriage relations established between a particular group and other groups.

extended household: a household containing more than one family (husband, wife, and children); sometimes called a multiple family household. Among the Rashaayda: a collection of families who migrate and camp together.

habitus: a social setting that enculturates people—so that they internalize abstract categories, ideas, values, and contrasts (e.g., guest/host, sacred/profane, generous/stingy)—by connecting them with tangible bodily or spatial distinctions (left/right, inside/outside, up/down).

household: the group of people who live in one residence, share in its meals, repair it, clean it, and organize it. Often its members pool their incomes and cooperate in daily tasks such as childrearing, caring for livestock, and tending crops. Its members need not all be relatives.

idealist explanation: an attempt to explain the existence and characteristics of a social practice in terms of ideas; for example, explaining exogamous marriage as the result of obedience to an abstract rule ("Thou shalt not marry a blood relative").

in-law avoidance: a custom in some societies according to which a person must not speak to, eat with, or sit near a relative by marriage (especially the parents and siblings of a spouse).

life-crisis rituals: rituals that mark an individual's passage from one stage in his or her life to a new stage. Weddings, bridal showers, and bachelor parties, for example, mark the passage from unmarried to married life in American society.

lineage: a group of consanguineal ("blood") relatives who can all trace descent through either the male or female line to a named common ancestor.

male initiation rites: rites designed to dramatize the difference between "boys" and "men" (as conceived by a particular society), teach "boys" how to live like "men," and socially confirm their new male identities.

marriage rules: statements about the forms of marriage (with cousins, nonrelatives, or people of high or low social status) that a particular society encourages or discourages.

Marxist analysis: the description and explanation of social practices in terms of the economic and political interests of social classes. For example, a particular tax law can be explained as a device created by the ruling class to protect its interests or exploit other classes.

materialist explanation: an attempt to explain social practices as the results of material needs; for example, explaining exogamous marriage as a strategy for creating social ties with nonrelated families who have valuable resources such as farmland or livestock.

mode of production: a kind of production found in particular historical and ecological circumstances, which depends on specific social relations and technological knowledge; for example, the feudal mode of production, in which land is cultivated by serfs, owned by monarchs, and defended by lords, so that subsistence crops can be grown.

nomadic pastoralists: pastoralists (see **pastoral production**) who migrate seasonally from one region to another in search of fresh natural pastures for their animals.

pastoral production: raising livestock by exploiting natural pastures and so obtaining animal fodder for free.

patrilineal descent: tracing descent through the father and father's male ancestors only.

patrons: See **client.**

political economy: a people's political and economic relations, which determine the kinds of goods they can produce, the ways in which these goods circulate or are distributed, and the means by which goods can be transformed into stable kinds of wealth or political power.

polygyny: marriage by one man to more than one woman at any given time; as distinct from polyandry (marriage by one woman to more than one man at the same time) and as a variety of polygamy (marriage by one person to more than one spouse at a given time).

practice: a meaningful social act that is directed toward other people and that can be interpreted or evaluated in the light of a society's customs and ideals. Some American practices are Halloween, Thanksgiving dinner, Fourth of July picnics, dating, football practice, spelling contests.

residence rules: the answers given by the members of a society to this question: "Where should a newly married couple live after the wedding?" Some possible answers: with the husband's parents; with the husband's maternal uncle; with the wife's mother; by themselves (in an independent household).

sexual division of labor: the allocation of tasks to men and women solely on the basis of sex (rather than according to ability, experience, age, etc.).

sexual division of space: the division of space into an area for men, an area for women, and perhaps a neutral area for children.

subsistence production: production of food and goods for household consumption or exchange; the opposite of commodity production.

teknonym: a name for a parent derived from the personal name of his or her child. It frequently takes the form "Father of (X)" or "Mother of (Y)."

unilineal descent: tracing descent through either the male line only or the female line only to a known male or female ancestor.

worldview: image of the world as seen through the eyes of a particular social group or society.

Bibliography

Sources on the Rashaayda and Sudan

Ahmed, A. G. M. (1979). "'Tribal' elite: A base for social stratification in the Sudan." In S. Diamond (Ed.), *Toward a Marxist anthropology* (pp. 321–335). New York: Mouton.

Ali, A. I. M. (1972). *The British, the slave trade and slavery in the Sudan, 1820–1881.* Khartoum: Khartoum University Press.

al-'Ariifi, Ṣ. A. (n.d.). "*Al-Badw wa al-badaawa fi al-Suudaan* [Bedouin and the Bedouin way of life in Sudan]." In A. G. M. Aḥmad (Ed.), *Tanmiya wa istiqraar al-ruḥal [Development and the sedentarization of nomads]* (pp. 52–75). Khartoum: al-Majlis al-Qawmi li al-buḥuuth.

Asad, T. (1970). *The Kababish Arabs: Power, authority, and consent in a nomadic tribe.* New York: Praeger.

Baaniqaa, S., & Aḥmad, M.A. (1959). *Al-Rashayida.* Khartoum: Maṭba'at miṣr-suudaan Limited.

Beachey, R. W. (1976). *The slave trade of Eastern Sudan.* New York: Barnes and Noble Books.

Cunnison, I. (1966). *The Baggara Arabs.* Oxford: Oxford University Press.

Ḥasan, A. (1974). *Al-Turaath al-sha'bi li qabiilat al-Rashaayda [The folk heritage of the Rashaayda tribe].* Khartoum: University of Khartoum, Institute for Asian and African Studies.

Hasan, Y. F. (1967). *The Arabs and the Sudan.* Edinburgh: Edinburgh University Press.

Ḥasan, Y. F. (1975). "Hijrat al-Rashaayda ila al-Suudaan [The migration of the Rashaayda to Sudan] 1846–1910." In Y. F. Ḥasan (Ed.), *Dirasaat fi ta'riikh al-Suudaan [Studies in the history of Sudan]* (pp. 24–42). Khartoum: Daar al-ta'liif wa al-tarjama wa al-nashr, University of Khartoum.

Hassan, H. M. (1974). *An illustrated guide to the plants of Erkowit.* Khartoum: Khartoum University Press.

Ingham, B. (1982). *Northeast Arabian dialects* (Library of Arabic Linguistics Series, Monograph No. 3). London: Kegan Paul.

Johnston, N., & Werner, L. (Directors). (1989). *Voice of the whip* (Ethnographic Film). New York: Museum of Modern Art, Circulating Film Library.

Johnstone, T. M. (1967). *Eastern Arabian dialect studies.* London Oriental Series: Vol. 17. London: Oxford University Press.

Munzinger, W. (1864). *Ostafrikanische studien.* Schaffhausen: Fr. Hurtersche Buchhandlung.

Perlez, J. (1992, March 5). "For Bedouins of Africa, sands are running out." *New York Times International,* p. 4.

Sadr, K. (1991). *The development of nomadism in ancient Northeast Africa.* Philadelphia: University of Pennsylvania Press.

Schweinfurth, G. (1865). "Reise an der Küste des Rothen Meers von Kosser bis Suakin." *Zeitschrift für Allgemeine Erdkunde, 18,* 131–150, 283–313, 321–360.

Shaked, H. (1978). *The life of the Sudanese Mahdi.* New Brunswick, NJ: Transaction Books.

Toledano, E. R. (1982). *The Ottoman slave trade and its suppression: 1840–1890.* Princeton: Princeton University Press.

Trimingham, J. S. (1965). *Islam in Ethiopia.* London: Frank Cass & Co.

Turki, Ḥ. Ṣ. (1978). *Aritriya wa al-taḥaddiyyat al-Miṣriyya [Eritrea and the Egyptian challenges].* Beirut: Daar al-kunuuz al-adabiyya.

von Oppenheim, M. F. (1952). *Die Beduinen. Vol III. Bearbeitet und herausgegaben von Werner Caskel.* Wiesbaden: Otto Harrassowitz.

Woidich, M., & Behnstedt, P. (1980). "Zum Sprachatlas von Aegypten." *Zeitschrift für arabische Linguistik, 5,* 176–192.

Young, W. C. (1984, November/December). "Ethnohistorical research: A supplement to documentary evidence and a stimulus for historical discovery." Paper presented at the eighteenth meeting of the Middle East Studies Association, San Francisco.

Young, W. C. (1987). "The effect of labor migration on relations of exchange and subordination among the Rashaayda Bedouin of Sudan." *Research in Economic Anthropology, 9,* 191–220.

Young, W. C. (1991). "Review of Johnston and Werner, *Voice of the whip.*" *American Anthropologist, 93*(1), 260–261.

Young, W. C. (1994). "The body tamed: Tying and tattooing among the Rashaayda Bedouin." In Nicole Sault (Ed.), *Many mirrors: Body image and social relations* (pp. 58–75). New Brunswick, NJ: Rutgers University Press.

General Sources/Recommended Reading

Antoun, R. (1972). *Arab Village.* Bloomington: Indiana University Press.

Asad, T. (1979). "Equality in nomadic social systems? Notes towards the dissolution of an anthropological category." In Equipe écologie et anthropologie des sociétés pastorales (Ed.), *Pastoral Production and Society* (pp. 419–428). Cambridge: Cambridge University Press.

Barth, F. (1961). *Nomads of South Persia: The Basseri tribe of the Khamseh confederacy.* Boston: Little, Brown.

Black, J. (1972). "Tyranny as a strategy for survival in an 'egalitarian' society: Luri facts vs. an anthropological mystique." *Man, 4,* 614–634.

Bourdieu, P. (1990). *The logic of practice* (Richard Nice, Trans.). Stanford: Stanford University Press.

Bulliet, R. W. (1975). *The camel and the wheel.* Cambridge: Cambridge University Press.

Chelhod, J. (1978). "Kabila [tribe]." In E. van Donzel, B. Lewis, & C. Pellat, (Eds.), *Encyclopaedia of Islam* (pp. 334–335). Vol. 4. Leiden: Brill.

Cribb, R. (1991). *Nomads in archaeology.* New York: Cambridge University Press.

Dahl, G., & Hjort, A. (1976). *Having herds: Pastoral herd growth and household economy.* Stockholm Studies in Anthropology, No. 2.

Eickelman, C. (1984). *Women and community in Oman.* New York: New York University Press.

Evans-Pritchard, E. E. (1940). *The Nuer.* London: Oxford University Press.

Finkelstein, I. (1988). "Arabian trade and socio-political conditions in the Negev in the twelfth–eleventh centuries B.C.E." *Journal of Near Eastern Studies, 47*(4), 241–252.

Fried, M. H. (1975). *The notion of tribe.* Menlo Park, CA: Cummings.

Keenan, J. (1977). *The Tuareg.* London: Allen Lane.

Khuri, F. I. (1990). *Tents and pyramids: Games and ideology in Arab culture from backgammon to autocratic rule.* London: Saqi.

Lancaster, W. (1981). *The Rwala Bedouin today.* Cambridge: Cambridge University Press.

Lavie, S. (1990). *The politics of military occupation.* Berkeley: University of California Press.

Lewando-Hundt, G. (1984). "The exercise of power by Bedouin women in the Negev." In E. Marx & A. Shmueli (Eds.), *The changing Bedouin* (pp. 83–123). New Brunswick: Transaction Books.

Lewis, I. (1961). *A pastoral democracy.* London: Oxford University Press.

Mernissi, F. (1987). *Beyond the veil.* Bloomington: Indiana University Press.

Sahlins, M. D. (1968). *Tribesmen.* Englewood Cliffs, NJ: Prentice-Hall.

Wolf, E. (1982). *Europe and the people without history.* Berkeley: University of California Press.

Yanagisako, S. J., & Collier, J. F. (1987). "Toward a unified analysis of gender and kinship." In J. F. Collier & S. J. Yanagisako (Eds.), *Gender and kinship: Essays toward a unified analysis* (pp. 14–50). Stanford: Stanford University Press.

Youssouf, I. A.; Grimshaw, A. D., & Bird, C. S. (1976). "Greetings in the desert." *American Ethnologist, 3*(4), 797–824.

Index